Fashion Branding Unraveled

fb

Fashion Branding
Unraveled

KALED K. HAMEIDE
Montclair State University

FAIRCHILD BOOKS   NEW YORK

Vice President & General Manager, Fairchild Education & Conference Division: Elizabeth Tighe

Executive Editor: Olga T. Kontzias

Assistant Acquisitions Editor: Amanda Breccia

Editorial Development Director: Jennifer Crane

Development Editor: Abigail Wilentz

Creative Director: Carolyn Eckert

Production Director: Ginger Hillman

Senior Production Editor: Elizabeth Marotta

Project Editor: Jeff Hoffman

Copyeditor: Susan Hobbs

Ancillaries Editor: Noah Schwartzberg

Photo Researcher: Ken Cavanagh Photography Services

Illustrator: Andrea Lau

Cover Design: Carolyn Eckert

Cover Art: Front Cover: D&G Perfume, Louis Vuitton Store, Dior Watch, Calvin Klein Show, and Guess Jeans: Courtesy of *WWD*; Chanel Bag: © Stephen Mark Sullivan

Back Cover: Vans Shoes, Target Store, Revlon Lipstick: Courtesy of WWD; Versace Window: © M.Flynn/Alamy

Text Design: Carolyn Eckert

Composition: Alicia Freile, Tango Media Pty Ltd

Library of Congress Catalog Card Number: 2010925368

ISBN: 978-1-56367-874-5

GST R 133004424

TP08

Title Page: Photo by Stephen Sullivan
TOC: Courtesy of WWD/Stephane Feugere
Page 9: Courtesy of WWD
Page 11: Courtesy of WWD

Chapter Openers:
1: © Frédérik Astier/Sygma/Corbis
2: Courtesy of WWD
3: Image courtesy of The Advertising Archives
4: Time & Life Pictures/Getty Images/James Keyser

5: © Justin Kase zsixz / Alamy
6: Courtesy of WWD
7: Courtesy of WWD/Steve Eichner
8: Courtesy of WWD

Part Openers:
Part 1: Photo by Carolyn Eckert
Part 2: Courtesy of WWD
Part 3: © Adrian Lyon / Alamy

Contents

V

Extended Contents

Preface

The term *brand* is probably one of the most frequently used in the world of marketing and, even more so, in the world of fashion. This book attempts to unravel the mysteries and misconceptions of the concept, establish a road map to brand creation, and examine the impact of new technologies on the future of branding. After reading the book, the reader will have gained an understanding of what a fashion brand is, how to develop one, the different categories of fashion and retail brands, as well as the challenges and opportunities technology is holding for brands in the twenty-first century. It is important to emphasize that although the book focuses on the fashion industry, highlighting its characteristics, segments, and marketing strategies, its topics and discussions regarding the brand concept and branding process can be referenced in general branding and marketing courses as well.

The book adopts a step-by-step approach and utilizes examples and case studies to clarify the terminology and demonstrate real-life applications to the theory. From an organizational perspective, the book is divided into three sections. Part 1 presents an overview of the concept of branding and the dynamics of the branding process. It is a crash course on branding, brand management, and branding strategies as they are currently practiced and understood. Part 2 examines the applications of concepts covered in part 1 in the world of fashion. It identifies and analyzes different fashion brand categories, such as luxury brands, private labels, and so on, exploring consumer profiles and strategies, as well as examining relevant characteristics and challenges pertaining to each segment. Part 3 focuses on the future of fashion branding in the twenty-first century, exploring new technologies that will redefine the industry and branding as we know them. New concepts will be highlighted, together with the challenges and opportunities they bring. Concepts such as mass customization and M-branding will be discussed and various examples examined. Technologies such as radio frequency identification (RFID) and their influence on retail branding will be examined and explored as well.

While reading this book, the reader should be aware that this is not a general marketing book but one specifically on branding; therefore, basic marketing principles and theories are not covered here unless they are directly needed to emphasize or complement a specific branding issue. Approaching this book with the expectation that it covers all marketing and fashion merchandising principles will not be fair to the book or the reader Thus, if covered in the book, marketing topics have a specific purpose and focus that are meant to support an argument and are not meant to be examined as they would be in a principles of marketing or merchandising book.

In addition, most chapters are written with enough references and information to make the reader understand the relevant topic if he or she decides to skip chapters and read them independently. However, it is highly recommended that the book be read in the sequence of its sections because there is a certain logical build-up to its argument. Thus, chapters 1, 2, and 3 should be read in order, and together they form the launching pad for reading the chapters in part 2. In the same manner, chapter 8 cannot be totally appreciated without reading chapter 7, and although the reader of both chapters would easily comprehend the message and concepts addressed, he or she would gain more benefit from reading the earlier chapters first.

One of the major challenges of studying branding is its relevant terminology. There are so many concepts associated with the terms, such as *positioning*, *identity*, and *image*, just to name a few, that the main challenge lies in how each of these terms is used and defined. Listening to experts or reading marketing books demonstrates how these can be defined and interpreted in many different ways depending on the backgrounds of the users and their business perspectives. Thus, one recommendation for the reader of this book is not to focus solely on the labels of these terms, but rather on their essence and the way each relates to the general branding process. This way, even if the terminology changes from one book to the other, the concept itself will remain relevant and applicable.

In conclusion, this text has been written to fit within a logical structure, taking a direct approach to the concepts of brand management and marketing. I hope to take the reader on an enlightening voyage of discovery, during which he or she, whether a student or an industry professional, will gain valuable knowledge and understanding of the branding concept, even if this concept has been totally unfamiliar thus far. Enjoy the journey.

Acknowledgments

This project wouldn't have been possible without the support and collaboration of many great individuals. Everyone at Fairchild Books has been amazing, and to each and every member of this wonderful and professional team of editors, designers, and marketing specialists, I send my thanks and sincere appreciation.

Special thanks go to Executive Editor Olga Kontzias for believing in the project from day one, Jennifer Crane for her constructive feedback and superb coordination, as well as to Elizabeth Marotta and Noah Schwartzberg for their amazing work and efforts.

There are two people who have been so special and instrumental to this book. First is my editor Abigail Wilentz. Simple words cannot express how much I appreciate her professionalism, patience, and contribution. She is a superb partner and a tremendous asset to this project. The second is photo researcher Ken Cavanagh, my "photo guru," who always found ways to accommodate my endless requests with his diligence and positive input. The three of us communicated on a daily basis, and we made the perfect team. It was a real honor working with them, and I thank them both with all my heart.

I would also like to thank my reviewers for their support, encouragement, and constructive feedback: Phyllis Greensley, Illinois Institute of Art (Chicago); Amy J. Harden Leahy, Ball State University; Beth Hinckley, FIDM; Wi Suk Kwon, Auburn University; Dudley Blossom, LIM College; Soo H. Kim, Savannah College of Art and Design; Roger Kramer, University of Arizona; and Denise Morano, Art Institute of San Diego.

I thank my students for enriching my life and making me smile, and my colleagues for their warm support.

Finally, I would like to thank my family, who are the most precious people in my life, for their unconditional love and support; and above all, I thank God.

TIFFANY & CO.

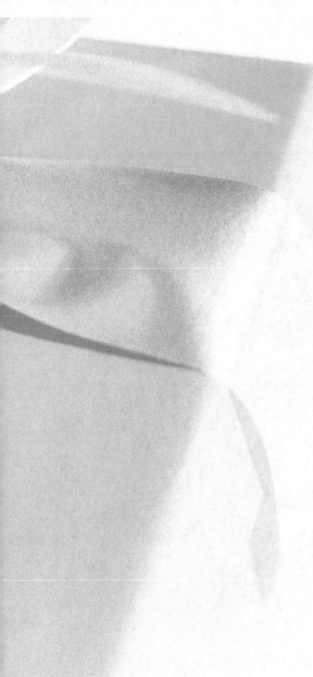

PART 1

Understanding the Brand

**Products are
created in
the factory.
Brands are created
in the mind.**
—Walter Landor, founder of
Landor Associates

1 The Brand

The word *brand* comes from the Old Norse *brandr*, meaning to burn,[1] in reference to how owners stamped their livestock so they are distinguished from others' cattle. That process became necessary among traders to identify the quality of animals based on the name of the farm stamped on them. In that sense, both the term and its function have developed.

However, we can trace that need for distinction back to ancient times. There is evidence that the Greeks attempted to identify and distinguish their quality pottery products through the use of a stamp, a signature, or some symbol. Similar attempts were made in Roman, Ancient Egyptian, and Asian societies as well. It is interesting to note how those times mirrored many of today's branding issues and trends. There was first the need to distinguish and "brand" a product, and then came the use of symbols (or logos rather than just names or signatures) that seemed easier to identify. There has even been evidence of ancient attempts to copy or imitate the works of skilled craftsmen to produce counterfeit replicas and cheaper imitations of their "brands," just like we witness today.

By the eighteenth century, rigid laws were put in place to protect products and give purchasers more confidence. The move was in response to the increased volume of manufacturing and trade in products, such as tapestry, furniture, and porcelain, as well as the rise in the hallmarking of gold and silver objects.[2]

But it was the industrial revolution of the nineteenth century that redefined branding in modern times. The industrial revolution

CHAPTER OBJECTIVES

* Present the background of branding.

* Define the term *brand*.

* Highlight the characteristics of the brand.

* Explore ways to evaluate the brand.

* Demonstrate the value and importance of the brand for the company and the customer.

* Identify different brand types.

introduced machines, which in return facilitated assembly-line production, enabling the ability to produce the same product in large quantities and identical forms in a way that could not have been achieved in the earlier days of workshops and craftsmanship. With mass production came mass marketing and the birth of monster consumer brands. Mass production meant large quantities of sameness, which in turn created the need to distinguish these new products from their competitors; making products easier to identify helped brands to achieve more successful marketing, through which they could gain consumers' trust and loyalty. Hence branding emerged as a marketing necessity. And again with branding came the need for more protective legislation that allows for the creation and protection of trademarks.

Although the Industrial Revolution could be credited for the birth of branding in modern times, it wasn't until the second half of the twentieth century that branding as we know it today exploded in the business scene. Technological advancements in communication and marketing tools together with flourishing economies and increases in consumerism made branding the buzzword of the eighties. Everything became branded, to the point that many have accused big brands of consumer and labor exploitation as they grew into dominating world markets under the umbrella of globalization.

Whether these accusations are valid or not, the reality remains that branding is a major force in business, and brands play a very important role in our lives. And in the world of fashion, it is not any different.

In this book, we will take a journey that explores fashion branding as we know it today and how it may develop in the future.

Figure 1.1

A brand is more than a name or a logo.

The Brand

Today, the term brand is one of the most utilized and referenced terms in marketing and business literature. Yet if you ask any number of people to define the term, you will most likely get as many different definitions. This is mainly because

professionals usually approach the term from different perspectives, depending on where they stand on the marketing spectrum. For instance, a brand may be defined as a registered trademark from a legal perspective and an asset from a financial one. Another source of confusion arises from the way scholars and professionals alike use and interpret various terminology related to the concept. It is common to find alternative terms (such as image and identity, or values and benefits) used interchangeably in one case whereas they mean different things in another.

However, the biggest misconception about a brand remains the belief that a brand is simply a name or logo given to a product or a service (see Figure 1.1). This simplified view of a brand is common, even among business professionals who happen to have a direct impact on the decision-making process that affects their own products. Yet as we will discover, that definition does not capture the true meaning, purpose, or impact of the brand and what it truly means to its creators and users.

Thus, we will spend some time in this chapter dissecting the term and exploring its essence before we move to outlining the branding process in chapter 2. A good starting point for our journey is to define the term and understand its elements. So let us begin.

Brand Logic

Brands exist mainly to reduce risks for consumers by encouraging them to buy a *branded* product that they can trust as well as anticipate its level of quality and service. In this light, brands make it easier for consumers to make safer choices that will eventually satisfy their needs as promised by the brand, and in the process provide a certain reward or value that can be either emotional or rational.

Brands are also built on the premises of differentiation and bringing something new and different that other competitors in the market cannot, such as a new idea or concept packed with a mix of offerings and features that are different and unique. If the concept is not different, it will neither attract the customers' attention nor convince them to take the risk of giving up what is already familiar for something that is new and seemingly riskier. In other words, a brand is meant to shout out to you, "I am the only one (or the best one) that can do *this* for you." The more unique and distinctive the idea, the more legitimate and valid the brand is, as well as the more attractive.

When a brand is recognized and appreciated by the customers, it aims at keeping them attached and loyal by consistently living up to their expectations and remaining relevant and fresh.

The Definition

Now that we understand the logic behind having a brand, we should be ready to put together a definition that captures that rationale as well as the essence of the term from a holistic perspective:

A **BRAND** is an entity with a distinctive idea expressed in a set of functional and experiential features with a promise of a value reward relevant to its end user, and an economic return to its producers *(through the building of equity)*. A successful brand has a strong identity *(mentally and physically)*, is innovative, consistent, competitively positioned, and holds a matching positive image in the consumer's mind.

By examining this definition, notice a few key concepts that reflect the essence of the brand. They are:

- Entity
- Distinctive features
- Idea
- Promise of value
- Return
- Equity
- Relevance
- Identity
- Positioning
- Innovation
- Consistency
- Image

Now let us take a closer look at each of these terms in order to get a better understanding of the definition.

Entity

In most cases, the term *brand* refers to a product or service, yet many would argue that a brand could be almost anything: a product, a person, a country, and so on. Others may find this notion disputable given that a brand must possess, for instance, features that are open for change, which is not totally true in all of these cases. Nevertheless, it is true that many things can be *branded*. Accordingly, we prefer to use the term *entity* instead of *product* or *service* for two reasons when defining what a brand

is: the term *entity* is more inclusive and has both a legal insinuation and a reference to a potential market value and financial worth, which should be true for any brand.

Ideas, Features, and Values

The three terms *ideas, features,* and *values* are closely related, yet carry different connotations and meanings. Thus, it is recommended that we approach them under one heading to examine the meaning and relevance of each concept to the brand and to each other.

As previously mentioned, any brand is supposed to be built on the premises of differentiation through a concept that is meant to bring something new, offer a better solution, or introduce a new technology. In all cases, a brand is born as an idea—better yet, a distinctive one.

The **IDEA** is the concept; it's the vision of the brand or the initial dream upon which an entire venture is created. Any product (or service) is meant to solve a problem or satisfy a need. Thus, the idea usually regards a proposed solution for a certain problem or to satisfy a need the targeted user may have. For these to occur, the idea needs to materialize or be expressed in a set of tangible, physical, **DISTINCTIVE FEATURES,** as in the case of products, concepts, or facilities in terms of services to fulfill this task. (Note: for the sake of our discussion as well as simplicity, we will focus on product brands unless otherwise stated.)

Therefore, any brand is a product at its core. And any product is built on a feature or set of features that solve a problem or satisfy a need. These features are eventually augmented by choices of attributes relevant to the finished product and its market, such as a specific price and location of distribution. It is the mix of these features and attributes that generates the product's benefits and differentiates the product from those of competitors. Based on these offerings, customers can make buying decisions. Accordingly, the benefits created by the product mix (features and attributes) generate some reward or value to the user, such as getting the best value for money or encouraging the buyer to feel that he or she is a smart shopper.

Every brand has a product in its core, but a *product* and a *brand* are not the same thing. As a matter of fact, it is common to have a one-brand-many-products strategy, as in the case of most fashion brands. No wonder that brands can outlive their products.

But the question remains: if the product and its features are the core of the brand, and they create those benefits that solve our problems as consumers, *then why do we need to brand the product?* We will answer this question as we proceed in examining the key terms we highlighted earlier.

One important term that we need to examine further at this point is that of *value*. The notion of value is essential in our discussion, as well as the distinction between a value and a *benefit*. Let us examine this example: Every black wool sweater is meant to solve the same problem and offer the same benefit of protecting us from cold weather, just as every car is there to take us from point A to point B. However, although the benefit is the same, the real value that we get from each one may be different.

So what makes the experience different? And what would make us pick black sweater A over black sweater B? Although both sweaters are identical—basic, black 100 percent wool—their mix of offerings may be different. For instance,

sweater A may be wool and black, but cheaper; or easily available through a larger number of conveniently located stores. If this is the case, then both sweaters are not really identical. Sweater A does have a differentiator as part of what we have already called its product mix. Thus, it is essential to remember that a product is more than just its physical and tangible features. There are other attributes that shape or complement the product (such as price and distribution), and it is through its mix of features and attributes that a product attempts to differentiate itself and consequently attract our attention as consumers. Therefore, if sweater A does offer an advantage through any of its attributes, it is an added value that is rational and hard to ignore.

The other reason we may have picked sweater A over sweater B is our belief that sweater A is a better status symbol, or would make us feel cooler, smarter, or even sexier than sweater B—at least that is what our friends and peers would think. It had to be something that the producers have done or said to enforce this message that sweater A is more than just a black wool sweater. If this is the case, then we are getting more value from sweater A than protection from cold weather. We are getting an added value, which in this case is emotional and hard to ignore.

A value, therefore, is that extra thing that is meaningful to us and satisfies us both rationally and/or emotionally, which we are made to believe the brand will deliver like no other and even convince us to pay the extra dollar for it, if needed.

Thus, values can be rational, derived from the functional features or attributes of the product core and our interpretation of what they mean for us, or they can be emotional, usually developed as a result of branding that product. Brands need to identify and focus on this value that is relevant and more meaningful for its target customer while promoting the brand. Choosing which value depends on many factors, such as type and segment of the brand. In general, mass-market and budget brands are bought for rational reasons, so rational value derived from the brands' product features and functionality is more common. On the other hand, luxury brands are usually bought for emotional values that are derived from elements added to the product in the branding process, as we will examine in future chapters. Therefore, both options are valid as differentiators and generators of value.

However, one problem with relying on features and attributes as your core differentiator and source of value is that it diminishes the purpose of branding to simply identifying the product and guaranteeing the delivery of the value. While this is valid and more than a product by itself can deliver, it is usually a short-lived competitive advantage because features are easily copied in a faster and cheaper manner than they were initially developed.

A quick reminder not to forget is that, so far, our black sweater from the previous example is still just a *product;* we have yet to identify all the other elements needed to transform it into a brand.

So far we have established the following:

- A product and a brand are not the same thing.
- Most brands are built around a product in their core.
- A product is a set of tangible features put together with the goal of delivering certain benefits that would ultimately deliver one or more values that are meaningful to the end user.

- The more unique and exclusive the features are, the more competitive, stronger, and relevant the brand will be.
- It is apparent so far that although products compete on the basis of features and benefits, brands can compete on the basis of other values they create.

Promise of Value

If there is any one simple definition of a brand, this would be it: *A brand is a promise.* It is a promise that it will deliver a value in the best, most efficient way and will always do so. A promise is a contract, a guarantee, and a reducer of risk, so accordingly the **PROMISE OF VALUE** ensures that the values attributed to the brand will be delivered. As we mentioned earlier, one of the most important advantages or reasons for having brands is their role in minimizing the risk in decision making. It makes it easier and safer for us to choose.

Values are the ultimate reason for our purchase and the answer to the most important question: "Why should I buy *this* brand?" Values can be about self-esteem or a sense of belonging to an elite group as in the case of luxury and designer brands (Rolex, Porche, Louis Vuitton), value for money as in the case of mass-market and budget brands (Walmart, Old Navy), or search for heritage and leadership (Coke and Levi's 501). In the end, a brand delivers some rational or emotional rewards in a way that an unbranded product does not. Obviously, the significance of these values is highly dependent on many factors, including the brand's segment, our experiences, culture, and so on, as will be examined shortly.

Earlier we mentioned that brands usually outlive their products. As time goes by, products develop and change or get substituted by newer products through the process of growth and innovation. *So how does this affect the brand?*

Brands are dynamic entities, pretty much like human beings; they live and die and constantly need to grow and stay relevant. Thus, brands are encouraged to continuously develop and upgrade their products and their technical features and, in many cases, even introduce new products. What this means, however, is that the product offering keeps changing, so if a brand was really nothing more than a product with a name or a logo, then every time the product changes, so does the brand and its meaning to us. This does not make a lot of business sense, given that brands are meant to live long, especially as it takes time and effort to develop them. Therefore, a brand has to be about something more stable and consistent. Accordingly, the essence of the brand goes beyond the product, and although products change and evolve (and they should), the core value (which it promises to deliver) should stay consistent. *This* is what branding is really about. Core values define the brand to such an extent that if they are lost, the brand (not the product) ceases to exist.

If a brand producer decides to redefine its core values, it will alienate its loyal customers; however, there may be some situations in which a brand needs to change as part of a strategy to reposition itself in the market after it loses steam or relevance with its customer base.

Relevance

Every brand is meant to appeal through its promise of value to a targeted customers' segment. Whether they are rational or emotional values, it really comes down to how relevant these values are to the consumer. **RELEVANCE** is a key word for the success of any brand. It confirms that what the brand is promising as a value makes sense to consumers, and that it is a proposal convincing enough to make them purchase the brand, selecting it over its competitors.

In the nineties, Harley Davidson attempted to expand the brand into different segments to benefit from its strong brand recognition and very loyal customer base. Among their attempts was to introduce a Harley Davidson cologne and aftershave (see Figure 1.2), along with many other extensions (including ties!). Because of its disconnect with the brand's personality, the attempted brand extension failed terribly. The proposed products did not fit with the Harley Davidson personality and values of rugged, strong masculinity. The products were simply irrelevant to the customer, and although extending the brand is a legitimate strategy, doing so in a category that did not reflect the core value was disastrous.

As demonstrated, relevance is extremely crucial in connecting the brand with the customer. It is also clear that the notion of a targeted customer and relevance are strongly related; through its offerings, a brand may not be relevant at all to one group of consumers, but extremely relevant to another.

Segments and Brand Values

If I ask you, "Why would you buy a product from a luxury brand such as Gucci and be willing to spend extra cash for one of its bags or shoes?" your answer could be "because they are quality products," or maybe "because with a quality

expensive product I also get great customer service," and so on. This explains why you are willing to pay the cash to buy a luxury brand in general as opposed to a mass-market brand, but it still does not explain why you would choose Gucci over Prada, for instance. If it were about quality, customer service, and so on, then every brand in the luxury segment would promise and deliver (albeit in its own way).

Therefore, in addition to these *segment-specific* values, there must be other *brand-specific* values that would make you pick one brand over the other. For example, Gucci's identifies its values in its "high quality, innovation, and craftsmanship *(segment-related)*, as well as its own heritage and the power behind the made-in-Italy notion *(brand-related).*"[3]

Thus, we can deduce that brands may offer a mix of values, some of which are segment-specific that may be shared by other brands within the same segment, such as high quality and service among luxury brands. In addition, each brand should deliver brand-specific values. These values are what distinguish one brand from its competitors in the same segment. The unique mix of these values (among other elements) builds a unique personality to the brand and generates a core value that is the ultimate reason for choosing and buying the brand. In most cases, this core value is emotional and strongly linked to the brand's personality. It could be that Gucci is a sophisticated brand with an Italian heritage or Chanel is the ultimate female brand with a French linkage that means something to you and makes you feel a certain way or, in your opinion, reflects a certain status symbol.

So back to our question: Why Gucci and not Prada, for instance? It may be because of the brand's:

- *Good quality:* True, but it should be also true for Prada. If it isn't, they are not competitors in the first place.
- *Good design and taste:* For sure this is a major differentiator and a unique feature especially at

the luxury level where every collection is meant to be unique and creative. However, if the same collection is offered to you with no label, would you still have made the same decision and have bought it without knowing it was from Gucci? What if the same garment was offered to you with a Christian Dior label instead? Would you have bought it? There is a chance you would have not.

- *Italian heritage:* Very important for sure, but Prada is also Italian and a valid competitor.
- *Ability to make you feel sophisticated in a different way:* Now we are getting closer. If Gucci makes you feel special and sophisticated like no other brand does, then that is the ultimate reason why you are buying it. It is how this luxury brand makes you feel and what it means to you.

It is the end result of the brand's combination of values such as luxury, Italian heritage, quality, unique design, and so on. If you have chosen a Gucci product over another brand, then Gucci has succeeded in utilizing its values as a luxury brand and created a unique mix of offerings at the brand level that is meaningful and relevant to you. It created a dream, an experience, or a story for the brand to which you relate and would like to belong. This is really what branding achieves, as we will discover in chapter 2. Even if you buy this basic black sweater from Gucci, which may not be that unique, you will still feel special and sophisticated. That is the core *value*.

Identity

If brand value is what a brand *means* to consumers, then an **IDENTITY** is what it *says* to them. It describes the brand and enforces its differentiation proposition. At this stage, it is very important

to understand that how the brand proposes to present itself may not necessarily be how the consumer ends up seeing it. (We will later refer to this as the image.)

There are two elements, or components, that create a brand's identity: *personality* and *symbols* (we can also call these symbols *attributes* or *visual/ audio identity*). Obviously these two elements work hand in hand and complement each other to form the brand's identity.

The concept of brand identity is similar to that for humans. If I ask you to identify someone, the first thing that comes to mind would be that person's name. A name makes it easier to identify "John" within a crowd of people. However, a name with some other attributes, such as the color of his eyes or hair, will make it not only easier to find John but to remember him as well. Although this information makes it easier to pinpoint John, it does not tell much about who he really is as a person. For this we need to learn more about his personality and character. We can learn about his personality from the way he acts and thinks, his values, and the decisions he makes. This is exactly what an identity does to a brand. After all, a brand is a dynamic entity, just as humans are!

Consumers often define brand identity in terms of very concrete, palpable, and tangible attributes. So the basic elements of brand identity and consumer choice are partly physical (i.e., tangible),[4] which we will call symbols or attributes. Remember our black wool sweater from earlier examples. So far, it was just that—a black wool sweater with no name or identity. If put in the market with other sweaters, it will be highly indistinguishable. We need symbols, such as the name, logo design and color, packing, and so on, to create

Figure 1.3a–c

Identity symbols
in branding:
(a) The unique
shade of Tiffany
blue has become
an international
symbol of the
brand.
(© Amy Strycula /
Alamy)
(b) Hermès
classic Kelly bag
is synonymous
with the luxury
brand and one
of its most
sought-after
products.
(© 2008 Fairchild
Fashion Group)
(c) The
Ferragamo
signature as an
example of a
typographic logo;
Timberland's
tree symbol as
an example of
a graphic logo.

also contribute to the brand's need to look different and unique. However, a brand is not meant to just *look* different, but to *feel* different as well. The "feel" dimension is achieved through the brand's personality.

It is important to remember that although creating and adding these attributes are essential in the branding process, they are not enough to create a brand (see Figures 1.3a–c). A product with a name and a logo is simply that, and not a brand. There must be a meaning behind it all.

Identity Symbols

In addition to names, logos, and color, a brand can be physically and mentally identified through an item or product that stands out as a symbol of the brand. This can be looked at as its *buzz* note.

Examples may include:

- *A color:* Tiffany's light blue, Valentino's hot red, or LV's brown
- *An item:* Mont Blanc pen, Chanel suit, Kelly bag
- *Packing:* Tiffany blue box, or Godiva's chocolate box
- *Graphic (logo):* Timberland's tree or Lacoste's alligator
- *Typography:* Salvatore Ferragamo signature-like font

Contrary to common belief, choosing the right name, color, or logo design for the brand is no easy task. Companies may spend thousands of dollars researching and seeking the help of consultants in their pursuit of a suitable name or logo that is recognizable, memorable, legally available, and creative. We will examine different guidelines for choosing effective attributes as we discuss the branding process in chapter 2.

visual (and sometimes audio) signals or expressions that help us identify the brand physically and aesthetically, as well as mentally. Attributes simply put a name and a face to the brand, creating a high level of brand awareness and recognition. They

Personality

The personality is the brand's character and what humanizes the brand by giving it human references such as fun, boring, exciting, conservative, and so on. The personality thus adds an emotional aura or dimension to the brand and is more or less developed through time and practice. It is a summation of how the brand behaves, its culture, stories, vision, decisions, even how its employees act. The personality is such a personal thing that it is usually hard to emulate or imitate.

It is, therefore, the combination of a brand's visual symbols and personality that form the brand's identity; in turn, this identity allows us to easily identify the brand both visually and mentally while differentiating it from other brands.

Positioning and Image

POSITIONING is generally defined as how the company proposes the brand should be perceived in reference to its competitors, or as emphasizing the brand's distinctive advantages so that it stands out in the market and differs from specific competitors. However, one very important point to remember is that positioning is really a proposal or a strategy, and again, it does not mean that this is actually how the consumer will end up perceiving the brand.

Positioning is all about identifying and highlighting brand differentiators and competitive advantages. That is why positioning becomes even more important when products are almost indistinguishable. But what about products that are, for the most part, inherently different, such as in fashion? Is drafting a positioning strategy for these products still relevant and necessary? We explore that question as we proceed.

Positioning

A brand can be positioned at two levels—the product level and the brand level. At the product level, the brand is positioned based on its product mix or any of its attributes. For example, a brand can be positioned based on its features, functionality, or creativity (such as luxury brands), or it can be positioned based mainly on its price, distribution outlets, and so on, or a mix of these attributes. At the brand level, positioning is driven by identity, mainly by the brand's personality and what it means in terms of emotional values. The Gucci statement we've seen earlier demonstrates how Gucci positions itself not just on the basis of its unique and innovative designs (a product level element) but the perceived values from its Italian heritage and the lifestyle it depicts (a brand level element).

Positioning solely based on product features or one of the other attributes can present a few challenges. First, these features are easily copied and eventually will be ineffective as differentiators. Second, it ignores the values added and created through the branding process. To demonstrate this let us examine the brand a little closer based on previous discussions.

Brands play a number of roles:

- A brand creates a visual identity and a mental reference to the product.
- A brand offers a promise of a certain value and a contract or guarantee that it will be consistently delivered.
- A brand makes our choices easier and less risky.
- A brand allows us to identify with and belong to a certain lifestyle or image.
- A strong brand can create an entry barrier for competitors to enter the market and challenge it.

Figure 1.4

**The anatomy
of a brand.**

(*© 2008 Fairchild*

Fashion Group)

ANATOMY OF A BRAND

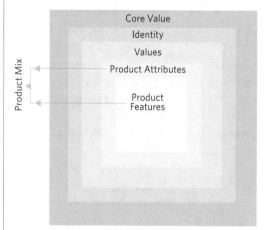

- the product can differ in its level of service (comes with a better warranty or after-purchase support); or
- the product can differ in any combination or mix of these attributes.

The more unique the comparative advantage mix, the more competitive the brand. Thus, features and attributes are strong and important differentiators, especially when a rational decision is needed.

In this case, the benefits from branding the product would be to:
- easily identify the product among competitors,
- build confidence toward the effectiveness and reliability of these features, and
- build trust and support behind the product.

Positioning at this level triggers mostly rational incentives for buying the brand, such as convenience, value for money, efficiency, and so on. Walmart, for instance, positions itself as a consumer advocate, one that offers reasonably priced products and true value for money. The strength of the Walmart brand lies in the fact that it consistently delivers on that promise. Competing solely on the basis of low price is not a bulletproof strategy because you may reach a level where you cannot lower your price any further, so you get outbid by competitors and end up being stuck with a price too low to make financial sense. Yet this strategy works for Walmart (or similar stores such as Target) because of its size and reach. But even Walmart and Target can only support this positioning proposal through an identity derived from the retailing experience they offer as a brand.

On the other hand, a brand can also be positioned at the brand level based on its identity.

Based on these points, a company has the option to position and market the brand at the product level, meaning based on the product's features and attributes (see Figure 1.4). We can refer to this combination of elements as the *product mix*, which can be defined as follows:

**Product Mix = Features + Price +
Distribution + Support**

Because positioning is about identifying and highlighting differentiators, any single attribute or a combination of the four attributes can be chosen as a product differentiator and the driver behind the product positioning. For example:
- the product can differ from competitors in its price (it's cheaper);
- the product can differ in relevance to where it is sold and distributed (convenience or exclusivity);

However, by looking at the following diagram, we see that the product is at the core of the brand and that the identity wraps around the product, so positioning based on identity does not mean it is an either/or situation. Identities are based on the product and everything else. Identities (which include personality) simply create a soul or a meaning to the product. Thus positioning based on identity does not mean that the product and its mix is not relevant; it simply means we take it a step further toward what that means emotionally as well as mentally to the consumer.

For example, why would you buy a Calvin Klein undergarment and not one from Fruit of the Loom, assuming that both are 100 percent cotton and may even look and feel the same? Probably because although they may look like the same product, Calvin Klein (although more expensive or maybe even because of it) makes you feel better and more accomplished. When Calvin Klein created a great buzz with his designer underwear in the eighties, he did not really revolutionize underwear as much as revolutionize its status and redefine its image. He managed to make underwear sexy, modern, and fashionable. In his provocative ads such as one featuring a Peter Lindberg portrait of Djimon Hounsou, Calvin Klein redefined underwear as an element of lifestyle (see Figure 1.5).

Thus, the way Calvin Klein positioned and marketed his underwear was not really based on its functionality but on its creative design and how that complemented the new status, image, and identity. Buying this underwear was not necessarily a rational decision, but rather an emotional one.

There are different tactics to the positioning strategy, but the previous examples show us that positioning strategies can take place at two different levels. Although a positioning strategy can be based on a main element or differentiator, a brand, which is more than just a product, needs to be positioned with both levels in mind.

This shows that you can position based on product features (the product level), but you can also position the brand in terms of its identity and the emotional value it creates (the brand level). The choice is determined by the market situation, the company's size and strategy, and the brand's segment.

Therefore, a brand such as Chanel can be positioned based on its designs and the value derived from its exclusivity and creativity (a product feature), or the relevance of these designs as expressed by its identity as *a very feminine brand* of *timeless elegance* developed through its French heritage, history, and strong personality (another branding feature).

Positioning through identity and personality is usually harder to emulate than elements of the product mix previously mentioned, but can be challenging at times. Think of Chanel: Have you ever wondered why Chanel never offered a full-fledged menswear line? Many analysts believe it is because of its strong established identity as the ultimate woman's brand. The brand, its heritage, and the persona of Coco Chanel were all about feminism and the liberation of women. The personality is so strong and rooted that it was difficult to stretch beyond this concept.

There are many cases where the fashion designers are both the founders and/or the main or sole creative force behind the brand (as opposed to a team of product developers) and, as such, they are a major part of the brand's identity. In the case of luxury brands, which symbolize a certain lifestyle, designers embody that identity and lifestyle. They become the symbol and, in many ways, *they* become the brand.

Why is it that when a great designer retires or passes away, questions about the brand's future start to be raised regardless of its long history and heritage? His or her death should not affect the level of quality, price, or customer service. But it may affect the level of creativity (a product feature relevant to luxury brands) and/or the brand's personality and identity in general (a brand feature);

because these are the two strongest elements for positioning a luxury brand, his or her death or departure imposes a threat for sure.

Based on how we described positioning so far, we can think of positioning as the case for the brand. It's a strategic proposal for how the consumer is meant to perceive the brand. And we have seen that as a strategy, positioning can take different approaches, but in all cases it needs to focus on something meaningful and rewarding for the consumer.

Thus, from an organization's perspective, positioning is a strategy that is inclusive of all its activities with the aim of getting the consumer to see the brand (and create an image for it) exactly the way the organization intends it to be viewed. However, this may not always succeed, and there may be discrepancies between the proposed position and the actual one. These discrepancies can be due to many factors, both internal and external, such as:

- misunderstanding of the true potential of the brand and what it can and cannot deliver,
- failure to live up to the promise and/or be consistent about it,
- misunderstanding of competitors,
- misunderstanding of consumers' needs and priorities, and
- predetermined perceptions that the brand failed to address.

The last point refers to how consumers may have predetermined perceptions that may challenge the positioning strategy. For example, made-in-China brands have been perceived as cheaper and of lower quality than those manufactured in places like Italy or France. Therefore, a Chinese luxury

Figure 1.6

A master of
innovation,
Apple CEO
Steve Jobs
discusses a Nike
shoe that makes
use of the iPod.
(*Associated Press/Paul
Sakuma*)

brand may have a hard time positioning itself as such. Also, a first-time luxury product buyer will have different preset expectations of the brand than does a regular luxury shopper. These external influences can create disrupting "noise" that should not be ignored. Accordingly, it is safe to conclude that the consumer is really the one who defines the actual position of the brand.

Image

An **IMAGE** is how the consumer ends up seeing or understanding the brand. It can coincide with or differ from what the brand had planned. Images created by customers can be positive or negative, and successful brands are those for which the targeted positioning and image coincide.

The image the customer develops is affected by his or her own experiences with the brand and its competitors; the customer's cultural, religious, and economic background, as well as many other external influences. As we've seen,

a brand cannot totally control these external influences and experiences, but it tries to create the conditions and incentives that may result in a more positive experience.

Innovation and Consistency

A brand needs to be in tune with the times, and in sync with customers' needs and aspirations. It needs to respond to economic, technological, and generational needs and developments.

Innovation

As we've mentioned, a successful brand needs to be a dynamic entity that evolves, usually through **INNOVATION**. A key area of competition in the twenty-first century, innovation is an absolute necessity for any brand's survival (see Figure 1.6). Innovation can:

- enable the brand to respond to changing customer needs,
- enable the brand to stay relevant and compete on stronger basis, and
- create new business opportunities and possibly attract new consumers through enhancing existing features or introducing new ones. As features generate benefits, they create values in return, and eventually entice consumers to purchase your brand.

Consistency

CONSISTENCY is another key factor for the success of any brand. If a brand is a promise or a contract that guarantees delivery of a specific value to the consumer, then the consumer needs to see that the brand is serious about its offerings and will consistently deliver the promise. Without consistency there is no customer loyalty, which at the end of the day is the ultimate goal for any brand and a measure of good performance.

From a marketing perspective, it is always believed that the goal for any brand is not just to sell a product, but to sell it again—meaning to make sure that the customer was satisfied enough to return and purchase the same brand again and again. Loyal customers are great assets and great champions of the brand. They are also less costly to service and retain than bringing over new customers. And customer loyalty can be much more rewarding to a company. Customer loyalty is a stamp of approval and success, and it cannot be achieved without honesty and consistency in every aspect.

However, the concepts of the terms *innovation* and *consistency* may seem a bit contradictory. Whereas innovation is about change, consistency seems to be all about standardization and conformity. In reality, the two terms complement each other perfectly. Brands have life cycles where they start small, grow, and can eventually die if not well-nourished and rejuvenated. Usually, as a brand gets older, its life cycle becomes a series of smaller cycles whereby, after some time, the brand needs to be rejuvenated and then goes through the process again. Therefore, if not flexible enough to innovate and respond to new technologies and opportunities, brands cannot stand the test of time and the challenges of technological and cultural changes, as well as changing customers' needs and buying habits. So how can a brand strike this balance between innovation and consistency? The answer lies in deciding on *what to innovate and what to maintain as consistent.*

If a brand is the sum of features, attributes, identity, and values, then what should not change, unless seriously needed, is the *value* because this is the main purpose of the brand and what is at its core. Consistency in value demonstrates that the brand is trustworthy, reliable, and serious. What could and should be innovated are the other elements such as the tangible features or intangible support services like customer service, and so on.

Identity symbols such as logo design, color, and so on, can change over time but with serious consideration and research to avoid confusion and customer backlash. As for the personality, which is a major contributor to the core value, there is a big difference between changing or redefining, rejuvenating, and realigning it to correctly complement and enhance the brand's image.

Equity and Market Valuation[*]

Although it costs a lot of money to develop a brand, brands never should be treated as mere expenses on financial statements. In reality, brands are probably the most valuable asset a company might have. And one of the great advantages of branding is that indeed it adds to the market value of the product. But *why*?

A brand's market value is a function of the brand's **EQUITY** that it accumulates. The greater the equity, the more valuable the brand. This equity is in direct proportion to the brand's ability to retain current customers and attract new ones. To the extent a brand does these well, it grows stronger against its competition and delivers more profits to its owners.[5] In addition, a strong brand

---

[*] In this discussion the word "value" refers to market or financial value. So to avoid any confusion, we will refer to it here as "market value."

usually creates barriers for competitors to enter the market and challenge it.

The problem with brands, however, is that the additive and accumulated gains from branding are mainly intangibles, which has always been a true challenge for traditional accounting practices to measure. In accounting, the concept of goodwill was introduced as a balance sheet entry to reflect that intangible market value of brands, but this concept never sufficed, as we will see later in this chapter.

If you examine the current market value for many of the world's famous brands, you will be amazed by these market estimates. For example, according to Interbrand (a marketing consultant agency that publishes a list of the world's top 100 global brands every year), the market value in 2009 was over $21 billion for LV and $15 billion for H&M. This market value is obviously much higher than the actual value of all the company-owned assets. It reflects the brand's market power, level of awareness, and appreciation by the consumer.

However, measuring the brand's market value remains a great challenge. There have been various approaches and techniques introduced. We will briefly examine a few of these methods to get a quick understanding of the issue without being too technical because covering all the financial details and formulas is beyond the scope of this book.

Traditional Accounting and the Concept of Goodwill

Accounting has introduced the concept of goodwill as an entry on the balance sheet to measure the intangible market value of companies and brands. However, this approach has not succeeded in capturing the essence of the concept.

CRITICISM OF THIS APPROACH

A major problem with traditional accounting in general is that it is historically based. It only measures activities in the past. On the other hand, the general consensus is that the main strength of a brand lies in its future potential.

Accounting does not propose a clear way to measure or anticipate the value of this goodwill, and there have been many inconsistencies in the valuation techniques used; thus, unless the brand or the company is actually sold in the market or evaluated for a merger or a similar market activity, this value will never be truly known.

We can, therefore, conclude that the goodwill approach proposed by traditional accounting does not always reflect the real value or importance of the brand to the organization and the shareholders.

The Finance Approach

The finance approach is based on the simple premise that a brand is able to generate more market value than generic (no-brand) products because it can command a price premium. So this price premium represents the base for the brand's market value because this is what differentiates it from the market value it would have as a no-brand, generic product.

The finance approach, therefore, measures the brand's current market value as the net present value (NPV) for those future price premiums a brand would command over its generic equivalent. (These future gains are discounted back to measure their NPV, which means how much these future gains would mean today, given a certain interest rate.)

CRITICISM OF THIS APPROACH

This method assumes that all brands demand premium price, which is not always true, especially for nonluxury consumer brands. Whereas many mass-market brands may still cost a bit more than generic ones, they mainly rely on volume (for example, Walmart) rather than price to generate profit.

This method is based on the principles of comparison (you compare a branded product to a similar nonbranded one), which makes the comparison even harder given that a brand by definition is meant to be different from competitors, let alone from generic products.

Some would argue that brands don't necessarily generate more market value because of their price premiums. Rather, it is because of their potential to secure consistent future flow of income due to customer loyalty, which is a major reward from branding that this approach (and others) seems to ignore.

Other Notable Approaches
CUSTOMER EQUITY

As a result of the flaws in the previous two approaches, the concept of consumer equity was introduced as an alternative. This new approach puts into consideration the relative value of the consumer and what could be the most important driver for a brand value: consumer loyalty. The concept is based on the following premises:

- Customers do have financial value, and customer loyalty may be more significant in generating value and sustainable profitability than previously realized.
- Revenue should be evaluated relative to consumer value. For instance, the cost of retaining current customers is lower than the cost of acquiring new ones.

Calculating customer equity can be a complex process and is beyond the scope of this book. But we can highlight the following principles:[6]

- the need to differentiate between profitable and nonprofitable customers;
- the need to consider factors that drive customer profitability, such as life cycle, retention, or referrals;
- the need to understand how customer life cycles determine where customers stand in the relationship with the brand and the strength of that relationship (new, inactive, defected, and so on);
- the need to collect more data regarding the cost of acquiring or retaining customers, as well as the amount and cost of services offered to them down the line. (Some services decline as the consumer becomes familiar with the offerings.)

CONSUMER BEHAVIOR APPROACH

This approach is market-research based, and it helps identify equity through consumers' attitudes and perceptions toward the brand. It recognizes that a brand delivers something more than a generic product, and it looks at equity as that *something* attached to a brand that adds value over and above the objective characteristics of a product.[7]

Instead of approaching value purely in financial terms or specifically in the form of the financial gain it delivers to the organization as a result of its price premiums, this approach focuses on the consumer and market's attitudes toward the brand. Thus, if we can understand what factors create this market attitude toward the brand, and if we can measure these elements, then we can appreciate the brand's market value.

THE INTERBRAND APPROACH

Interbrand is an acknowledged branding consulting company. Each year they publish a list of the top 100 global brands based on a set of criteria they have developed. The methodology is endorsed by *BusinessWeek* magazine, which publishes the list every year. According to Interbrand and *BusinessWeek* magazine, the methodology could be summed up as follows:[8]

- A brand must derive at least a third of its earnings from outside its home country.
- It must be recognizable beyond its base of customers.
- It must have publicly available marketing and financial data.

- The method calculates sales and determines how much of earnings are derived from the power of the brand. It then discounts future earnings against many variables, such as the brand's risk profile and ability to cross geographic and cultural borders.

Interbrand ranks only the strength of individual brand names, not portfolios of brands, (for example, Louis Vuitton and not LVMH). Those criteria eliminate private companies as well as companies such as Walmart, which sometimes operates under different brand names internationally.

Table 1.1 lists fashion and fashion-related companies (such as cosmetics) that appeared on the 2009 top 100 list.

TABLE 1.1	TOP GLOBAL FASHION BRANDS		
RANK	**COMPANY**		
16	Louis Vuitton	73	Harley Davidson
21	H&M	76	Tiffany & Co.
26	Nike	77	Cartier
41	Gucci	78	Gap
44	L'Oréal	86	Nivew
50	Zara	87	Prada
59	Chanel	88	Armani
62	Adidas	91	Lancome
68	Rolex	97	Puma
70	Hermes	98	Burberry
		99	Polo/Ralph Lauren

Source: Interbrand, "Best Global Brands 2009 Ranking,"

http://www.interbrand.com/best_global_brands.aspx?year=2009&langid=1000

Observations (on the various market value measuring approaches)

The previously mentioned variety of approaches, when aiming to measure brand equity and determine the brand's true market value, demonstrate the difficulty of the task, mostly due to the intangible dimension of branding. Yet at the same time, they highlight the importance and significance of the brand.

The other significant observation is the importance of the future impact of branding. We've seen brands that may be losing money yet still have high market values, whereas other brands are cancelled in spite of their market value simply because they lack future potential. Thus, branding, from a business perspective, is an investment that needs to warrant some future **ECONOMIC RETURNS**, which we may hypothetically call a *return on branding*.

No wonder many professionals argue that a brand's strength is more important than market share because a brand's strength has a long-term future impact. In determining a brand's value, we have also observed the importance of brand loyalty.

Brand Issues

Now that we have examined the key elements of a brand, let us put them all together and sum up our brand story (refer to Figure 1.4)

1. All products are built with a set of features and attributes referred to as the *product mix*. These features are meant to perform functions that, in return, solve problems for the user. Features are expressed in design, material, trims, and so on, which determine the functionality of the product and are designed to solve a problem or satisfy a need.

2. A product is more than just its set of features. An integral part of the product mix is what we have called *attributes*, such as price, distribution, and location (type, number, and location of stores), as well as complementary service and support.

3. These attributes and features are differentiating tools at the product level, so every product is meant to be built with a mix of features and attributes that makes it different, attractive, and competitive.

4. These features and attributes generate benefits to the user, which in return translate into values. Values based on features and functions are for the most part rational values, such as value for money, convenience, and so on. These values are a source of differentiation and can be the focus of a positioning strategy.

5. At this point, we have created a product with a unique set of features but not yet a brand. We have the following problems to solve:
   - This product has no name and no visual identity to make it easier to refer to.
   - So far the customer's relationship starts and ends with that particular product. It does not extend to any other products nor does it develop a clear mental reference to it.
   - The other issue we may face is that other competitors may quickly copy our set of features if it proves to be successful and attractive to consumers. In such a case, consumers who bought our product based solely on its features may quickly switch to any other product with any added slight advantage.

6. To overcome these issues, we will start by creating an identity for the product. First we give it a name and a visual identity (such as a face or a look) that makes it easier to refer to. However, although a name, logo, or look makes it easier to visually identify the product, it does not create any true viable incentive to purchase it and pick it over competitors.

7. What the product really needs now is a *personality* that adds an emotional meaning to the product and maybe associates it with a lifestyle that the user aspires to have. The personality is created through behavior, stories, and culture that we develop around the product. It is translated in every decision, vision, and symbol used.

What we have now accomplished through developing the identity is the following:

- We created an atmosphere of confidence for the consumer, emphasizing that what we offer is real, consistent, and fully backed up with our support.
- We established that this level of value will be carried over to any other product we produce or add to our family of products so the customer could expect the same standard of service and quality.
- We have created a story, a dream, an imaginary world to which this product belongs, and with which the user would like to be associated.
- Most important, we created a social reference or meaning to the product.

In essence, *we have created a brand*. This brand, while it delivers the values created by the product features, managed to create a new set of values. Such values might include confidence (remember what we mentioned earlier in this chapter about the promise), security, and any other emotional core values that consumers can appreciate and relate to, such as a certain level of social acceptance, a sense of personal achievement, a feeling that they are smart, sexy, beautiful, or that they belong to a certain lifestyle.

Who Is Responsible for the Brand?

If a brand is indeed a story, then who is responsible for writing this story and creating its storyline? Is it simply the manufacturer or producer of the brand?

The brand story is actually cowritten by three main partners:

- The company
- The consumer
- The culture (and external environment)

So far we have talked about the role of the company and will explore that even further in chapter 2. It is the major player and the one that will assume all the financial and marketing risks; however, it is not the only contributor in determining the brand story.

The company creates a brand for financial gain by consistently satisfying customer needs. As a matter of fact, no brand can be built without fully understanding who its customers are and what their needs may be. Customer needs and wants are shaped by many cultural, social, and economic factors. Consider pop culture and the influence of teenagers to decide what is currently considered cool in a wide range of brands. Technology is also a factor because it introduces new solutions and creates new desires. Economic downturns and

Figure 1.7

A breakdown
of the family of
LVMH brands.

(© Nicholas Felton)

A GUIDE TO THE PRINCIPAL HOLDINGS OF BERNARD ARNAULT.

Bernard Arnault
CHAIRMAN & CEO, LVMH

Groupe Arnault

HOLDS STAKES IN

- **Carrefour**
- **Cheval Blanc Vineyard**
- **Seloger.com**
  (Real Estate Site)
- **Betfair.com**
  (Gambling Website)
- **Belle International Holdings**
  (Giant Chinese Shoe Retailer)
- **Viagogo.com**
  (European Ticket Site)
- **Mongoual sa:**
  (Parisian Real Estate Firm)

OWNS

- **Go Voyages**
  (Online Travel Agency)
- **Hotel Cheval Blanc**

70% Ownership

Christian Dior SA

Dior Couture

42% Ownership

LVMH

FASHION & LEATHER GOODS

- **Donna Karan**
- **Thomas Pink**
- **Louis Vuitton**
- **Loewe**
- **Celine**
- **Berluti**
- **Kenzo**
- **Givenchy**
- **Stefanobi**
- **Fendi**
- **Eluxury.com**
- **Emilio Pucci**
- **Marc Jacobs**

WATCHES & JEWELRY

- **Tag Heuer**
- **Zenith**
- **Fred**
- **Chaumet**
- **Hublot**
- **Montres Dior**
- **De Beers**

PUBLISHING & MEDIA

- **Groupe Les Echos**
  » Les Echos
  » Serie Limitee
  » Enjeux-Les Echos
  » Investir
  » Capital Finance
  » Radio Classique
  » Connaissance Des Arts
  » Le Monde De La Musique
  » Les Editions Arlea
  » La Fugue
  » La Salon Des
    Entrepreneurs
  » Eurostaf
  » Sid Presse

WINES & SPIRITS

- **Champagnes**
  » Moët & Chandon
  » Dom Perignon
  » Veuve Cliquot Ponsardin
  » Krug
  » Mercier
  » Ruinart
  » Montaudon
- **Spirits**
  » The Glenmorangie
    Company
- Glenmorangie
- Ardbeg
  » Millenium
  » Belvedere
- Chopin
  » Hennessy
  » Wenjun
  » 10 Cane
- **Wines**
  » Chateau D'yquem
  » Estate Wines
- Domaine Chandon
  California
- Bodegas Chandon
- Domaine Chandon
  Australia
- Cloudy Bay
- Cape Mentelle
- Newton
- Terrazas De Los Andes
- Cheval Des Andes
- Numanthia Termes

PERFUMES & COSMETICS

- **Parfums Christian Dior**
- **Parfums Givenchy**
- **Parfums Kenzo**
- **Perfumes Loewe**
- **Parfums Fendi**
- **Guerlain**
- **Benefit Cosmetics**
- **Fresh**
- **Make Up For Ever**
- **Acqua Di Parma**

SELECTIVE RETAILING

- **DFS**
- **Miami Cruiseline Services**
- **Sephora & Sephora.com**
- **Le Bon Marché**
- **Samaritaine**

OTHER

- **Royal Van Lent Shipyard**
  (Netherlands
  Yacht-Making Company)

Groupe Arnault Owns a 5% Stake of LVMH, Independent of Christian Dior SA

upturns have a direct impact on consumers' decisions and priorities as well. These accumulated forces shape brands and create the environment in which they are meant to live and grow.

Types and Levels of Brands

There are different types or *levels* of brands that can be adopted, based on marketing strategies. The most common are:

- *Corporate brands:* This is a case when the company or the corporation is the brand, and the products are an extension of the company's image. The corporate brand's visual identity is placed on all of its various products (such as Nike or, beyond fashion, 3M). When the company is the brand, the customer looks for the company (and all its activities) to deliver the value, which in return becomes the company's responsibility and it is held accountable for it. This strategy makes it easier to create focused marketing activities that may also be easier to adopt globally. In addition, it creates a large umbrella for a wide range of products.
- *Independent brands:* In this approach, the company creates separate brands and promotes each individually as a separate entity (for example, LVMH; see Figure 1.7). In many cases, customers may not even know the name of the mother company. How many people know that Givenchy is now owned by LVMH? Or that Jean Patou is owned by Procter and Gamble? This strategy makes it easier for companies that made a strategic decision to target various markets and segments with different price points. This is also the strategy adopted by designer brands when they

introduce new, cheaper, ready-to-wear lines under a new brand (such as DKNY or CK).

There are some cases where both strategies co-exist, as in the case of LVMH where the organization itself has a strong presence in the market as much as the various brands under its umbrella. Apple, along with individual brands iPod & iMac, is another example outside the fashion industry.

There are many other variations to this structure:

- The case of Gap, for instance, is both an independent brand with its own line of products, as well as a corporate brand that acts as an umbrella for other independent brands such as Banana Republic and Old Navy.
- PPR owns two group branches: the luxury branch—the Gucci Group, which includes Gucci, Bottega Veneta, Yves Saint Laurent, Balenciaga, Boucheron, Sergio Rossi, Alexander McQueen, and Stella McCartney—and the sports branch, which includes PUMA.
- In the case of Giorgio Armani, all brands are actually sub-brands branching off the mother brand, where all have the name "Armani" attached: Armani Exchange, Emporio Armani, Armani Casa, Armani Jeans, Armani Junior.

In general, factors such as source of value (for example, heritage), growth strategies, and product nature work together to determine the brand-level strategies adopted.

National vs. Private Brands

In addition to the types and levels of brands, fashion brands can also be categorized based on their distribution strategy as national versus private label brands.

- *National brands:* Brands owned by a manufacturer and distributed through national store chains not owned by the company.
- *Private brands:* Brands owned and distributed through an exclusive chain of stores or boutiques (such as The Limited, Gap, J. Crew).

Categories Based on Segment

Another way to categorize brands is based on their segments or positioning strategy, such as luxury versus mass-market brands.

- *Mass-market brands:* These include Gap, Mango, Esprit, and so on. These brands offer more rational values, such as value for money and affordability, accessibility, and wider distribution with an acceptable level of quality and support. Even within this segment, brands can be categorized according to their price points such as budget, bridge, contemporary, and so on.
- *Luxury brands:* These are brands that promise a high level of quality, creativity, and exclusivity and demand a premium price in return. Luxury brands can be old brands rooted in a heritage of craftsmanship (example: Gucci) or designer brands (most American luxury brands) built on aspiration and the premise of a lifestyle. Luxury brands can offer either haute couture, ready-to-wear collections, or both (examples include Louis Vuitton, Armani, Dior, Gucci, and Neiman Marcus).
- *Premium brands:* Also known at times as the new luxury (or new luxe), premium brands are ones that borrow elements from both the luxury brand and mass-market brand categories. They are at the top of the mass-market spectrum in terms of price, yet at the same time they are more accessible than luxury brands (for instance, Victoria's Secret and Zara).
- *Private label brands:* Brands created by retailers rather than manufacturers. They are sold exclusively within their own chains, but can exist side by side with other national brands. A few examples are INC and Club Room by Macy's and Arizona and American Living by JCPenney. They are meant to compete with existing manufacturers' brands mostly on the premise of comparable quality and lower price, so they offer a better value for money. They are not usually trendsetters and are not associated with a famous designer name. In many cases, brand names are simply made up with a French or Italian sound to them to imply certain emotional values (such as Alfani by Macy's).

Most of these strategies will be discussed in more details in later chapters.

Brand Life Cycle

In marketing we learn that products have a life cycle (see Figure 1.8), but how about brands?

Brands are indeed dynamic living entities and thus should have a life cycle similar to that of a product in which they grow, expand, and contract. However, a brand's life cycle is generally longer than that of the product. Brands can outlive products. Brands that are built around one product may have a life cycle and life span that are more or less attached to that of its products. But brands that act as umbrellas to many products have the capacity to survive way after any of their products' failure or demise.

In addition, brand growth through innovation and extensions keep the brand longer in its stage of growth. A brand like Walmart most likely cannot grow any further; however, it aims to remain alive, relevant, and far from the decline stage through continuous innovation and adaptation.

Older brands, such as many of the luxury brands, tend to have a life cycle that is a series of shorter life cycles whereby the brand is expected to reinvent and revitalize itself after a certain period of decline. In essence, we observe successive cycles of relaunching the brand.

During their life span, brands face a number of challenges:

- Long life cycles can divert the brand's focus and result in a loss of interest or steam.

- Some brands become victims of their successes by turning into generics. Think of Xerox, whose name overshadowed the product and the brand, or Polyester, which, despite the fact that there are many polyesters, turned into a generic term with specific insinuations.
- Brands can lose relevance or fail to innovate. Pierre Cardin lost relevance due to overlicensing the brand, as did Burberry before its recent repositioning.
- As brands get older, they risk failing to deliver new significant differentiators.
- Long-existing brands face the challenge of maintaining their values and vision.

Figure 1.8
The product life cycle.
(Illustration by Andrea Lau)

PRODUCT LIFE CYCLE CURVE

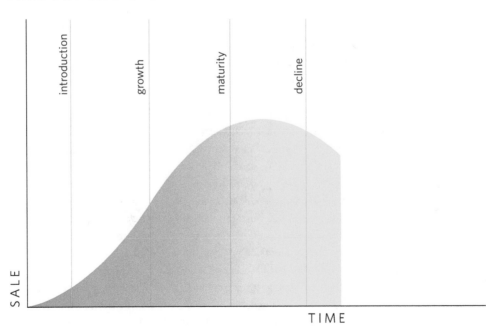

- Brands could choose the wrong methods and channels to communicate with their customers.
- External factors, such as competition or economic downturns remain to be major challenges for the brand.
- One of any brand's greatest challenges is succeeding in having the potential customer actually perceive the brand as proposed by its positioning strategy.

Brands and Ethics

The relationship between brands and ethics is of the utmost importance, given that brands and the process of creating and globalizing them have a strong social and economic impact on the lives of those who consume their products as well as those who produce them. It's a relationship that has been highly scrutinized and evaluated. It is either highly praised or strongly critiqued.

To Brand or Not to Brand?

In recent years there have been many debates on the pros and cons of brands and branding in our lives. Few scholars and activists (such as Naomi Klein) have raised arguments against *the brand*, focusing on the malpractice of many multinationals in the name of brand dominance and globalization. Child labor, poor working conditions, and sweat shops are among the issues raised as examples of labor abuse in mainly third world countries, where workers are usually mistreated and underpaid in the pursuit of brand domination and higher profits. They highlight the fact that garment workers who represent the base of the industry get the smallest share of financial benefit. The cost of labor is typically 2 to 5 percent of the retail price, so for a garment that sells for $100, less than $2 may go to the workers, if not much less (see Figure 1.9).

And it is not only labor abuse that occurs but also consumer abuse by promoting global products, shopping habits, and lifestyles that ignore domestic cultures and local sensitivities.

Nike, the Gap, Abercrombie & Fitch, and Adidas were among the many apparel and sports brands accused of producing their brand products in conditions that were described as "unethical" where workers toiled long hours in unhealthy environments, being underpaid and mistreated, in addition to numerous accusations of child labor violations that seem to be a consistent problem in developing countries where most of these products are produced. A few of the numerous examples are:

- Nike was accused in 1996 of contracting factories in places such as Vietnam that were better labeled as sweat shops. They treated their workers in a manner that was once described by a CBS television network report as both mentally and physically brutal, where workers suffered serious health problems as a result of very unhealthy and unsafe conditions due to their one goal of fulfilling their quotas.
- Adidas was accused of working with Indonesian factories that used child labor and forced them to work a minimum of 70 hours a week, while female workers in Thailand had reportedly worked 12-hour shifts, 7 days a week for a pay as low as U.S. $1.50 per day.
- In an NBC *Dateline* episode that aired in 2005, an undercover investigation showed the tough working conditions in garment factories in Bangladesh. The investigative report showed how these factories are under continuous

BRAND AND RETAILER

$75

$10 Material

$5 Factory Operations Cost

$5 Quotas/Taxes

$4.5 Purchasing or Trade Company's Profits

Including Up
to $1.75 in
Workers' Wages

$0.5 Transportation

pressures. There is often fear that the factories will lose their lucrative and sizeable American clients who could easily take their business elsewhere, if these factories do not meet their deadlines or lower production costs. As a result these factories are forced into lowering their costs and imposing on their workers low wages, unpaid overtime, long working hours, and tough working conditions. One factory owner in Bangladesh claimed that he had asked Walmart, one of his major clients, to pay one cent more per garment so he could use that increase to enhance the working conditions for his poor workers. Yet Walmart reportedly replied by asking him to lower his cost two cents instead. Walmart described the accusations as unsubstantiated and their pricing policies as fair. They also defended their tough negotiation strategies as part of their position as advocates for lower prices for their customers.

- The island of Saipan is part of the Commonwealth of the Northern Mariana Islands in the Pacific Ocean, which is a self-governing U.S. territory where tourism and garment manufacturing are the main industries. However, the reputation of the over $1 billion garment-manufacturing industry on the island has been tarnished with accusations of deplorable unsanitary working conditions, low wages without overtime pay, labor abuse, even involuntary servitude. Yet, the clothes these workers sew carry "Made in the U.S.A." labels and, of course, final consumers are ignorant of what takes place behind these labels. In recent years, anti-sweatshop movements launched a campaign of lawsuits against these conditions in a publicized manner that affected the image of reputable clothing makers such as Levi Strauss, Calvin Klein, Brooks Brothers, Abercrombie & Fitch, Talbots, Nordstrom, JCPenney, and Target, among others. Since then, many of these brands have either phased out their manufacturing contracts in Saipan (such as Levi's) or have agreed to impose further measures on local manufacturers to ensure their compliance with legal working conditions and codes of conduct through surveillance, unannounced visits (such as Nordstrom has done), as well as establishing independent monitoring in collaboration with human rights organizations.

So, why have brands? The issues raised in this section are important and worth serious attention by the industry as a whole. However, how much of this can be blamed on branding and the quest to establish global competitive brands is very debatable. Many scholars and branding professionals would highlight some important facts that support the other side of the argument, which refutes the role of branding in these issues. For example:

- By definition, a brand is meant to be born with the consumer welfare in mind, and thus the accusations of cultural insensitivities or cultural domination seem too exaggerated and contradictory.
- Many of these factory malpractice cases in developing countries, although valid, cannot solely be blamed on branding or globalization, but rather on weak local policies (or lack thereof).
- These factories create what local workers need the most, which is jobs. Garment production is among the leading industries in developing countries due to being labor intensive and not very technically sophisticated.
- Most of these so-called sweatshop factories that produce products for multinationals and global brands, in reality, pay significantly above average wages in the countries where they are located, and by putting things in perspective, these factories may be offering a more attractive option compared to many other local firms.
- Statistics show that the same developing countries where these mishaps have taken place have demonstrated a decrease in the level of poverty, an increase in standards of living, and economic growth due to increase in trade and outsourcing from these countries, including that from the garment industry.

Nevertheless, these issues remain major challenges for the apparel industry, especially in today's global environment (see Figure 1.10). And, if anything, this debate proves once again the importance and impact of brands in our lives one way or the other, while raising the issue of the relationship between brands and ethics at the same time.

Figure 1.10

The pyramid
of power, from
retailers at the
top to garment
workers at the
bottom.

(Illustration by
Andrea Lau)

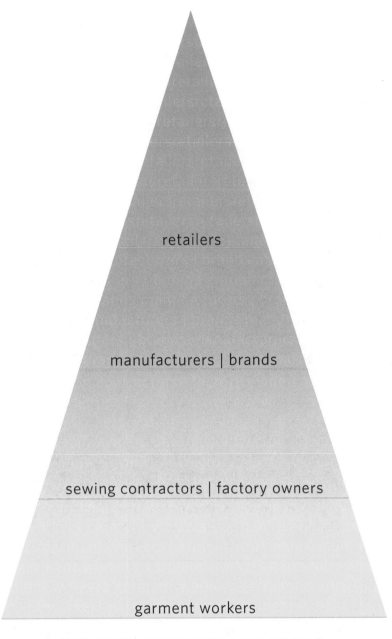

retailers

manufacturers | brands

sewing contractors | factory owners

garment workers

PYRAMID OF POWER AND PROFIT

Corporate Ethics and Social Responsibility

Like any business venture, brands need to operate ethically in order to survive and retain a long-lasting space in our lives. Brands develop an emotional relationship with their users. It's a relationship that is built on trust, support, and allegiance. Unethical practices are, in a way, a breach of this trust and brand contract. And as we have seen, this issue becomes of greater importance given the high level of global integration the apparel industry has witnessed, where clashes of cultures and business practice standards challenge global brands all the time.

ETHICS is generally defined as *the moral standards or what we perceive to be right and wrong.* Brands are dynamic entities with a strong presence in our lives and a high level of interactivity within the markets where they exist. Thus, the way they behave is critical to their image and the relationship they develop with the customer and the community as a whole.

The topic of brand ethics can be approached at two levels: corporate ethics and social responsibility. Although some tend to use both terms interchangeably, they are different in their approach, application, and line of responsibility. The primary goal of corporate ethics initiatives can be seen as prevention of *bad* actions or harm, whereas the objective of social responsibility is to do *good* and establish the organization as a good corporate citizen. Accordingly, corporate ethics strategies are generally protective and reactive in nature whereas social responsibility strategies are proactive. Ethics programs also have an internal focus and are usually reflected and expressed in published documents known as codes of ethics or codes of conduct, which aim to create a consistent reference point especially in a global working environment. On the other hand, social responsibility practices have an external community focus with a wider scope of stakeholders. Ideally, these two concepts are meant to complement each other, and they should be embedded in corporate culture and a set of values from day one.

It is essential to remember that social responsibility represents a step ahead of what we may call social responsiveness, which refers to a situation where an organization does good simply because it is a popular thing to do or because it is expected to, and not because it is inherently embedded in its values.

Most of the brands mentioned in this chapter in association with cases of manufacturing malpractices have taken serious measures to overcome any association with these practices and to reinforce that they happened behind their backs and against values they stand for as an organization and a brand. In essence they were trying to convince their stakeholders that any measure they were taking was more than just responsive; rather, it was a course of correction to realign values and actions with their established ethical standards that are rooted in their culture.

One example is Nike, who established a code of conduct that in many ways stipulated measures and conditions that surpassed acceptable local laws and standards in countries where it manufactures its products. It accepted responsibility for working with its contractors to put these measures in place, prevent such harmful working conditions, and ensure that they abide by the company's code of conduct including safety and health standards as well as unfair wages and overtime. In addition, the company initiated cultural sensitivity training programs for its supervisors. And in Pakistan, Nike took a creative approach to the problem of child labor in factories that produce soccer balls by paying to educate those children rather than letting them work. Nike thereby broadened its level of responsibility beyond merely preventing harm to promoting child education and better working conditions in the international communities in which it operates.[9]

There are many other examples and initiatives that demonstrate a sincere desire for brands and corporations to have a positive impact on the lives of their customers and communities. Here are a few more:

- Target gives back 5 percent of its income to the community through grants and sponsorship of various education and services programs.
- PPR Corporate Foundation for Women's Dignity and Rights is a foundation that "promotes women's rights and empowers women to fully contribute to the development of their communities. The Foundation will develop partnerships with local and international NGOs, award grants to social entrepreneurs, and support awareness-raising campaigns. The Foundation will also combat the economic marginalization of women by promoting their integration into the workforce and facilitating their access to micro-credit financing."[10]
- Designer Linda Loudermilk's business and design philosophy is built on the concept of luxury eco™ (a term that she trademarked). As described on her Web site, "The Linda Loudermilk brand is design with a higher purpose." One that respects our earth and delivers products that are "created by meticulously researched sustainable business practices and fair labor standards," Laudermilk attempts to blend her designs with eco-responsibility by working with scientists and researchers in developing new fibers and textiles that are environmentally friendly, have not been subject to pesticides or toxic processes, and most notably have a positive effect on the earth. She uses organic textiles that are woven from natural sources like bamboo, seaweed, and sasawashi. Among her other initiatives is donating 17 percent of the proceeds from selling pieces of accessories and garments dubbed "mission wear" to clean water initiatives around the world. She also developed The luxury eco™ stamp to be given to "the top echelon of certain products, services and business processes."[11]

Chapter Summary

- The brand is, in essence, an old concept, yet it became
  a differentiating and competing necessity in modern times
  as a result of the similarity of mass-produced products that
  flooded the markets after the Industrial Revolution.

- The brand is created on the premise of creating value for
  the consumer and financial gain for the producer.

- Whereas a brand proposes and strategizes its market positioning,
  it is the final user who determines its real position and develops
  the ultimate image.

- Whereas brands have market values, they are hard to measure.
  A brand value is about anticipated future gains.

- Brands, like products, have life cycles.

- There are three authors of the brand: culture + company + customer.

- Brands need to operate ethically in order to survive and retain
  a long-lasting space in our lives.

Chapter Questions and Issues for Discussion

1. Explain in your own words why we need brands.

2. The promise of value is an important element of any brand.
   Explain the concept and its relevance to the brand.

3. *Innovation* and *consistency* may seem to be two contradicting
   notions. What does each term mean in relevance to the brand,
   and how do these terms work together in defining it?

KEY TERMS

BRAND

CONSISTENCY

DISTINCTIVE
FEATURES

ECONOMIC
RETURN

ENTITY

EQUITY

ETHICS

IDEA

IDENTITY

IMAGE

INNOVATION

POSITIONING

PROMISE OF
VALUE

RELEVANCE

ENDNOTES

1. Clifton, Rita, et al. *Brands and Branding* (London: Bloomberg Press, 2003), 13.

2. Ibid, 15.

3. Reference Document 2005, PPR (Paris: PPR, 2006), 4.

4. Jean-Noel Kapferer, *Reinventing the Brand* (London: Kogan Page, 2001), 34.

5. Scott D. White, "Brand Equity," Ezinearticles. com. March 16, 2005. http://ezinearticles. com/?Brand-Equity&id=20703

6. Nick Werden, *Profit Brand* (London: Kogan Page, 2005), 72.

7. J.N. Kapferer, *The New Strategic Brand Management* (London: Kogan Page, 2008), 120.

8. "Picking the Winners Methodology," *BusinessWeek*, September 17, 2009. http://www.businessweek.com/magazine/content/09_39/b4148050507775.htm

9. Juliet Altham, "Business Ethics Versus Corporate Social Responsibility: Competing or Complimentary Approaches?" *International Business Ethics Review*, 4, no. 1 (2001): 2.

10. François-Henri Pinault, Editorial, PPR Corporate Foundation for Women's Dignity and Rights. http://www.ppr. com/front__sectionId-592_Changelang-en.html (accessed June 24, 2009).

11. www.lindaloudermilk.com

2

THE BRANDING PROCESS PHASE ONE:

The Brand Decision and Positioning

To avoid any confusion resulting from the use of terminologies, we shall focus our branding discussion in this chapter on the branding of products and will discuss retailing services in another relevant chapter.

A product is simply defined as *a commodity offered for sale or as a sum of features that are meant to solve a problem (and is offered for sale).* An unbranded product that possesses the needed features will serve the purpose of solving a specific problem; add a name to it, and it becomes easier to identify. However, apart from its functional capabilities, it still does not mean much to the consumer. There aren't any mental or emotional references, it does not "click," and the consumer has not yet developed an emotional interest in the product—that is left for branding to achieve.

Initially, we need to establish a few key points. The first is that a product and a brand are not the same thing and that developing a brand is different from developing a product. Second, branding has been generally approached as a marketing activity and as being the sole responsibility of the marketing department in any organization. Although it is true that there is a strong marriage between marketing and branding from the early stages of brand development, if we examine our definition of a brand from chapter 1 and step back to look at the big picture, we will realize that branding is a much larger and more inclusive process than being a function of just one department or discipline.

- **Define the branding process and develop a roadmap for creating a brand.**

- **Differentiate between the *product* and the *brand*.**

- **Appreciate the role of management and other departmental activities in the branding process.**

- **Identify the relationship between branding and the different facets of marketing.**

- **Understand the purpose of developing a positioning strategy and closely identify its components.**

The problem with the notion that branding is solely the responsibility of the marketing department is that it isolates or diminishes the role of many functions and key players from participating and contributing what would be an essential role in the branding process, especially top management. It also diminishes the importance of the brand's meaning to the organization from being the most valuable asset the organization possesses to a divisional activity. If we go back to our definition of a brand, we realize that in reality the brand is the responsibility of everyone within the organization. And given that a brand is the most important asset, it has a strategic significance and a direct link to all other activities, making it the focus of all functions and decisions. Therefore, when we look into branding as a process, we should keep in mind this strategic dimension and significance.

The third point is that not all brands are the same or exist in similar circumstances. The products to be branded are different; external environments are different; and organizational structures and strategies are different. Sometimes you will have a new product to brand, whereas in other cases you need to re-brand an existing one. Thus, there is no single branding solution or universal model for branding. However, what we will establish here is a logical framework or roadmap that will capture the

BRANDING PROCESS

38 PART ONE: UNDERSTANDING THE BRAND

essence of branding, so that even if in some cases the sequence of events may slightly differ, the concept remains intact.

So What Is Branding, Really?

We can start by defining branding as follows:

> **BRANDING** *is a multifunctional process that highlights a proposed value for a product and transforms it into a real consumer experience. Thus, we can say that a brand starts with a* concept, *that is meant to solve a problem and add a certain value to the consumer, the concept is transformed into a* product whose features aim to materialize the concept, *and the product is given an* identity that distinguishes it and reflects its values, which are communicated to the potential customer through various marketing channels. The whole process starts with a vision that identifies the need and the purpose for the brand to exist.*

The branding process is a roadmap that can be demonstrated by the diagram in Figure 2.1. According to the diagram, the branding process has the following steps:

1. The brand decision
   - The brand vision
   - The brand concept
2. The positioning strategy
   - The product mix (features + attributes)
   - The brand identity (symbols + personality)
3. The brand communication
4. The brand audit and evaluation
5. Growth or brand repositioning

In this chapter we will examine the first two steps (brand decision and positioning strategy), as they represent phase one, where the branding strategy is developed. And in the following chapter we will examine the remaining steps, as they represent phase two, where the brand is communicated and evaluated. It is important to remember that both phases together form the complete branding process.

Through this process we should be able to answer the following eight questions:

1. *The brand purpose*: *Why* does the brand need to be created now? What purpose or need does it satisfy?
2. *The brand level*: *What* type of brand is it (private vs. corporate brands)?
3. *The brand focus*: *Which* marketing segment is the brand targeting (mass-market vs. luxury)?
4. *The brand identity*: *What* is the brand's personality, name, feel, and look?
5. *The brand position*: *Where* does the brand stand in the market relative to competition?
6. *The brand scope*: *How* far reaching the brand will be (domestic vs. global and various growth options)?
7. *The brand awareness*: *How* can the brand be introduced and communicated?
8. *The brand sustainability*: *How* can the brand be evaluated, innovated, and maintained?

General Observations on This Model

The process seen in Figure 2.1 reflects a branding model that demonstrates the flaws in the common belief that branding is simply a marketing function and that you can create a brand by simply putting a name and a logo on a product. Although the marketing department might be in charge of developing and supervising the execution of the brand (usually through a dedicated team headed by a brand manager), the strategic decision and vision for the brand concept should be proposed or at least endorsed by top management. Marketing activities are essential to identify market needs through market research and data analysis, but the interpretation of data and its financial and strategic impact should be a shared responsibility by many departments. Sensing an opportunity within a market cannot be isolated from the strategic goals and mission of the organization, which in return are defined by top management. Branding is a long-term strategy that requires entrepreneurial sense and vision. That is why most brands are usually born in the minds and imaginations of top managers, entrepreneurs, or visionary designers. Finally, given its strategic impact, the branding process requires the full dedication of the organization and a multi-functional collaboration. From a disciplinary perspective, branding is clearly a multi-disciplinary function that incorporates, among other factors, marketing, management, finance, and design in one process.

Now that we have established a framework for the branding process, let us examine the model in more detail.

The Brand Decision: The Vision

Legally, a brand is born when it is given a name and is copyrighted. However, as we learned from chapter 1, a brand is more than just a name. A brand is a **VISION**, a concept, and a story coauthored by many partners. And the starting point is realizing that there is a necessity for the brand to exist and a potential for reward.

Based on our definition, a brand has two strategic goals:

1. To bring value to the consumer while satisfying a need
2. To generate economic return to its owners

Thus, the branding decision starts by recognizing that there is both an external and internal need for creating the brand. An internal need means that it is a potentially profitable endeavor for the organization that promotes its strategic goals and vision. A branding decision, therefore, cannot be made in isolation from the organization's financial and marketing goals. Answering questions such as

- *Who are we?*
- *What kind of business are we in?*
- *What are our strengths and what are we all about?*
- *What is our mission?*
- *What is our vision for the company?*

is essential to making strategic decisions that work to achieve your goals. These goals are usually laid out in the organization's mission and vision statements or interpreted through the owner's vision for the business.

Mission and Vision Statements

Generally, the mission statement mainly targets an internal audience. It directs the strategic decisions and answers the important questions of why are we in business and what kind of business are we in.

Figure 2.2

Vermont Teddy
Bear needed
to shift its
mission when
it realized
the core of its
business was
not selling
teddy bears
but bear-grams.
(Courtesy of the
Vermont Teddy Bear
Company)

Example of a Mission Statement

Nike as a brand has always identified itself as the "athlete in you" brand. This concept is reflected in every design, advertising, and decision made by the brand. Every employee understands and works toward that goal. This is clearly reflected in their mission statement:

> *To bring inspiration and innovation to every athlete in the world. If you have a body, you are an athlete.*[1]

On the other hand, the vision statement targets the outside world. It is usually concise and long-term oriented. It also presents a framework for future decisions while maintaining the flexibility to respond to future changes.

Example of a Vision Statement

DuPont is a chemical company that is a leader in supplying the fashion industry with innovative man-made fibers and protective finishes, such as Kevlar. Their vision statement reads:

> *The vision of DuPont is to be the world's most dynamic science company, creating sustainable solutions essential to a better, safer, and healthier life for people everywhere.*[2]

Identifying external market needs is not always an easy task. It is even more difficult when the product is not a mere necessity, as in the case of fashion—although clothing is necessary, fashion may not be so. After all, does the world really need a new brand of jeans? The goal of the branding process is to convince the world that it does. But it takes vision, leadership, and creativity to forsee such potential and transform the dream into a necessity that consumers want to be a part of. It

also requires good business sense and willingness to take a risk. No matter how creative the idea, it still must make business sense. As we've mentioned earlier in this chapter, understanding what the company is all about is instrumental in making the right and relevant decisions to lead the organization toward growth and success. Vermont Teddy Bear Company is in the bear-gram business (see Figure 2.2). Customers can send specially designed and crafted teddy bear telegrams that suit every social occasion as an alternative to sending flowers. However, a few unsuccessful decisions in its road to success made it reevaluate its strategies and realize that in spite of the fact that teddy bears are their main product, Vermont Teddy Bear Company is not really in the teddy bear business. It is in the bear-gram business. That it is not a toy company, but rather a direct marketing company that happens to use teddy bears as the vehicle. This revelation was essential in order to compete and achieve strategic growth. This strategic shift in focus reflected a better understanding of the company and its mission. And accordingly, every business decision and promotional activity was designed to reflect this focus and highlight it as their mission and competitive advantage.

Decision Making in the Fashion Industry

In the fashion industry, the nature of the decision-making process and the relationship between top management and the creative department varies according to the type of brand and its segment. One difference between luxury brands and mass-market brands lies in the power and role of the designers. Luxury brands live on creative superiority and trendsetting. In many cases, full control and creative authority are given to the designer. As a matter of fact, in many luxury brands, the position of brand managers does not exist. On the other hand, mass-market brands are, for the most part, trend followers. In most of these companies, design is handled by teams of young designers or product developers whose main role is to emulate fashion trends proposed by luxury brands' designers. Accordingly, mass-market brands have a more marketing approach to design and almost always have brand managers. They also tend to be created by entrepreneurs, whereas fashion trendsetting brands are commonly envisioned by designers.

Fashion brands draw a large amount of their legitimacy from their association with a talented designer or a craftsman who ends up enjoying a highly publicized star status. However, these designers at some stage need to team up with a business partner to turn the vision into a viable business venture. This marriage of skills becomes especially necessary as the business grows and starts to encounter business and market realities. It is usually this partner who possesses the necessary appreciation and sensitivity needed to balance creativity with sound business decisions. There are many examples of such level of collaborations, such as that between Tom Ford and Domenico de Sole, Valentino and Giancarlo Giammetti, Calvin Klein and Barry Schwartz, Yves Saint Laurent and Pierre Bergé, Nicole Miller and Bud Konheim, Marc Jacobs and Robert Duffy, and Giorgio Armani and Sergio Galeotti (see Figure 2.3a–b).

The turnaround in companies such as Gucci (the team of De sole and Tom Ford) and Burberry (the team of Rose Marie and Christopher Bailey) manifest the importance of a strategic vision working hand in hand with a creative power. It was not just Tom Ford's designs that rebuilt the Gucci brand, although they were the core (as all products are) around which other activities and decisions circulated; it was his designs that successfully captured and revitalized the true spirit of the Gucci brand together with the vision and managerial support he got from De Sole that led to the mobilization of the necessary resources needed to rebuild and showcase the brand.

Top management's continuous support for the brand throughout the process is essential, as the brand calls for the collaboration of various functions within the organization from allocating finances, to marketing, distribution, and product design. All forces need to collaborate within the larger organizational framework.

There is another element of top management support that is essential for the branding process, and that is the need to establish a brand culture within the organization. In reality, the brand is the responsibility of everyone within the organization. Everyone must understand it, believe in it, and support it. Managers need to become brand champions, promoting the brand internally before they do externally; managers also need to make sure that the whole organization is *living* the brand. They need to not only mobilize resources but rally employee support and understanding of the brand's purpose as well. This is achieved through what is known as internal marketing.

Branding and Marketing

As we mentioned, the relationship between branding and marketing is strong and essential. Marketing supports the development of brands in all of its stages; it plays an integral role in the creation of the emotional value through the shaping of the brand personality and then communicating it to the outside world through its various communication channels. We can categorize many of these marketing activities into internal and external activities.

Internal Marketing

The concept of **INTERNAL MARKETING** is of the utmost importance. It refers to the need to sell and market the brand's concept inside the organization before you attempt to do so to the outside world. If the brand concept is not understood and not embraced by everyone in the organization, how can they speak for it, market it, or support it? The main purpose of internal marketing is, therefore, to overcome any internal resistance to new ideas or strategies as well as make it easier to implement them. It also creates a higher level of communication and commitment toward shared goals.

The tools for internal marketing can be the use of training programs, seminars, e-mails, special events, internal newsletters, word of mouth, leading by example, or internal focus groups. It is essential that every activity within the organization supports the brand and that everyone understands it and believes in it. Everyone involved must be a brand advocate.

Figure 2.3a, b
The most successful ventures usually consist of a partnership of visionaries in design and business, such as (a) Tom Ford and Domenico de Sole and *(Getty Images)* (b) the team of Marc Jacobs and Robert Duffy. *(WireImage)*

a

b

As an example, Vermont-based Burton is a world leader in snowboarding equipment, accessories, and clothes. The Burton team of employees is like a big fun family of snowboarders. Everyone understands and relates to the sport. The company's working environment is open and friendly (employees are welcome to bring their dogs to office), but most important, everyone speaks the same brand language and, in one way or another, lives it. There is no confusion among the team about what the company is all about, what the product is, or who the customer may be.

External Marketing

EXTERNAL MARKETING refers to external interaction with the market. This interaction starts at the early stages of market research as well as the later activities aiming at marketing and selling the brand concept to the rest of the world. Known promotional activities are common in showcasing the brand and making the case for it. Market research and market analysis is meant to allow organizations to identify target markets and segment them based on many parameters, such as consumer motivations, usage patterns, geography, and demographics, among others.

External marketing also allows companies to identify a market niche that will distinguish them from their competitors. Marketing is a two-way street or a bidirectional exercise; as much as it pulls a wealth of market information inward toward the organization, it also pushes necessary information and signals from the organization to the outside, allowing it to introduce the brand to the world and facilitate its penetration into these external markets. Thus, marketing activities are essential throughout the life span of the brand,

even as companies need to redefine and reposition themselves when times change and technologies and markets develop. In all cases, an organization is better off if it is able conceptually and logistically to offer specific solutions for specific problems, to specific customers, and with specific levels of expectations. For example, retailers can decide to change the nature of their business from brick and mortar to an online operation, or a manufacturer can decide to switch from couture to ready-to-wear. In these cases, the organization will need to restate its mission statement and envision its new identity and role in the market. It is through both internal and external marketing activities that these changes can be effective.

Determining the Brand Level

We have established that there is strategic and financial significance in deciding to introduce a new brand. We have also established that such a decision has to be taken at the highest organizational level with the full support of the whole organization.

Yet the question remains: brand what? In general there are two options:

1. Brand and promote the organization itself as an umbrella under which many products are sold (e.g., NIKE). In the case of designer fashion brands, it can also be promoting the designer as the institution and the brand at the same time (e.g., Giorgio Armani).
2. Create separate brands, and promote each individually as a separate entity. This strategy makes it easier for companies that made a strategic decision to target various markets segments with different price points and different consumers to focus on brands and not on companies.

In all cases, a brand has to be built on a concept or an idea. The concept or idea needs to be fresh and unique enough to convince potential customers of its role and significance in their lives. It is true that well-orchestrated marketing campaigns play a significant role in the process; however, a brand with no substance is doomed.

The concept could be in the form of a different proposal to solving a problem: a new use of fabrics, a new distribution system (the Internet rings a bell?), a new interpretation or marriage of styles, and so on. In high fashion where brands are mainly trendsetters, the unique creative style of its head designer is a fresh proposal in its own right. However, it takes more than creativity or a design concept to be marketable and have branding potential. Isaac Mizrahi was heralded in his early days as a creative genius; however, his business never increased—his brand did not flourish because it did not "click" with consumers or make marketing sense at that time. For concepts to work for an organization, they must always be in sync with the mission statement of the business and remain relevant to customers. This is also one of the reasons why Mizrahi was very successful later with his work for Target.

We decided in chapter 1 that the brand concept is determined and co-penned by three major partners: the company, the customer, and culture.

The Company

Although we have agreed that the company is not the sole author of the brand, it remains the sole *legal* owner of the brand and all its copyrightable elements such as the name, logo, or technology. The company is also the brand's major investor and financial backer (through its owners and shareholders). Accordingly, it is also the major risk taker from a financial, marketing, and social perspective.

The Customer*

The customer plays an important role in the shaping of the brand throughout the branding process:

- The brand is meant to address a user's need. Thus, every brand is built with a target customer or group of customers in mind. Marketing principles have established various segmentation criteria, such as demographic (age, income, gender, and so on), geographic, psychographic, lifestyle, usage habits, and so on, as the basis of choosing and targeting markets and potential users. Bases of segmentation may differ based on the product type (such as women's wear, children's wear, activewear) and brand category (luxury vs. mass market). In all cases, it is about targeting and satisfying unmet customer needs, whether these needs are functional or emotional (such as status).

- We have also established that it is the customer who actually ends up determining the brand's true market positioning. Brands propose a position and design a strategy to achieve that position, hoping the users will see the brand in a way the company intended. However, how the end user understands and interprets that message and actually sees the brand can be totally different.

---

* In branding we prefer to use the term "customer," rather than "consumer" because although you may consume a product you actually experience a brand.

Figure 2.4

An illustration
of common
patterns by
which different
groups of con-
sumers adopt
new trends.

(Illustration by

Andrea Lau)

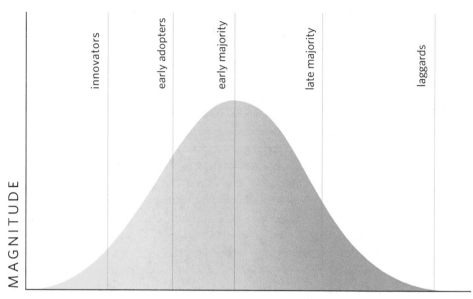

CONSUMER ADOPTION PATTERN

innovators | early adopters | early majority | late majority | laggards

MAGNITUDE

TIME

- The manner in which the user sees the brand and the image he or she mentally creates are subject to many influences, such as their experiences with the brand and its competitors, as well as other accumulated cultural, social, and economic influences.
- A customer's verdict on the brand is also a major catalyst in the evolution of the brand. User behavior and response toward the brand determines whether the brand is ready for growth, re-branding, or demise.

Product consumers differ in their backgrounds, habits, and the pattern by which they adopt a brand. Figure 2.4 shows the different customer adoption patterns.

The consumer adoption curve demonstrates that consumers' adoption patterns for products differ in size and timing. Whereas innovators such as the celebrities, socialites, and fashionistas are eager to buy new trends off the runway and are willing to pay a premium price to be among the leaders and the trendsetters, the "late majority" or "laggards" adopt a trend at its decline stage when it becomes available at discount retailers at cheaper prices.

How Buyers Make Purchase Decisions
Understanding how buyers make purchase decisions is an essential step in the branding process. After all, the brand is meant to create value for

a group of targeted customers, and it is through their support and adoption that the organization achieves its planned financial returns.

The diagram in Figure 2.5 demonstrates the following basic steps of a purchase decision.

1. *Problem recognition.* This is the stage where a person perceives that he or she has an unfulfilled need. A need is generally understood as *the difference between where you want to be and where you actually are.* This gap represents your need. Needs can be actual or perceived, functional or emotional, and in all cases they are the main focus for branding and marketing activities. Marketing is not designed to *create* needs but to *respond* to them. What marketing can do is activate this need, alert you to its urgency, and then direct you to where you can find the solution.

2. *Information search.* After people realize the need, they start to search for the best options and solution to fulfill it. The source of information can be either internal or external.
   - *Internal* Internal sources refer to the person's own experiences with different products and brands relevant to that need. It is an effective, cheap, and less risky source of information.
   - *External:* External sources of information can be friends and family, consumer reports, or promotional sources, such as advertising, publications, and salespeople.

3. *Alternative evaluation:.* With various options to choose from, individuals start to evaluate the alternatives based on the nature of the need and their own priorities. Decisions can be made based on rational, objective criteria (such as functionality) or emotional, subjective ones (such as status or prestige).

4. *Purchase decision:* The decision based on evaluation of alternatives can be to buy or not to buy. If a brand is better positioned to satisfy the need, the buyer may decide to make the purchase. The decision involves making a series of choices, such as where and when to buy. Strong positioning and marketing should make these decisions easier to make.

5. *Postpurchase behavior:* It is always essential from a marketing point of view to understand that the relationship with the buyer does not end when the actual purchase is made. The same is obviously true from a branding perspective. It is at this stage that the buyer actually experiences the brand and develops a verdict based on his or her level of satisfaction

PURCHASE DECISION PROCESS

Perception of need or problem	Information research: Seeking value	Identify and evaluate alternatives versus needs	Purchase	Post-purchase evaluation

and the level of success the brand has achieved in meeting its promises. This is when the user forms an opinion and creates an *image*. The ultimate goal is that the buyer will have a positive experience, that the image he or she creates coincides with the proposed positioning strategy and promise of value, and that eventually the buyer will decide to repeat the purchase. To facilitate this, marketing responded by introducing what has been known as "relationship marketing." Relationship marketing, as the name implies, aims at building a strong and long-term relationship with the buyer postpurchase. It involves after-purchase services such as follow-ups, warranties, reward programs, and so on.

Culture and External Influences

Social and cultural changes are instrumental in shaping the needs and aspirations of every generation. The aging of the baby boomers and the rise of generations X, Y, and recently Z (also known as the Google generation) reflects the ever-changing social scene and structure. Consumers' purchasing habits and decisions are defined by the social forces and cultural influences around them. One clothing retailer once said "teenage shoppers today run in packs. If you sell to one, you sell to everyone in their class and everyone in their school." In addition, with the existence of the largest-ever teenage population in the United States in an environment of the Internet and digital revolution, it is inevitable that such a consumer group will have different aspirations and significant influences. **COOL HUNTING** is a marketing research practice concerned with identifying what is perceived to be currently "cool" among

teenagers. The practice aims at spotting potential trends that emerge among teenagers and identifying their marketing potential. This information is essential in helping organizations develop the right products and brands that target such an important and hard-to-predict segment. Cultural influences and interests, such as music, Internet activities, video gaming, and so on, are all signals of what may be cool, which is especially relevant to this important segment.

The rising interest in the Internet's social networks, such as Facebook and Twitter, or the indispensable cell phones, have all reshaped social habits and cultural interests. The impact on marketing and branding, as will be discussed in more details later, is clear and strong. They reshape how marketers can now reach and talk to consumers, how brands are defined, and how consumers interpret and respond to marketing activities. Thus, not only have purchasing habits changed, but the decision-making process has evolved as well. Consumers are more informed, empowered, and in control. Consumers "hijacked" the brands and in many ways took over the marketing process through *viral marketing* practices, such as sharing views and comments on YouTube, Twitter, or the blogosphere. It is a totally new environment and ball game where the rules have changed, and unless brands understand and adopt them, they will lose.

The Positioning Strategy

Think of **POSITIONING** as the *case for the brand*. Positioning is a process, and, according to marketing scholar J. N. Kapferer, the positioning process can be summarized in the following four questions:

1. *What:* What is the benefit and purpose of the brand? The brand promise and value to the consumer need to be clearly identified.
2. *Who:* Who is the target, the potential customer?
3. *Reason:* What are the differentiators that support and can create such a benefit?
4. *Against whom:* Who is the competition?

Needless to say, *positioning* and *position* refer to two different things. *Positioning* is a process and a strategy, which may or may not succeed, whereas the *position* is the actual mental slot where the consumer places the brand relevant to others, based on all the factors we mentioned earlier. Position is translated into a mental image the consumer creates for the brand. The distinction between the two is important because how the company hopes and plans to position the brand may be totally different from how the consumer actually does position the brand.

Positioning is for the most part product driven. The product mix is at the core of any branding strategy. However, we have already learned that brands can be positioned at two levels: its product component level, highlighting its competitive features or attributes; and the brand level, mainly through the personality component of its identity. In reality, both work well together and complement each other. A product mix is the physical manifestation of the identity, whereas the personality reflects all that is proposed and offered by the mix, bringing it to life and transforming it into an experience.

In all cases, any positioning strategy must have a clear focus. No brand can be everything for everyone. And because positioning is built on differentiation, these differences need to be relevant and meaningful to the customer, or positioning will be ineffective.

The Product Mix: Product, Price, Service, and Distribution

A brand idea has been chosen. It is now time to transform the idea into a brand-ready and saleable product. The product is the core of the brand. Brands are not created in a vacuum; they are built around a product (or a service). The product constitutes its physical, tangible, and functional component and features. However, it is not wise when dealing with and analyzing a product to isolate it from its three major attributes: *price, location (or distribution), and service.* Together with the product features, we have our product mix. The product mix concept recognizes that when a person buys a product, even if unbranded, the decision and experience is not isolated from its price, where it is sold, and the service (if any) that comes with it. At the same level, decisions about the attributes are directly linked to design decisions. Fashion products can be categorized based on features like design or attributes, such as price and distribution. The same collection, for instance, can be categorized as "sportswear" based on its design level or as "bridge" based on its price.

The Product

The product's designer or design team has the job of creating a product that captures the spirit of the brand, translates the concept in a way that makes sense to the consumer, and satisfies a need. Thus, at this stage, many decisions are to be made in terms of the features and product segment. A fashion product is built on many elements of design and features, such as silhouette (including length and shape), fabrication, color, and trims. All of these elements have aesthetic as well as functional purposes.

Fashion products differ according to their categories or segments. Examples of common categories are menswear, womenswear, misses, childrenswear (toddler, teens, and so on). In addition, there are special categories like plus size, bridal, maternity, uniforms, and more.

There are different segments within the fashion industry, but most would fall under the umbrellas of luxury and mass-market.

LUXURY PRODUCTS

The trendsetters, these luxury products are characterized by a high level of creativity, craftsmanship, quality, and service, in return for a premium price. These groups of products can be either haute couture or ready-to-wear.

Haute Couture

Translated to English as "high fashion," this is the embodiment of fashion luxury. There are certain criteria for fashion houses to be considered haute couture, such as:

- Design made-to-order garments for private clients, with one or more fittings.
- Have a workshop (atelier) in Paris that employs at least 15 people full time.
- Present a collection each season (that is, twice a year) to the Paris press, composed of at least 35 outfits for both day wear and evening wear.
- Be a member of the Chambre Syndicale de la Haute Couture.

Haute couture is also characterized by its high level of handwork, exquisite craftsmanship, and creativity (see Figure 2.6). Today there are only a couple hundred true haute couture clients, so most of these houses have shifted their focus to producing ready-to-wear (or prêt-a-porter) collections.

Ready-to-Wear (RTW)

As the name implies, these are garments that come in standardized sizes and are bought off the rack in retail shops rather than in couture salons, although usually through a controlled distribution network in exclusive chains of stores. Luxury RTW is factory produced for the most part, as opposed to the workshop-produced products of the past (see Figure 2.7). They are still considered luxury and expensive, although priced lower than haute couture. With the contraction of the haute couture market and decrease in number of its clientele, most designer houses (such as Chanel, Dior, and so on) have introduced RTW lines. Although they may still do couture, this mainly serves marketing and publicity purposes by creating the media buzz needed to place a brand in the spotlight and promote its other lines, such as cosmetics, RTW, and accessories.

MASS-MARKET

These are the trend followers. They follow the footsteps of luxury brands and are meant to sell to a larger market at a more moderate price. However, even within this category there are many subcategories that widely range in their price points:

- *Budget:* lowest price and quality (for example, Wrangler).
- *Moderately priced:* Priced slightly higher than budget, but with more attention given to

Figure 2.6

Designer
Christian Lacroix
on the Paris
runway with a
model in one
of his designs
demonstrating
haute couture's
handwork.

(AFP/Getty Images)

syling and quality (for example, the Gap is a moderately priced brand, priced above budget brands such as Wrangler, but below better market brands such as Banana Republic).

- *Better market:* priced higher than moderate, but lower than bridge (for example, Tommy Hilfiger is a better market brand, just above the moderately priced level, such as Gap. See Figure 2.8).
- *Bridge:* Just above the better market, one notch under designer RTW in terms of style and price. These are the most stylish of the non-luxury brands. Some fashion designers have decided to create bridge lines that represent a more marketable and accessible option to address and attract a newer and larger group of customers (for example, DKNY by Donna Karan—its comparatively attractive price point can bring in more customers than its signature luxury line, Donna Karan).
- *Premium:* At the top of the mass-market spectrum in terms of price, quality, and taste, and borrows elements from luxury brands without being true luxury. Examples include Zara, Coach, Victoria's Secret, and most of the RTW designer brands. The category emerged as a result of many economic and social changes seen in the past years that were responsible for the rise of a new wealthy group of customers that emerged from the middle class looking to live a better life and adopt a higher-end lifestyle (see Figure 2.10).

PRIVATE LABELS

Private labels are brands produced not by manu-facturers, but rather by retailers. The term covers brands produced by retailers and sold in their

Figure 2.7

Haute couture
designers often
present a ready-
to-wear line
as well. Here,
a runway look
from Dior's
Spring/Summer
2010 collection.

*(Getty Images/Karl
Prouse/Catwalking)*

stores alongside other manufacturers' brands, such as Alfani and INC produced and sold by Macy's. It also covers brands sold solely through their own chain of independent specialty stores, such as the Gap or Victoria's Secret. Private labels have grown tremendously in recent decades and evolved from being a low-quality, low-priced alternative for manufacturers' brands to a very competitive alternative with comparable and sometimes superior quality. Private labels may have created some tensions among retailers and manufacturers, but they are regarded by retailers as an important tool to differentiate among other competitors and stand out in a sea of retail sameness and boredom. Although profitable due to their higher margins, private labels are limited in distribution. They may also impact sales of other brands available in the store and thus affect overall revenues. Examples of other store private labels are Macy's' Club Room and Style & Co. and JCPenney's Arizona (see Figure 2.11).

THE NATURE OF THE FASHION PRODUCT

The fashion product is a seasonal product. An interesting and challenging aspect of the fashion product is the speed and frequency by which it needs to be updated or even replaced. Like any other products, fashion products have a life span. These life spans differ from one product to the other, and in the apparel industry, the more "fashionable" the item, the shorter its life span.

FASHION COLLECTIONS, LINES, AND SEASON

Fashion products are produced in lines and collections. A collection is a group of different but coherent items that are meant to have a specific mood and image. Collections are more common with fashionable, trendy lifestyle brands because they are meant to tell a story and emphasize a vision or a concept that can be built around a style, a color theme, or fabrication. One mistake made by many young designers is failing to understand the concept of the collection and ending up offering a mishmash of unrelated styles and ideas on the runway.

On the other hand, a product line can focus on one fashion item produced with variations in colors and sizes, such as a line of jeans or shirts. Thus, fashion lines are built on separates rather than on coordinates. A company can produce a group of lines such as a line of pants and a line of shirts that can be mixed and matched. They might create themes with specific color palettes and fabrication story and, in a way, create sub-collections within their lines. This approach allows them to target specific consumer groups (for example, professional women) by offering

them options and ideas that fit a certain need, look, or lifestyle and fall within a specific price range. The number of lines and the range of items produced are highly dictated by the type of the product and production requirements, such as lead time, sourcing, and seasonality.

The number of lines produced follows the number of seasons the company adopts. Traditionally, the two major fashion seasons are Spring/Summer and Fall/Winter, for which major fashion houses produce and show their new collections. However, many companies produce as many as six lines a year. The number of seasons obviously depends on the category produced; whereas high fashion is usually offered twice a

Figure 2.10
Coach is an example of a premium brand, the top of the mass-market segment.
(© Richard Levine / Alamy)

year, women's and men's sportswear lines have additional seasons. Table 2.1 demonstrates examples of different fashion seasons.

The number of seasons seen in Table 2.1 demonstrates how the production cycle for apparel is back to back and almost nonstop. With most production taking place overseas, crucial issues such as quality control and sourcing as well as lead times and delivery deadlines become especially challenging.

Price

Price is an integral tool in positioning a brand. In general, one of the advantages and purposes of branding is demanding a premium price as compared to nonbranded products. This does not mean that all brands are expensive; mass market and discount store brands are not, but compared to nonbranded products they have the capacity, and *supposedly* the legitimacy, to ask for higher prices.

Choosing the right pricing is a major strategic decision that could make or break the brand. If the price is set too high, it will alienate potential customers and shift the brand to a segment where it does not really belong. On the other hand, a price set too low may raise suspicion about the quality

and credibility of its products and still alienate potential customers. Thus, it is essential to choose the right price and the right strategy.

In general, price is calculated by determining your cost and adding a reasonable markup (MU) that is big enough to cover your costs and generate profit.

$$Price = Cost + MU$$

Deciding on the right MU in itself is a function of many aspects, such as cost (direct and indirect), competition, market conditions, and your positioning strategy. For instance, would you want the brand to be perceived as the cheapest option in a certain segment? When Burberry embarked on revamping and repositioning the brand, the goal was to introduce Burberry as a luxury brand that is aspirational but functional and at a lower price range than other lifestyle brands such as Gucci and Prada.

The perceived value plays an important role in determining the price as well. For mass-market brands where value for most of them is the driving force behind buying the brand, prices are set with a ceiling they cannot surpass. Thus, if MU levels are not met, lowering costs is usually the main course of action. Luxury brands, on the other hand, are highly sold on the merits of their emotional values and exclusivity, permitting the assignment of significant premium prices.

Price is a critical decision because it directly determines income. Therefore, choosing the right price is essential to ensuring that it generates enough income or revenue to keep the brand afloat. This is not always easy given the high costs of creating and maintaining brands. In fact, choosing the right or wrong pricing strategy can make or break the brand.

PRICE STRATEGIES

Price is an integral component of the product mix. As the product goes through various stages in its life span, it may be deemed necessary to adopt various pricing strategies in relation to its segment and stage of growth (whether it is in a launch, growth, or repositioning stage). Pricing strategies differ in their focus. Some brands may aim to increase market share by lowering prices and profit margin per item in return for volume. Other policies may focus on combating competition, while still others adopt a premium price to maintain a certain image.

Examples of pricing strategies are:

- *Price skimming:* Introducing the product at a premium price (skimming profits). This strategy is common with new, innovative, and exclusive products, Customers known as "the innovators" are always willing to pay the premium price in order to be the first to try something new and exclusive. The demand at that price point should be high enough to cover initial production costs

in the short period of time before competitors can enter the market and force prices to fall (for example, True Religion jeans).

- *Price penetration:* This policy is opposite of the skimming approach, whereby a product is introduced at an attractive low price to achieve a faster market penetration and gain market share. This policy is more common with budget mass-market products. A variation of this strategy is the "market trial" strategy, whereby products are introduced at a trial low price with the intention of increasing it as consumer awareness increases and customers get hooked (for example, Walmart).
- *Everyday value pricing:* As the name implies, this is a strategy that focuses on the concept of value for money, where prices emphasize the amount and value a customer gets for his or her dollar (examples include Walmart and JCPenney).

While adopting these strategies, companies can adopt various pricing policies:

- *Price lining:* Pricing all items the same (for example, One Dollar Stores).
- *Price zoning:* Creates a price floor and ceiling (for example, minimum and maximum).

TABLE 2.1 | **FASHION SEASONS**

SEASONS	DATES IN MARKET	DELIVERY TO WAREHOUSE
Spring	October	Late December – Early March
Summer	January	March – April
Transition	January/February	June – July
Fall (Winter)	March	July – October
Holiday	August	October – November
Cruise/Resort	August	November – December

they should be regarded as an integral part of the product mix. The level and type of support obviously differs by brand segments. When customers purchase a branded product at a particular price range from a specific location, they expect a level of service that reflects these elements. Not surprisingly, services offered by (and expected from) a luxury brand are at a much higher level than those provided by a mass-market one. However, in all cases, good marketing practices recommend that the relationship between the brand provider and the customer continues after the customer purchases the product, no matter what branding segment it belongs to.

Branding is a long-term relationship. It is about building confidence, consistency, and, above all, establishing loyalty. The goal is not just to sell (more of a salesman mentality) but to sell again and again (a branding mentality).

None of the above is attainable without a certain level of ongoing service and support. In marketing, this is sometimes referred to as *relationship marketing*, which basically aims at establishing long-term relationships with customers through a series of activities and initiatives to maintain and appease customers while securing their loyalty.

- *Odd pricing:* Uses non-round, uneven amounts for their psychological effect (for example, $1.99). See Figure 2.12.
- *Markdowns and promotions:* Offers special and promotional pricing (such as sales, clearances, "buy one get one free").

Service and Support

Support refers to the auxiliary services offered by the brand before, during, and after the purchase. They include customer service, after-purchase service, alterations, return policies, warranties, loyalty clubs, and so forth. These services are fundamental and equally important to the customer's perception of the brand; in fact, they are part of what you pay for with your purchase, so

Distribution

Deciding on the distribution channels of the brand's products and where they will be sold is another important strategy to establish.

There are basically three levels of distribution:

1. *Exclusive distribution:* This form of distribution can be either through stores owned by the brand's manufacturers or through an exclusive distribution agreement

Figure 2.13

This flyer for a DKNY and Fetty product exemplifies co-branding through exclusive distribution.

(Courtesy of Alter/ Tommy Cole designer)

with a specialty retailer. This approach has a strong impact on the brand's exclusive image as demonstrated by the case of luxury brands. It allows the brand to distance itself from competitors, and in the case of stand-alone stores owned by the brand, to display its full range of products and lines exactly in the manner and atmosphere it is envisioned (see Figure 2.13).

2. *Limited distribution:* As the name implies, this approach allows the brand to be sold in one or more stores, chain of stores, or selective department stores that suit its targeted positioning strategy and image. There is still a high level of control and selective distribution, but this approach is more relaxed than the totally exclusive option.

3. *Mass distribution:* Distribution is available to almost any retailer willing to carry the products. These are usually budget products that generate profit through high sales volume.

Within each of the these levels are many options for distribution channels and store types

that vary in their ownership level and business model. From traditional brick-and-mortar stores to e-tailing on the Internet, the options are truly variable.

CHICO'S PASSPORT PROGRAM

Chico's loyalty program, known as the "Preliminary Passport" program, is free and offers its members the following benefits:

- Be the first to know about newest collections, sales, and offers
- Preview new collections via e-mail

Passport (with merchandise of $500 or more) benefits may include:

- 5% off every merchandise purchase
- Birthday bonuses
- Double discount days
- Invitations to special parties and events
- Private sales

- *Self-owned stores:* This model of ownership refers to stores that are fully owned and managed by the brand producer as opposed to being franchised. They could range in size, from boutiques to bigger flagship stores, and could be one or more stores. Although they tend to be specialty stores, their business model (for example, type and range of merchandise) could vary as well (one or more—can be boutiques and flagship stores).
- *Specialty stores:* Specialty stores are retailers that focus on one category of products, such as men's sportswear, women's lingerie, and so on. Although these stores carry a narrow range, it is usually deep in assortment of color and size. Specialty stores can be independent stand-alone stores or a chain of stores. In all cases, they tend to be trendier and fashion oriented, carrying designer brands and exclusive lines (examples include Ann Taylor, Banana Republic, and Talbots). See Figure 2.14.

Another example of these stores is *boutiques*, which are usually smaller stores with niche market clientele, carrying trendy and avant-garde merchandise. The trendy and exclusive image associated with boutiques has paved the way to the creation of in-store boutiques in department stores that feature designer brands. It is, in a way, a store within a store, as adopted by Ralph Lauren or Tommy Bahama, among others (see Figure 2.15).

- *Category killers:* This is another form of specialty store that offers the largest range of products in a specific category and at competitive prices.
- *Department stores:* Technically a *department store* is a retailer that sells both soft goods (apparel) and hard goods (appliances and furniture). Thus, whereas Macy's is a department store, Neiman Marcus should be classified as a specialty store. However, there has been a tendency to refer to any large store with many departments and large number of employees as a department store, so Neiman Marcus can be referred to as a specialty department store. Many department stores are chain stores. They all offer a wide range of products but can differ in their market focus; for example, JCPenney and Sears are known for their moderate prices.

Department stores have played a major role in the American retailing scene since the late nineteenth century. In the 1980s, a major wave of mergers and consolidation took place that enabled Federated (Macy's owner at the time) to acquire some of the nation's prominent department stores, such as Marshall Fields and Rich's, among many others. Today Federated is known as Macy's Inc., and it operates Macy's and Bloomingdale's. Recently, there has been a lot of cynicism about the future of department stores in the face of specialty stores, especially those opened by manufacturers of designer brands to showcase their full collection range in

Figure 2.14

Talbots is a specialty retailer chain offering its own exclusive line.

(© 2010 Fairchild Fashion Group)

Figure 2.15

Ralph Lauren's
flagship New
York store pro-
vides customers
with the full
experience of
the brand.

(© Catherine Karnow/
CORBIS)

an environment and atmosphere that allows customers to fully experience the brand as intended,
for example, the Ralph Lauren store located in
a historic mansion on Madison Avenue in New
York. (See Figure 2.15.)

- *Discount stores:* These are stores that sell known
  brands at discounted below-market prices.
  These no-frills stores offer minimal services
  and in-store experiences in return for cutting
  costs and passing these saving to customers.
  They adopt a low margin/high volume policy.
  Discount stores come in different forms:

- Off-price discounters, such as Ross and
  Marshalls (see Figure 2.16)
- Factory outlet
- Membership clubs such as Sam's and Costco

- *Mass merchants and hyper-stores:* The major
  distinction between these stores and other
  department stores is that in addition to a mix of
  hard and soft merchandise, they sell groceries
  as well. They are also value oriented with a
  wide range of inexpensive products, centralized
  checkout points, and self service.

- *E-tailing:* The Internet or "click-and-shop"
  model has introduced online retailing, or
  e-tailing, through a virtual store environment.
  Many retailers have established Web sites
  with shopping capabilities in addition to their
  traditional brick-and-mortar stores, whereas
  others have decided to switch totally to the
  electronic format. Online shopping offers a lot
  of opportunities for the manufacturer and buyer.
  It is available 24/7, can be easily and quickly
  updated, and offers a wealth of information.
  However, there have been many challenges with

Figure 2.16

Inside Marshalls,
where customers
search the
racks for great
bargains.

(© Jeff Greenberg/
Alamy)

Today's Special
081·588
NFL
Faux Leather
Colorblock
Jacket by G-III
Retail Value
$75.00
HSN Price
$64.95
Today's Special
$49.95
S&H $7.21
2 flex $24.98
800·284·3100
hsn.com
NFL 2pk of Bolster Pillows 332-275
30 day money back guarantee   7108 sold   2:50

Figure 2.17

Television
shopping net-
works such as
HSN and QVC
are available in
many markets
(© Jeff Greenberg/
Alamy)

online shopping, such as security concerns and the inability to touch, feel, and try the product, which is a major hurdle for apparel brands. Retailers try to offer solutions to these concerns through free, fast shipping and return policies to allow for product trial, as well as adopting sophisticated encryption technology and privacy policies to minimize security concerns. In fashion, many shoppers express more comfort shopping online for products that they know or have already seen and experienced earlier in a store.

- *Catalogs:* Selling through printed catalogs has proven to be a major business. It is estimated that almost 20 billion catalogs were mailed in the United States in 2006. Some catalogs are independent (such as L.L. Bean), whereas others belong to retailers (like Sears). Catalogs are convenient and offer a full range of products and occasional exclusive items. There has been some cynicism about the future of catalogs as well with the inception of the Internet, which happens to be more accessible and easy to update on daily basis. However, the 20 billion catalogs that were mailed in the United States show that catalogs have managed to co-exist and even benefit from the Internet as a complementary alternative for placing orders. These companies managed to successfully exist

on- and offline due to their already-established distribution infrastructure, which happens to be essential for the success of online retailing.

- *TV shopping:* The power of television shopping shouldn't be underestimated: massive audiences nationwide can purchase featured products without ever leaving their homes. Home shopping networks (such as ShopNBC and QVC) and infomercials are attractive options to many consumers. TV shopping allows for better product demonstration and also runs all day long. Today with interactive TV, the experience promises to be more engaging and exciting (see Figure 2.17).

Identity

Brand **IDENTITY** can be simply described as the "meaning of the brand." In our discussion in chapter 1, we delved deeper into the term and realized that a brand's ultimate identity is a result of its personality expressed in a set of visual attributes. We also realized that an identity contributes to the positioning strategy. Identity is also affected by the image established by the user for the brand, which is an aspect the brand cannot directly control. The image is a mental perception of how the buyer sees and understands the brand's identity and value. It is a function of many external factors, such as competitors and all other circumstances in which the buyer encountered the brand. An image can distort an identity or emphasize it.

The mix of visual and physical attributes represent graphic, visual, audio, and verbal identities, or **SYMBOLS,** that are meant to communicate the personality and soul of the brand and aim to trigger specific mental associations and signals. They may take various forms, such as a name, logo, color, and packing design. A strong visual identity, therefore:

- Makes it easier to visually identify a brand in a market full of competitors
- Makes it easier to recall a brand from memory
- Makes it easier for consumers to buy a product
- Makes it easier for sales personnel to sell a brand

Identity Symbols

As discussed in Chapter 1, a brand can be physically and mentally identified through an item or product that stands out as a symbol of the brand—an identity symbol. Identity symbols include names, logos, typeface and typography, color, packing, and personality.

NAMES

Because the brand name is the first point of contact between the consumer and the brand, it is a very important choice to be made by the brand's producers. Names do not need to be direct (contrary to popular belief) and unimaginative, but they need to be memorable and play a role in evoking all the intended associations that make up the brand. Successful branding transforms a name into a trigger by which consumers can recall a brand identity and mentally decipher a brand's connotations and personality from memory.

An important point to emphasize here is that although names are important to any brand, they do not *make* the brand. As we mentioned in Chapter 1, it is a common mistake for people to define a brand as simply a name or a logo given to a product. By now we should understand that this is far from the reality. A name alone does not tell us much about a brand, unless it is backed by a clear personality and meaning.

There are many ways to approach choosing a suitable name for the brand. Sometimes it happens by accident—the classic Kelly bag by Hermès was so named because it was carried by Grace Kelly. In the past, names were assigned or picked simply as an identifier, without any intended meaning. However, as the branding concept evolved, the significance of name choice became more apparent. In most cases, it requires some market research to determine the level of uniqueness, ingenuity, and suitability of the name. It is not uncommon for companies to hire consultants and pay lots of money to find a name that is appropriate and can be legally protected.

Criteria for an effective name can be:
- Easy to remember.
- Easy to pronounce. This issue is even more important in the case of global distribution (for example, the letter R and L are sometimes indistinguishable in Japanese).
- Appropriately significant. If it is not a person's or place's name, then it is important to choose a name that does not have any negative connotations. Again, this is significant for global distribution. The famous examples of the Chevrolet Nova (means "does not go" in Spanish) and Toyota MR2 (reads as a curse word in French if M-R-2 are pronounced in sequence) are good reminders of that.
- Anticipating potential growth. Designer names (real or made up) or initials allow for that, whereas specific names such as "American Apparel" or "Style.com" may limit any possible future branching into other business segments if needed. (Style.com will have a harder time branching into books or electronics than Amazon had with apparel and accessories, and it might be harder for American Apparel to diversify into home furnishings than it is for INC, for instance.)

- Works well with various media options such as prints, TV, and billboards.
- Available to be trademarked and legally protected.

Choosing a name is a long-term decision because names do not change as often as logos may. Thus, choosing a name has to be a balance between what it means to the brand both now and in the long term. A name that is chosen to reflect a present event or fad, for example, may not make much sense in the future as it does at the moment it was chosen.

Names can be:

- Descriptive (such as Oil of Olay or Nautica)
- A total invention (such as Boo.com or BeBe)
- Something that evokes certain emotions (Champagne Perfume) or mental associations (Payless Shoes)

In fashion there are different strategies that can be adopted for choosing a brand's name. For example:

- *A designer or founder name:* Choosing the designer's name to put on the label is probably the most common strategy, especially for luxury brands. This tradition is rooted in older days of craftsmanship. It's an effective option to differentiate a brand and identify it with a creative genius. Names can be combined (such as Dolce & Gabbana and Baume & Mercier) or initialized (such as YSL and DKNY).
- *A fake designer name:* This is more common with mass-market and private label brands that seek to give the illusion of a master designer behind the brand, when in most cases these brands are actually designed by a team of young designers who are virtually unknown to outsiders (such as Alfani by Macy's private

label and Massimo Dutti by Inditex). Even in the luxury segment, fake names can be used to imply specific connotations or heritage (such as Comme des Garçons by Japanese designer Rei Kawakubo, aiming to link the brand with French chic).

- *A descriptive name that is not a person's name:* This is more common in nonluxury, mass-marketed brands (such as American Apparel or Nautica). There was a time when descriptive names were seen as the best approach to brand naming because they minimize any possible confusion about what the brand is selling. However, as mentioned earlier in this chapter, one major disadvantage of this naming strategy is its limitations to diversification options.
- *An acronym or abbreviation:* These include names such as INC or DKNY. Some of these eventually transform into words themselves.

Figure 2.18

Logos can be initials, designers' names, or indicative of a particular lifestyle.

- *A meaningless, made-up name:* These include names such as Boo and XOXO. The advantage of these names is that they can be fun, catchy, easy to remember, unique, and flexible enough to allow for future growth and extensions.
- *A name that is metaphoric or implies a lifestyle:* These include names such as American Eagle, Polo, Tommy Bahama, and Nautica.

LOGOS AND INITIALS

Logos (see Figure 2.18) come in different shapes and forms that include:

- Monograms (LV and YSL, for example; see Figure 2.19a)
- Signatures (names in signature form like Salvatore Ferragamo)
- Names or abbreviations, such as Dior and Valentino
- Symbols and shapes, such as the Polo figure, the Lacoste crocodile, and the Nike swoosh (see Figure 2.19b)

The power of the logo lies in its ability to acquire an international appeal easier than a name can. In addition, some names may be hard to pronounce in different languages. Thus, logos are a strong and effective identity attribute or symbol for any brand. They are visual interpretations of the brand that may be much easier to remember.

Logos can be pure, colorful graphics or a combination of graphic, color, and content (words and typography). Some research shows that the brain acknowledges shapes first, then color, and then content, because words need some time and effort to be decoded and deciphered. That is why shapes are usually easier to remember than words, which is another reason why logos are effective communication tools.

Effective logos follow many of the principles mentioned earlier for effective names, in addition to the following:

- Need to be memorable
- Are easy to identify and recognize
- Provide an appropriate and consistent image of the brand
- Communicate the brand's personality
- Can be legally protected
- Work well across media in terms of their scale, form, and color, including a clear enough design to work in both color and black-and-white publications

Figure 2.19a, b

(a) The Louis Vuitton logo is a distinct identity symbol, here seen on the Fifth Avenue store in New York.

(© Kurt Brady/Alamy)

(b) The simple shape of the Nike Swoosh is recognized by all.

(Courtesy of Nike)

a

b

One important feature about logos is their ability to evolve and change in time. Successful examples include:

- Christian Dior transformed to simply Dior (see Figures 2.20a–b).
- Wal-mart became Walmart.
- Burberry's changed to Burberry.

Companies change their brand's logos for various reasons related to the marketplace. It can be due to competition or economic and social changes. Or it can be simply part of a strategy to revitalize the brand and make it look younger and more modern. Although some of these changes can be purely cosmetic, other cases can carry a more serious message.

In all cases, the amount of time and money invested in developing and marketing these logos proves that changing a logo is not really an easy or cheap task. Changing logos is a strategic decision with financial implications, as a new logo necessitates making changes on labels, products, packaging material, store fronts, published ads, and so on.

TYPEFACE AND TYPOGRAPHY

Relevant to logos are the typeface and typographic elements of the name. Issues to address here include what font is used; how legible the name is; what feelings they convey; how unique and different they are; if they reflect the brand personality and value (for example, luxury); and, again, how well they work in different media. For instance, the font's size, shape, and type used can carry a lot of signals and meanings about the brand as well as serve as a visual identifier. For many brands the font and typography is the core of its logo and visual identity. Think of the signature-like style of the Salvatore Ferragamo or Yohji Yamamoto's logos, the boldness and masculinity of the Hugo Boss font, the timeless classicism of BVLGARI (and the use of V instead of U) and Versace typeface, and the modernity of Calvin Klein. All these signals and meanings are embedded in the fonts and styles used (not to mention IBM recognizable cut letters, McDonald's yellow M, or Coca-Cola's font curves).

In general, round-edged fonts reflect a relaxed and calm message suitable for a romantic, even feminine brand, whereas basic, firm fonts convey professionalism, masculinity, and boldness, and so on.

COLOR

Color can be a component of the logo, name, or packaging. Colors are another strong visual attribute with strong connotations. And just like a name, color can help identify brands.

The ultimate achievement is when the brand manages to own a color—think of red for Coke, light blue for Tiffany's, and even Burberry's beige and brown tartan.

Colors have different meanings in different cultures and evoke different emotions. For instance, the color of prosperity in Chinese culture is the color red, whereas in another Asian country, Malaysia, it is green. Similarly, white is a color of purity in some cultures, and a symbol of mourning in others. Such cultural sensitivities must be kept in mind, especially for a brand aiming to reach global status.

There are other technical aspects to consider as well, such as how the color will look on advertising material, with various backgrounds, and in different scales. Or is the color equally effective in different media? The list continues.

PACKING

Packing is equally important as logos are. In many ways they are extensions of the previous attributes and a platform where other visual symbols are combined to clearly visually identify the product and associate it with the brand. No wonder that packing material such as boxes and shopping bags are great marketing tools. They are mobile forms of advertising that are as important as any other advertising medium. People may hold onto them for a long time and carry them in many places. As a matter of fact, many people use these shopping bags to demonstrate their association with the brand, especially with luxury brands. People love to carry a Saks, a Nordstrom, or Takashimaya shopping bag with their distinctive design and color, showing it off everywhere they go. The bag says a lot about your shopping style or one with which you would like to be associated (see Figure 2.21).

PERSONALITY

A **PERSONALITY** humanizes the brand and is developed through the accumulation of culture, vision, stories, product mix, and behavior. It sums up what the brand is all about and identifies

BOX 2.2   LACOSTE VS. CROCODILE: BATTLE OF THE LOGOS

French brand Lacoste has one of the world's recognizable logos: the crocodile, which was introduced in 1933. Hong Kong-based Crocodile Garments is an apparel manufacturer and retailer that produces a brand called "Crocodile," offering men's, women's, and children's casual apparel. Crocodile also uses the alligator as a logo for its sportswear Crocodile bands. The main difference between both logos is that the Lacoste alligator faces the right whereas Crocodile's faces the left!

In the 1990s, Lacoste fiercely opposed attempts by Crocodile to register the brand in the Chinese market. A long legal battle between both brands continued until a settlement in 2003 was reached whereby Crocodile Garments agreed to change its logo so that the tail is more vertical and scaly, and it has bigger eyes. As a result of this compromise, Crocodile Garments was allowed to compete legally against Lacoste in China.

Figure 2.21

Satisfied shop-
pers carrying
their Nordstrom
shopping
bags—a walking
form of adver-
tising and, to
many, a status
symbol as well.

(*Associated Press*)

service, or a mix of these. This approach is usually geared toward rational decision making whereby customers make decisions based on value for money, convenience, or functionality. In the mass-market segment where products are hardly distinguishable in terms of look and features, differentiation is greatly based on elements such as price or convenience.

the true emotional value and brand promise. Personality is the essence of positioning at the brand level because it represents the image you hope the customer will recall when the brand is mentioned.

According to retail expert Ko Floor, the desired personality scale of a brand consists of five basic dimensions with certain insinuations:

1. *Sincerity:* ethical, family-oriented, small-town, wholesome, real, ethical, old-fashioned
2. *Excitement:* trendy, exciting, outgoing, daring, cool, artistic, surprising, up-to-date
3. *Competence:* reliability, security, efficiency, seriousness, leadership, technical
4. *Sophistication:* upper class, glamorous, sexy, feminine, pretentious
5. *Ruggedness:* outdoorsy, masculine, active, strong, no-nonsense

Of course, the subtleties of each dimension may differ from one society or culture to the other.

Positioning on the Basis of Product Mix

This positioning strategy focuses on differentiating the brand on the basis of its product mix, which is basically its product features and attributes. It can thus be positioned based on features (such as design), price, distribution strategy, level of

Positioning on the Basis of Brand Identity

Branding adds a new dimension to the product as well as a new set of emotional values. In a way, it humanizes the product and establishes an emotional relationship with buyers. While buyers consume their products, they basically experi-ence the brand through its identity. Identity is a combination of the visual/audio symbols and the personality. Personality is the component of the identity with the stronger impact because it represents the philosophy and attitude of the brand and, as such, greatly shapes the other iden-tity choices. Personality develops and matures over time through activities, stories, decisions, and interpretations of the corporate vision and strategy. In many ways, lifestyle brands are posi-tioned highly on personality. Although lifestyles are built on the products and designs produced, they are really defined through the story weaved around these products by the branding process. Branding establishes the lifestyle as the soul of the brand through a clearly defined brand iden-tity. Brands tend to expedite the process through heavy advertising that emulates the personality and interprets the experience. Luxury brand advertising tends to strongly adopt this strategy. It usually offers minimal information and focus on the image, the lifestyle, and the meaning of the brand. In a Gucci ad, for instance, the focus

is usually on the brand's personality with a supportive role for the product. Compare that to an Old Navy ad, where the focus is most likely on the product (as well as the price in many cases) supported by the brand (see Figure 2.22a–b).

As mentioned earlier in this chapter, identities are created to reflect a product mix proposal as well as the brand's culture and attitude. So when Donna Karan, for instance, decides to introduce a new cheaper product with a more casual look, it has to be introduced under a new identity including a new name, DKNY, and personality. However, when marketed, the brand is not necessarily promoted and positioned as "the cheaper" brand but simply as a different proposal. Thus, positioning can be based on the brand's strong personality, which in return sums up the product and cultural proposal of the brand.

In fashion we always hear designers talk about their "signature look," which refers to their design philosophy and their personal way of seeing and interpreting fashion. You can easily recognize an Armani look, with its soft lines and elegance, or identify Miyake's fascination with new textures and fabrication. So, although their products and designs change every season, the signature look, unique style, spirit, and philosophy live long. That is the essence of identity and a sign of a strong personality. It is, to a great extent, what they are all about as designers, what distinguishes them as brands and guides them. This is a major contribution to branding and a major differentiator as well. Strong brands have a clear thread or message that ties their various products and creations together. It is important not to interpret this as a constraint on creativity or limitation on variety. On the contrary, what this means is a sense of direction and common meaning. It's a stronger and more focused message indeed.

If you are asked to describe what Chanel or Versace means to you, you may end up describing them as follows:

- *Chanel:* Timeless French elegance, or the ultimate women's brand
- *Versace:* Italian chic with a sexy risqué attitude

If these (or something similar) are the images you have developed for Chanel and Versace and how you see each positioned, then you have really described an identity that each has developed through design, country heritage, and strong personality. It is more than a design direction; it's a philosophy and an attitude that is expected to persist even when designs change. This simple example demonstrates how branding creates a meaning for the design and labels it, not just literally but psychologically and emotionally as well. *This is branding.* And this is why a positioning strategy that utilizes the power of the identity and the strong consistent message it implies confirms the notion of the brand promise and generates a strong proposed value. A *core* value.

Positioning Phases

J. N. Kapferer identifies five major phases for the positioning process:[3]

1. *The understanding phase:* This phase identifies all potential added values for the brand based on its identity, roots, heritage and prototypes in addition to an analysis of its customers, competition, and market.
2. *The exploration phase:* This phase suggests scenarios for the brand and finding the right platform. It is a process that requires time, eliminations, and adjustments to determine the brand's potential niche.
3. *The test phase:* This period is when scenarios are either refined or eliminated, which includes consumer studies to evaluate the credibility and emotive resonance of each scenario.
4. *The strategic evaluation:* Here a comparison of scenarios is based on criteria and economic evaluation of potential sales and profits, while taking into consideration the nature of the segment.

5. *The implementation and activation phase:* After the platform has been chosen and drawn up, the brand's values must be made palpable and tangible for the brand to become full active.

A closer look shows that this process mirrors our roadmap for developing and positioning the brand, which we built on:

- Decision making based on market analysis
- Product development
- Identifying differentiator and positioning strategies
- Developing an identity
- Introducing and communicating the brand

A New Positioning Approach?

As we have seen with a product mix and a strong identity, the brand uses many tools to establish a positioning strategy that differentiates and establishes its comparative advantage. We have also seen that there are different approaches to positioning strategies. Most of these approaches are built on the premise of competing against brands in the same segment or category. That has been the core premise of positioning strategies and the traditional approach. However, there have been attempts and suggestions to allow brands to adopt a new attitude to positioning and compete based on new premises. Accordingly, there could be two approaches to positioning: a traditional one shared by most professionals, and a newer one.

The traditional approach is built on the firm's ability to:

1. Identify a desirable position on the positioning map (the positioning strategy).

2. Develop a marketing plan to capture and dominate this desired position vis-à-vis other competitors in the category (execution of the positioning strategy).[4]

In other words, companies need to allocate a vacant slot on the positioning map that is not occupied by competitors. Companies hope to achieve that by developing their market leadership. Your market leadership (that is, your weapons to beat competition) should:

- Be based on real and deliverable strengths and values. A brand needs to live up to its claims.
- Be based on relevant values to the consumer.
- Be easily communicated and understood by the consumer.
- Reflect (or be in tune with) the financial and strategic goals of the organization.

Example of a Positioning Map

To use the positioning map, marketers need to identify two variables or criteria for comparison (see Figure 2.23). These two variables placed on each axis could be price versus quality, price versus convenience, and price versus image. Products are then mapped out in relevance to these variables. Accordingly, the map offers a visual representation of potential market positioning gaps that can be filled by the new brand.

The traditional approach to positioning has its own critics. The criticism lies on the notion that positioning through differentiation simply means doing what competition is not doing, which implies a couple of things: that competition's behavior is predictable and that positioning is a sure low-risk procedure. It may also force you to use competitors as standards and gauge your performance by

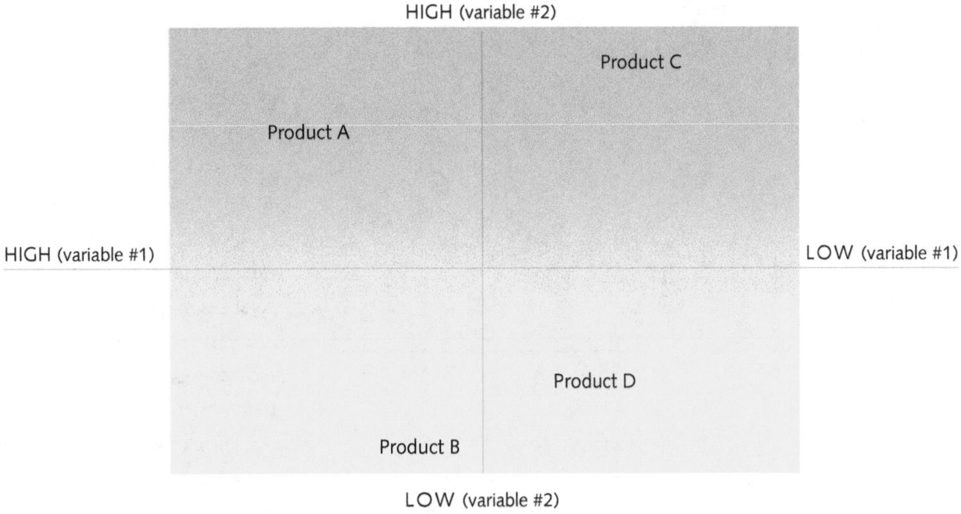

Figure 2.23

A positioning map requires the comparison of two variables.
(*Illustration by Andrea Lau*)

POSITIONING MAP

HIGH (variable #2)

Product C

Product A

HIGH (variable #1)   LOW (variable #1)

Product D

Product B

LOW (variable #2)

Figure 2.24

The classic
positioning
approach:
differentiating
from competi-
tors within the
same category.

(Illustration by

Andrea Lau)

CLASSIC POSITIONING APPROACH

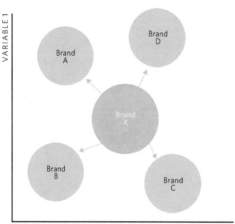

Figure 2.25

The disruptive
positioning
approach:
differentiating
from the entire
category.

(Illustration by

Andrea Lau)

DISRUPTIVE POSITIONING APPROACH

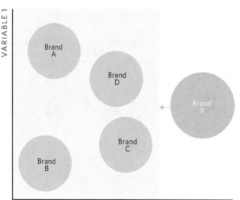

what they have achieved and not fully examine your potentials for innovation. Accordingly, scholars have proposed a different approach to positioning, one that is based on the idea that a company needs "to step back from the positioning map and look for ways to achieve differentiation from the category *as a whole* rather than from specific competitors within the category."[5] The approach is known as the "disruptive positioning approach." Traditional, or classic, and disruptive positioning approaches are illustrated in Figures 2.24 and 2.25.

There are different ways to adopt this strategy—by totally defying your own category (for example, IKEA created a new furniture shopping environment and experience), borrowing rules from another category (for example, Joe Boxers or Swatch introduced their products as they would a fashion item), or totally creating a new one (for example, Apple iPod). All approaches are based on the premise that instead of differentiating from a competitor or a group of competitors, you differentiate yourself from the whole category; in other words, you create a new playground where no competitors exist yet.

One example that demonstrates this strategy is the Swatch Watch brand. Swatch is referred to as a *breakaway* brand, which when launched did not compete with any traditional watch category or segment that existed at the time. Instead, it created a totally new category through borrowing elements from existing segments.

Prior to the introduction of Swatch in 1983, the watch industry was basically segmented into two major segments: "watches as jewelry" as in the case of most expensive Swiss-made brands being sold and repaired by jewelers, and watches as "functional tools" as in the case in other cheaper mass-produced brands, such as Timex, sold in department and drug stores.[6] Then came Swatch, and instead of competing within one of these two

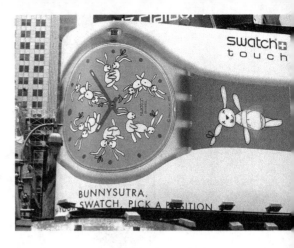

Figure 2.26

Swatch
introduced
the affordable
watch as a
fashionable
item, with
a sense of
humor, too:
"Bunnysutra" in
Times Square.

(*Associated Press*)

segments, it introduced, in many ways, a new sub-segment of "watches as fashion accessories," and endowed its product with a sense of fun. In other words, Swatch did not directly compete with individual brands in any of the existing sub-categories, but created its own sphere where no competitors existed yet. It stood solely (for a while) on its own map. (Who else but Swatch would place a "Bunnysutra" design on a massive billboard in Times Square? See Figure 2.26.) And by the time others followed, it had established itself as the category leader and benefited from early market penetration.

This model seems suitable for fashion brands because fashion brands are not only highly cat-egorized but highly tiered as well. Meaning that in addition to having mass-market brands and luxury brands within these levels or tiers, we can have sub-categories such as conservative luxury brands, trendy luxury brands, sexy luxury brands, and so on. What this does is to make distinctions a bit clearer and better defined. It also allows for personalities to clearly and distinctively position brands (think of Versace vs. Armani).

Other examples of this disruptive positioning strategy are Victoria's Secret or Zara. In the case of Zara, it was introduced as neither a traditional mass-market brand nor a luxury brand. It decided to take a different business approach and ushered in an era of premium brands with great success. Similarly, Victoria's Secret did not really compete with any lingerie manufacturer at the time—instead, it broke out from other lingerie brands by estab-lishing a new meaning and category of lingerie: lingerie as entertainment. Its highly popular cata-logs featured super sexy models (many of whom, like Heidi Klum, have become household names),

and every year its over-the-top fashion show is a massive, televised event. (See Figure 2.27.)

Although this positioning strategy comes with high rewards, it is not an easy task and obviously requires good timing as well as total dedication of effort and resources, in addition to a good understanding of the market.

The Positioning Statement

Some companies put together a positioning state-ment to reflect their positioning strategy. An effective positioning statement will identify the target cus-tomers, their problem, the brand's value proposition, and key competitors. Geoffrey A. Moore (ex-partner at Regis McKenna, Inc.) put together a format for what a positioning statement should cover:

- For [*target end user*]
- Who wants/needs [*compelling reason to buy*]
- The [*product name*] is a [*product category*]
- That provides [*key benefit*]
- Unlike [*main competitor*]
- The [*product name*] [*key differentiation*]

A well-constructed positioning statement is a good way to bring focus and clarity to the marketing strategy because every decision that is made regarding the brand will be judged by how well it supports the positioning statement.

Thus, we conclude that a positioning statement should at least cover the following four elements:

1. *Target audience:* The group of customers that mostly represent the brand's target market.
2. *Frame of reference:* The category in which the brand competes.
3. *Benefit and point of difference:* The most motivating benefit that the brand proposes relative to the competition.
4. *Legitimacy:* The most convincing reason to believe that the brand delivers what it promises.

Let us examine this excerpt from Bottega Veneta's strategy (positioning) statement:

> *Bottega Veneta is determined to reinforce its established positioning as a luxury lifestyle brand through innovation and the preservation of exclusivity for its flagship leather goods and its most successful activities, namely ready-to-wear, shoes, jewelry, and home furniture. Iconic bags represent the core business of Bottega Veneta and are to be protected.... All product launches are part of a well-planned and carefully executed strategy. Bottega Veneta is and will remain an exclusive luxury goods brand.[7]*

This statement has established a number of points.

- Bottega Veneta (BV) is an exclusive luxury brand. This implies all the attributes relevant to luxury, such as service, price, quality, and exclusivity.
- BV is an innovative lifestyle brand (thus expect product extensions).
- BV is an Italian brand (the name) with all the suggestive associations to an Italian heritage. (Note that *Bottega Veneta* means the "Venetian Workshop" in Italian.)
- BV's bags are its core product and differentiator: BV is known for introducing the first deconstructing bag that differed from the existing traditional rigid constructed French handbags.

So far in the branding process, we have established the *why*, *what*, and *how* to brand. Now it is time to examine the ways to communicate that to the outside world. This would be considered as phase two of the branding process, which we will discuss in the following chapter.

Chapter Summary

- A brand and a product are not the same.

- Branding is not just a marketing activity. It is usually a top management decision and the responsibility of every department and employee in the organization.

- The branding process starts with a strategic decision and a vision, and is executed through a positioning strategy.

- The positioning strategy shapes the product mix and identity of the brand.

Chapter Questions and Issues for Discussion

1. Describe the relationship between branding and marketing.

2. How does the decision-making process differ between that of luxury brands and mass-market brands?

3. Explain the meaning of "brand identity" and highlight its role in the positioning strategy.

KEY TERMS

BRANDING

COOL HUNTING

EXTERNAL MARKETING

IDENTITY

INTERNAL MARKETING

PERSONALITY

POSITIONING

SYMBOLS

VISION

CASE STUDY: Shanghai Tang: A Chinese Luxury Story

Perceptions of production quality have haunted Chinese products for years. China was never perceived as a place where reliable global brands were born, let alone a luxury brand. However, in 1994, a Chinese entrepreneur was on a mission to change this negative perception associated with the "Made in China" label. David Tang, a Chinese industrialist and entrepreneur, established Hong Kong-based Shanghai Tang with the goal of fusing traditional Chinese fashion with modern fashionable styles, interpreting the Qi Pao (traditional Chinese dress) and men's mandarin color suits in striking colors and with a modern twist. The bulk of Shanghai Tang couture was handled exclusively by the brand's tailoring facilities. In addition to fashion, the stores offered houseware items, such as silver frames, silk photo albums, and post cards, and accessories like watches and cufflinks with Mao's image. The flagship store in Hong Kong has managed to attract more than four million visitors since 1994, and the brand subsequently opened stores in London, Shanghai, Singapore, and New York.

Chinese Influence

In Tang's own words, Shanghai Tang's aim was to "create the first global Chinese lifestyle brand by revitalizing Chinese designs—interweaving traditional Chinese culture with the dynamism of the twenty-first century." In 1997, he opened a store on Madison Avenue in New York. However, the store closed in less than two years due to low sales. Never deterred, he opened a new store in 2001 at another smaller location on Madison Avenue, but it wasn't until CEO Raphael le Masne de Chermont and creative director Joanne Ooi joined Shanghai Tang in 2005 that the brand seemed to be heading at the right direction. (See Figure 2.28.) Ooi's role was to reinvent the brand and revitalize its image. Her goal was to maintain the strong Chinese cultural influence yet interpret it through bold modern designs that go beyond the traditional mandarin collars and Mao-style jackets. The new line of products was contemporary and sleek. The evident success triggered the opening of more stores

in Zurich, Tokyo, Bangkok, Milan, and Beijing. Of course, the fact that China is heading toward becoming the world's largest consumer of luxury goods bypassing United States and Japan did not hurt either. With a booming economy, China has gone from being the low-cost factory of the world to a purchaser of some big name brands to a stage where they create their own global brands built on local innovation capable of competing in quality, style, and prestige with designs coming out of the fashion capitals of the world. China is still a cheap place for production, which will be instrumental for home-grown brands to make financial gains that will allow them expand globally and compete with established brands. And with a more open society, more visitors are exposed to these brands and are getting familiar with them.

Design Strategy

Ooi chooses a new theme every season that may be new to international shoppers. She visits

1. What could have been the reasons for Shanghai Tang's initial failure in New York from a branding perspective?

2. What inherent forces allow Shanghai Tang to establish itself as a luxury lifestyle brand capable of competing with the likes of Gucci and Prada?

Figure 2.28

This Shanghai Tang boutique in Shanghai demonstrates Creative Director Joanne Ooi's goal to mesh traditional Chinese influence with bold modern design.

(© Lou-Foto/Alamy)

museums and reads history books for inspiration. She interprets characters, calligraphy, and other traditional patterns in her designs. One of her collections, for instance, was inspired by Mongolian and Tibetan nomads, offering fur-lined garments in the old tradition. In another collection, she was inspired by imperial symbols of the Qing dynasties from the fourteenth to early twentieth centuries, emphasizing the color yellow (a royal hue) and a five-clawed dragon (an icon worn only by the emperors). As Ooi describes the design philosophy, "We're not depending on zeitgeist. We're not the flavor of the month." Nowadays Ooi is supported by a team of designers located in London, Paris, New York, and China. Working with these teams located in different time zones is not the only challenge. As Ooi explains, the real challenge is to "make it look like it all came from the same person," referring to the importance of offering a coherent collection.

From the beginning, Shanghai Tang aimed at following the tradition of lifestyle luxury brands, such as Armani, Gucci, and Prada. As a result of its potential and success, luxury giant Richemont carried Shanghai Tang under its umbrella. The brand no doubt benefited tremendously from Richemont's experience in the world of luxury.

SOURCES

Broun, Samantha. "Designing a Global Brand," CNN. April 7, 2006. http://edition.cnn.com/2006/WORLD/asiapcf/03/15/eyeonchina.brands/index.html

Sauer, Abram D. "Shanghai Tang—Firmly Tongue in Chic." BrandChannel. November 5, 2001. http://www.brand-channel.com/print_page.asp?ar_id=42&section=profile

Shanghai Tang Web site. n.d. www.shanghaitang.com

Tischler, Linda. "The Gucci Killers." Fast Company. January 1, 2006. http://www.fastcompany.com/magazine/102/shanghai.html

ENDNOTES

1. Company Overview, Nikebiz.com. http://www.nikebiz.com/company_overview/

2. DuPont Vision, DuPont, http://www2.dupont.com/Our_Company/en_US/glance/vision/index.html

3. J. N. Kapferer, *The New Strategic Brand Management* (London: Kogan Page Limited, 2008), 207.

4. Youngme Moon, *Rethinking Positioning*, (Boston: Harvard Business School Press, 2005), 1.

5. Ibid., 1.

6. Ibid., 17.

7. Reference Document 2008, PPR (Paris: PPR, 2009), 47.

RALPH LAUREN

Blue Label

3

THE BRANDING PROCESS, PHASE TWO:

Communicating, Launching, and Evaluating the Brand

Brand **COMMUNICATION** refers to the promotional mix available for communicating the brand's presence, identity, and value through advertising and other channels. Refer back to the branding diagram in chapter 2 (Figure 2.1), and notice that there are two opposite arrows that connect communication to positioning. The reason for this is that although the communication strategy's major roles are to build awareness, confirm the brand identity, and reflect the proposed positioning, it also plays an equally important role in shaping this identity. As we mentioned in chapter 2, in addition to the sensual symbols, a major part of the brand's identity stems from its personality, which is shaped by the activities and emotions generated by the brand, including advertising and other promotional activities. Thus, there is a cause-and-effect relationship between the promotional mix and the identity, and, therefore, in positioning in general.

The Brand Communication

Communication channels play one or more of the following roles in the life of any brand:

- *Inform:* Deliver information about the brand, such as announcing the launch of a new product.
- *Remind:* Make people remember the brand.

CHAPTER OBJECTIVES

- Appreciate the role of communication in the branding process.

- Examine effective options and channels for communicating the brand.

- Introduce the VIP model.

- Understand and identify different branding growth strategies.

- Identify the difference among brand repositioning, relaunch, and revitalization.

- *Convince:* Attempt to convince people that the brand and its products are better than the competition (for example, emphasize the positioning strategy).

    Communication focuses not only on functional values, but emotional ones as well. For instance, most luxury brands' commercials do not focus on products and their features as much as they focus on the lifestyle and personality of the brand.

Revisiting the Four Ps

The marketing mix, also known as the Four Ps, has been the core of market analysis and communication strategies ever since the concept was introduced by Philip Kotler in the late sixties. The Four Ps stand for product, price, promotion, and place. The concept is built on the premise that any communication strategy is built on identifying product attributes, determining the right price, promotion mix, and channel of distribution. Evidently, the concept totally ignores the "brand" component and the emotional value created by the branding process. Although brands did exist at the time the concept was introduced, their role in our lives and in markets was not seen as significant. Today, brands bring a new meaning to marketing where the product is a component of a bigger entity (albeit an important one, of course). But brands create dreams, images, emotions, and positioning platforms that cannot be ignored. Accordingly, this concept of the Four Ps does not seem to be very relevant or at least inclusive from a branding perspective; for instance, it ignores the strong influences of the brand identity and personality on positioning and marketing strategies. Thus, new proposals for communication strategies need to be examined to replace this old approach. One proposal we introduce here is the VIP model.

VIP and VIPP Models

Based on the above and from a branding perspective, relying on the traditional Four Ps as the basis for your communication strategy falls short of embracing the essence of the brand. Therefore, the need for a new approach or concept is necessary. Our approach is a strategy based on what we may call the VIP concept, where V = Value, I = Identity, and P = Product Mix.

- *Value:* A core value is the brand proposal and ultimate reason for its existence and the purchase decision.
- *Identity:* This refers to both the visual identity or signals, plus the brand's personality.
- *Product mix:* The product mix is the product and its attributes.

    The VIP model endorses the product as the core of the brand and at the same time acknowledges the value-added elements introduced by the branding process. As a mix, it offers a good base for positioning, which in return is an effective base for any communicating strategy. It is also clear that this model acknowledges the Four Ps as an integral part of the product mix but not the sole driver of the communication strategy and marketing effort for a brand.

    If you examine the VIP concept closely, you will realize that it does embody the definition of the brand as being the sum of an identity and a value added to the product and its mix of attributes (V + I + P). That is to say that VIP in a way defines the brand or represents the "Brand Mix." By adding the promotion element (P) — which represents the suitable communication channels—we would complement the three basic elements and create the right "Brand Marketing Mix," which we may now call VIPP.

The VIPP model should be a more suitable marketing concept that embraces the brand, its value, and core elements. It is a more relevant and affective model in reflecting and communicating the brand than the traditional Four Ps marketing mix.

Communication Channels

The goal of communication is to convey the positioning proposal, polish it, and persuade the consumer to purchase the brand's products. To achieve that, a communication strategy is drafted to exercise the promotion mix adopted. The promotion mix determines the communication channels adopted.

The choice of the right channels depends on many factors, such as the brand's positioning strategy, cost, and available technology. Nowadays, the promotional mix options available are wide and variable and may include:

- Advertising
- Public relations
- Publicity
- Fashion shows
- In-store promotions

Advertising

Advertising is the most common channel for promotion. It usually delivers a focused message about the brand and its products, in addition to promoting the brand's identity. Mass-market brands that are built on rational values and positioned mainly on their product mix usually offer more information about the product as its competitive advantage, such as price, location, or functionality. Luxury brands, on the other hand, may still highlight a product's feature but tend to have a less cluttered message, presenting a strong visual and emotional message about the brand's personality and lifestyle.

For both types of brands, there are many channels available for advertising, each with its set of advantages and disadvantages.

Newspapers

Although newspapers are commonly used, the short lead time makes them more suitable for announcing special events, such as discounts and sale events, which are usually more frequent with budget, mass-market brands. Newspapers have also been commonly used as channels for distributing coupons and incentive promotion offers, mainly through weekend editions due to their outreach and high circulation. However, the fact that in recent years the news can be accessed and updated by the minute online has resulted in a drop in newspapers' circulations to the point where some have completely transformed to an electronic format. Even coupons can now be obtained and printed online in most cases.

ADVANTAGES

- Newspapers are usually cheaper than other media, such as magazines.
- It's possible to have wide national circulation.
- Specialized papers allow for targeting specific groups of customers.
- Newspapers require less lead time for submitting an ad when compared to magazines.

Figure 3.1

Although it
is certainly
cheaper to
advertise in
newspapers,
the print quality
is noticeably
inferior to
magazines.
(Image courtesy of The
Advertising Archives)

congratulations on one hundred years and never looking better

dunhill

DISADVANTAGES

- Print quality is inferior and not as attractive as in magazines (see Figure 3.1).
- Newspapers usually have a lot of clutter, so the ad can be lost among news articles and other ads.
- People usually discard a newspaper after it is read, diminishing an ad's longevity and exposure.

Magazines

Magazines play an important role in the fashion industry. They are a great channel for showcasing new designs and trends using creative and high-quality advertising as well as influencing readers through their editorial coverage.

Magazines are also suitable for different kinds and levels of brands. In the case of luxury brands, they are more commonly used than newspapers for the following reasons. In addition, as luxury brands are mostly lifestyle brands, they benefit from specialized magazines that promote certain lifestyles and consequently create direct associations.

ADVANTAGES

- Magazines have much better print quality than newspapers, allowing for more attractive and catchy advertising (see Figure 3.2).
- Advertising can be supported by editorial material.
- There are many specialized magazines, making them a well-segmented and focused channel.
- People usually hold on to their weekly or monthly magazines for a while, increasing the chances of viewing the ad.
- Running an ad in a magazine is cheaper than using other media, such as TV.
- Today's magazines allow for inclusion of sampling and gifts, such as creams and perfume samples.

DISADVANTAGES

- It is more expensive to buy a magazine ad than a newspaper ad.
- A longer lead time is needed to submit an ad for a magazine. The lead time and circulation frequency mean that magazines are not particularly suitable for quick and short-notice announcements of special events. Also, magazine advertising is usually part of a larger campaign.
- The cluttering of images can be a possible problem in magazine advertising.

Publicity

Publicity is non-paid, non-commissioned promotional activities, such as magazine editorials (see Figure 3.3) or word-of-mouth. Publicity usually responds to some company news or activities (see Figure 3.4). It is effective because it is perceived as unbiased and not self-serving. The notion that there is no such thing as bad publicity may be debatable, but it still highlights the strong influence of publicity on the public's opinion and perceptions—especially coming from what are perceived as respectable sources of influence, such as fashion editors and popular magazines.

Figure 3.2

Advertising in fashion magazines can be artistic and often provocative as well.

(Image courtesy of The Advertising Archives)

Figure 3.3

Louis Vuitton's ingenious feat of meshing parts of several Louis Vuitton bags into an almost Cubist design made its patchwork bag a star on the runway, with extensive coverage in fashion magazines.

(Getty Images/ Chris Moore/Catwalking)

TV (National and Cable)

TV advertising seems to be the most glamorous channel of advertising and the dream of every marketing manager. Although some may argue that TV has lost some ground to new media and digital options, it remains an attractive and mostly effective channel.

ADVANTAGES

- The biggest advantage of TV advertising is its entertainment value and demonstration ability.
- National TV has a very wide reach.
- Cable TV outshines national TV in being cheaper and highly segmented, making advertising more conceivable and effective.

DISADVANTAGES

- TV advertising is very expensive and, therefore, out of reach for small operations.
- TV has a lot of clutter, making it hard to recall most commercials. In addition, viewers have a tendency to skip commercials (especially with devices such as TiVo).
- Advertising on national TV doesn't make much sense to a local or regional operation.
- Usually a long lead time is needed.

No wonder that Anna Wintour, editor-in-chief
of American *Vogue* has more than once headed
the list of the most influential people in the
fashion industry.

Although publicity is a free activity, uncontrolled
by the brand, the organization attempts to stimulate
publicity and coverage through organizing events
(such as fashion shows; see Figure 3.5). and offering
samples, invitations to major events, and various

forms of VIP treatment. All of these are examples of
attempts to encourage editors to establish a positive attitude toward the brand.

Public Relations

Public relations (PR) refers to activities held by
the company to enhance the brand's image and
gain favorable publicity. PR activities are especially
important to minimize effects of earlier negative
publicity or clarify mishandled information. It can
also be used to establish the brand's image as a
socially conscious brand that is keen to contribute
to society (see Figure 3.6).

PR activities include press release kits and
special events, such as charities, speeches, and
product launches. The examples given in chapter 1
from Target and PPR demonstrate such activities.

Promotional Activities

Promotional activities such as coupons, sales, free
samples, and so on, are effective tools, especially

in the mass-market segment. However, choosing
the right promotional activity and the right timing
is essential. For instance, lowering your price
is effective only if price is relevant in the decision making. If price is not that relevant, then a
change in price may not only be ineffective, but
may backfire as customers question the decision
and perhaps even become alienated. Timing can
also be a factor of great importance; for instance,
though a luxury brand customer is not typically
motivated by price reduction, the recent global
recession hit many of the wealthy, and for the first
time we started seeing luxury stores and brands
offer promotional discounts and special offers.

P. H. Knight, founder of Nike, recalled a story
of a Nike product manager who decided that no
shoe in his line should sell for more than $39.95.
Knight explained how this decision was a tremendous error because it showed a complete lack
of understanding of what the brand as a whole
was all about and how it stands at the top of the
price spectrum of its category. Because of this
top-selling position, it had also managed to secure
endorsements from top athletes; otherwise, as
Knight put it, Nike would "have no reason to exist."

Celebrities and Fashion Promotion

Many fashion brands turn to celebrities to promote
their products. Celebrities range from movie
and TV stars to sports athletes and socialites
(see Figure 3.7). Celebrities can have various
promotional roles that include:

- *Endorsement:* Celebrities are asked to lend
  their name and face to a product for use in
  ads or in-store displays. Endorsements can
  also be made through a movie or TV character
  that endorses a brand.
- *Testimonials:* A celebrity supporting a product in
  a way that confirms its quality and benefits can
  be effective and persuasive and is an excellent
  form of publicity (see Figure 3.8).
- *Spokesperson:* Celebrities can be hired as
  spokespersons or faces of the brand. Making
  appearances is usually part of this strategy
  as well.
- *Product placement:* Product placement refers
  to the strategy of visibly integrating products
  into the scenes of movies as they are used or
  worn by the characters. This has been gaining
  tremendous popularity recently, and it takes the
  form of placing products in a range of media
  such as TV shows, movies, or music videos.

Jane Fonda for L'Oréal Paris

Products are always placed in a favorable way with a notable mention or display of the brand's name or logo. It has proven very effective when the placement appears to be subtle and an integral part of the script. James Bond movies are partly financed by such promotional activities, from 007's watches to his cars and, of course, his champagne. Similarly, the house of Halston staged a fashion show during an episode of *Desperate Housewives* in 2004. (See Figures 3.9a–b.)

Movies have always played an influential role in promoting fashion. Many stars, such as Audrey Hepburn (the little black dress) and Marlon Brando (bomber leather jackets), have been fashion icons that promoted trends. Movie characters have also inspired many trends and fads, such as the white suit from John Travolta's character in *Saturday Night Fever* or the oversized sweatshirts from *Flashdance*. Finally, it was really the movies that exploded Giorgio Armani's career in America, whether it was the red carpet's fascination with his designs or the infamous wardrobe he designed

for Richard Gere's character in the movie *American Gigolo,* in which he reconstructed and redefined menswear into a softer, sexier look (see Figure 3.10).

Co-Branding

CO-BRANDING is the practice of using multiple brand names together on a single product or service. This form of alliance can have potential economic and commercial rewards for participating parties.

Figure 3.10

Outfitting
Richard Gere in
American Gigolo,
Giorgio Armani
redefined
menswear.
(© Paramount Pictures/
Photofest; Photographer:
Ron Grover)

Figure 3.11

An advertise-
ment for Karl
Lagerfeld's col-
lection designed
specifically for
H&M, a highly
successful co-
branding effort.
(Image courtesy of The
Advertising Archives)

Co-branding examples

Stella McCartney by Adidas is an example of such collaboration. Typically, brand collaboration sees a more exclusive company hooking up with a larger, well-known brand, as Adidas has done in the past, and as H&M attempted when it created a limited collection with Karl Lagerfeld and Roberto Cavalli (see Figure 3.11).

Benefits of Co-Branding

Each collaborator hopes to gain something from the relationship without cannibalizing either audience; the parent brand earns credits and publicity, and the smaller name is exposed to a wider market

Co-branding agreements should cover marketing strategies, confidentiality issues, licensing specifications, warranties, payments and royalties, indemnification, disclaimers, and termination terms. They also include a lot of restrictions and provisions that regulate rights and obligations on all sides.

Co-branding is not a new strategy but has been a popular one lately, showcasing and communicating the brand in collaboration with another different company. Co-branding can be regarded as both a communication and growth strategy. It opens new venues to showcase the brand, and it also creates opportunities to expand and extend the brand through these collaborations.

Promotional Co-Branding

Promotional co-branding is the most common type of co-branding practiced by companies. It can enhance a brand's image and allows the brand to appeal to a new market through its association with other successful brands. Other than promotional reasons, co-branding can also present new investment and innovation opportunities through this close collaboration.

Coat
$149.00

Karl Lagerfeld
for
H&M

Launches November 12th in select H&M store
www.hm.com

while both benefit from an increase in sales and promotion. Here are some of the benefits.

- Presents the possibility of creating new products that benefit from the strong image of both brands and capitalizes on both brand's equities
- Benefits from resources and infrastructure of the partner brand in expanding into new markets and segments
- Offers a great channel for brand extensions
- Enforces positioning and image building through associations with a strong established brand
- Can form the basis of loyalty programs. In fact most of these programs are built on co-branding and collaborations between brands, such as the collaboration with credit cards
- Provides a new source of financing and income
- Allows for sharing of risk and marketing costs
- Increases customers' confidence and interest

Challenges of Co-Branding

On the other hand, co-branding does have its own challenges, such as the following.

- Lack of total understanding or compatibility between both partners
- Potential difficulty dismantling the co-branding association; each brand may find it hard to reestablish itself again in the market on its own
- The possibility that one brand might overpower and overshadow the other
- The fact that co-branding might work to the advantage of one partner and damage the
- other (for example, if it were handled badly, the association between luxury designer Lagerfeld and the mass-market brand H&M could have easily hurt the designer's image as a luxury brand)
- Legal headaches if anything goes wrong

- Difficulty predicting future economic and social changes as well as shifts in consumers' habits and their effects on the future of such partnership

Brand Launch

We have established that although a product is the core of the brand, a product and a brand are two different entities. We have also established that brands are long-term investments, and a brand outlives its products. Products come and go, are redesigned, updated, and replaced all under the same brand and the same value.

Thus, launching a new brand is more than just launching and introducing a product. A brand has to be introduced with its values and everything it stands for because you are launching the concept and establishing the platform or umbrella that will eventually cover and embrace all the products produced under the name. You are establishing the relationship or signing the intellectual and emotional contract with the potential customer. This demonstrates that launching a brand is about the experience rather than the item. It follows that during the lifetime of the brand there may be many product launches but only one brand launch. In the case of old brands, there may be the need to relaunch the brand after years of downturns and lack of interest. In such a case, the same process has to be repeated and followed.

Evaluation and Brand Audit

Evaluation is an essential stage in any planning process. In management, it is sometimes referred to as *control*. This **BRAND AUDIT** is the stage where the organization assesses the brand's performance and measures customers' reactions. Based on the evaluation outcome, many decisions can be made regarding whether the brand is on the right track or not. Has the positioning strategy been successful? Is the brand at a stage where it should consider introducing extensions? Or should it consider expanding to international markets?

Evaluation uses quantitative and qualitative data such as sales records, customer feedback, turnover, sales per square foot, complaints, returns rates, publicity, and so on. The main goal is to measure the level of success of the branding policy and positioning strategy, as well as measure the customers' actual perceptions of the brand (for example, the image the customer has developed for the brand), how they have experienced it, and how this relates to the positioning strategy. Based on the analysis, the brand owner decides to either continue the brand or revisit its strategy and/or consider various growth options.

Brand evaluation is also necessary because brands are meant to live long, but sometimes as time passes, managers lose focus of the brand's core values, the main reason the brand existed. Therefore, this form of brand audit is necessary to remind its owners of what the brand is all about, its values, strengths, target markets, personality, and all the elements that distinguishes it from other brands.

Growth Strategies

Fashion brands are an interesting breed of brands in that they are in a continuous state of innovation, transforming themselves at a constant rapid pace. Fashion products usually have a shorter life cycle than other products, and it is this level of innovation and creativity that brings excitement and interest to the brand. Innovation is always a source for growth.

A few growth options relevant to fashion brands are:

- Licensing
- Global expansion
- Brand extensions

Licensing

Licensing is a more than billion-dollar activity of the fashion industry. It is simply defined as an agreement through which the legal owner of a brand or a trademark (the licensor) gives another party (the licensee) the legal rights to use the brand's name and identity (or know how or their trademark), in return for a compensation often known as a royalty fee.

Royalty fees can be a percentage of net sales (which can range from 3 percent to 10 percent based on product, category, and arrangements), a combination of a royalty and a minimum annual fee, or a dollar amount paid for every item sold. Licensing agreements can also stipulate a minimum amount of sales volume. In addition, a licensing agreement can be drafted so that the licensee contributes to the advertising and promotion expenses as part of their licensing fee. These licensing agreements can stipulate certain geographic and commercial extents, limitations, and duration as well.

One interesting observation about the success of licensing is its relevance to the concept of branding. If a fashion brand does not manufacture

Figure 3.12

From T-shirts
and sweatshirts,
to jackets,
knapsacks, and
more, licensing
is big business in
children's wear.
(*Bloomberg via Getty
Images*)

or create more than 90 percent of products carrying its name, then the cornerstone role of the brand's owner is to establish the brand's identity and create the necessary dream as the prerequisite for the brand to flourish.

Licensing is fast becoming the major force behind brand growth and expansion. It is common in the premium segment and in recent years has gained more acceptance in the luxury segment as well. As a matter of fact, Christian Dior is regarded as the first designer to license his name. There are many advantages as well as challenges for this form of partnership as demonstrated in the following sections.

Licensing Advantages

For the licensor (the brand owner):

- Licensing allows them to expand their brand offerings beyond its initial line. As a matter of fact, most accessories such as glasses, wallets, belts, and so on, as well as other product extensions like jeans and underwear sold under designers' names are usually created through licensing agreements. This introduces new sources of revenue and market expansion when the licensor might not otherwise have had the expertise or financial capability to enter such markets (see Figure 3.12).

On the brand's part:

- Not only does licensing give the brand an opportunity for product extensions, but it also opens the door for distribution and market extensions.
- Possible contribution from the licensee in advertising and marketing campaigns can reduce the costs of these activities.
- Successful licensing partnerships and products can enhance the image of the brand and help transform it into a lifestyle brand.
- A partnership revitalizes the brand and in many cases can save or turn around a fading brand (see Box 3.1).

For the licensee (the purchaser of the license):

- The biggest advantage is using their resources (money, factories, and people) in producing a product under a name that is already established and has consumer following.
- Financially, being associated with an established brand enables them to minimize a lot of marketing and financial risks by cannibalizing on the brand's successes and market presence, and eliminating the need for start-up costs associated with brand development and promotions. The results could be better financial returns, bigger market share, and stronger competitive advantage.

Licensing Challenges

For the licensor:

- Licensing activities that are not closely monitored by the licensor could lead to a catastrophic impact on the brand. The case of Pierre Cardin is always referred to as a brand that went on a licensing spree for everything and to everyone, to a point where the brand lost its focus and damaged its image because the name appeared on almost every imaginable product, and quality inevitably deteriorated. Nowadays, most designers request full supervision and pre-approval on licensed products' quality and design before they are manufactured and hit the market.

For the licensee:

- While a licensee benefits from the status and success of the licensor's brand, it could easily be hurt by any failures and scandals that hit the licensor company.
- Licensing still requires investment and resource dedication on the licensee's part in order

to accommodate certain specifications or technology needs for the product.

- Licensing may place the licensee in a state of dependency on the licensor, which could have him in a weaker future negotiation position or in serious risks if the licensor faces financial troubles or bankruptcies, for instance.

Brand Extension

As mentioned earlier in this chapter, one of the main advantages of licensing is the opportunity it creates for expansion through brand and line extensions. **BRAND EXTENSION** refers to increasing the range and type of product lines

THE LICENSING OF CACHAREL

Figure 3.13

Cacharel's per-fumes like Anaïs Anaïs were so successful that fragrance became the focus of the brand.

(© Antiques & Collectables / Alamy)

Cacharel's brand identity changed as a result of its licenses and the way these licensed products overshadowed the original one. Originally a women's RTW brand targeting romantic women, Cacharel offered a perfume license to L'Oréal. The result was a streak of highly successful perfumes such as Anais, Noa, Loulou, and more. Eventually the RTW line vanished, and Cacharel has become primarily a perfume brand.

Source: Michael Chevalier and Gerald Mazzalovo, *Luxury Brand Management: A World of Privilege* (Singapore: John Wiley & Sons, 2008), 165.

Figure 3.14

The COS line
created by H&M
as a more
up-market
brand extension.

(Getty Images/ Karl
Prouse/Catwalking)

under the brand's umbrella. There is a difference between brand extension and line or product extension. Line extension means adding new product items to an existing line of products, like adding short-sleeved shirts to your line of shirts, or silk blouses to your line of blouses. On the other hand, brand extension refers to introducing new product lines or categories that did not exist before, such as introducing a menswear line to a previously known women's wear brand, or introducing a pants line when before the brand only offered shirt products.

Although extensions are usually easier and faster to launch and may require less research effort, they impose other challenges, such as usually being introduced on a smaller scale and therefore not benefitting from economies of scale (which refers to the concept that the more you produce, the less your total cost because your fixed cost is carried over more pieces). Of course, these new products also require an additional level of management and distribution, along with other logistics.

Corporate brands can also extend their brand through the creation of a series of sub-brands under related or unrelated names. Examples include Donna Karan and DKNY by Donna Karan, or Armani Exchange, Armani Collezioni, Emporio Armani, Armani Jeans, and Armani Casa by Giorgio Armani. This strategy can go either direction. The brand can trade up by introducing a more expensive luxury offering (H&M introducing its new line COS) or vice versa (haute couture luxury brands introducing cheaper, ready-to-wear premium lines). (See Figure 3.14.) However, this last approach is commonly regarded as brand creation rather than brand extension.

There are many obvious advantages to such growth strategies:

- Allow for better segmentation
- Offer more complete solutions for the consumer
- Allow for creation of supportive products, such as socks with pants
- Make the brands more visible and powerful
- Reach various markets and segments through trading up or down, without the need to reposition the initial brand, while attracting new customers and increasing market share in the process
- Can be a good strategy to respond to competition

However, such expansion strategies demand a number of preconditions.

- Brand extensions still require large investments.
- The brand needs to possess enough credibility and value as a lifestyle brand to extend into these categories and be accepted as such.
- Line extensions must make sense within the larger brand philosophy or they will fail; the Harley Davidson cologne is a good example.
- All extensions should follow the same rules of delivering value and a competitive advantage in the new arena as well.

Global Expansion

Globalization was driven by free trade, open markets, and telecommunication advances that allowed trade and cultural barriers to weaken. Global expansion is a geographic extension of the brand. Most brands start as local brands and then choose to expand globally as part of a growth strategy.

It is important in the beginning to differentiate between the two terms *international* and *global* because they are not really interchangeable.

- *International:* Any form of presence in foreign markets even if it is inconsistent in types of products or size of operation.
- *Global:* Having one branding proposal in all foreign markets with the option of some level of adaptation, but the brand more or less remains intact.

In fashion, most luxury brands are meant to be global brands. To them, global expansion is an economic and image building necessity. They are meant to be limited in quantity and exclusively distributed in markets where they exist, so they need to offset these limitations by existing in all major markets. In addition, their customers are affluent travelers who want to be able to find their favorite brands in all fashion capitals of the world (apart from fashion, Coca-Cola would be an ultimate global brand).

The degree of globalization depends on many factors, such as the universality inherent in what the brand has to offer, as well as its ability to offer its products or services in other markets at comparative prices. However, it remains essential to respond to local market needs without jeopardizing the brand's personality and value.

Going global creates new business opportunities and sources of revenue for the brand. A few other benefits include:
- Financial benefits from economies of scale
- Growth of reputation
- Boost of brand image
- New opportunities for other forms of extensions
- New market opportunities and resources
- Potential to overcome competitive pressures

In general, there are various patterns to going global.
- *Same brand—same product:* Implementing minor complementary adaptations to the brand offerings for different markets, such as change in sizes.
- *Same brand—adapted products:* Market differences, whether cultural, social, or economic, require some adaptation of the product offering. For instance, different designs or products may not be sold in other markets. This level of adaptation can affect the brand's visual identity, such as when there is a change of name or packing color. This approach

many not be common in the fashion industry, especially not in the luxury category where the brand is built around a consistent image and status. Also, the name forms a strong identity component that plays a major role in delivering the emotional reward of the brand. If people buy an Armani for status, it needs to remain the same in every market.

- *Same brand—different positioning:* Zara is a brand that is positioned differently in different markets around the world. Although it is considered a moderately priced brand in its home market, Spain, it is regarded as a premium one in many other markets. One of the reasons for these positioning discrepancies has to do with the pricing policy Zara adopts, which passes additional costs of distribution onto the consumer. Accordingly, the same Zara item could cost twice as much in Japan as it would in Spain.

Of course, going global requires a certain level of infrastructure and resources.

As with any strategy, there are advantages and challenges to global expansions:

- Standardization as an element of globalization reduces costs and generates benefits from economies of scale.
- Globalization allows brands to benefit from various talents and resources available worldwide.
- Going global opens new markets and enforces brand image.

And it does come with a lot of challenges:

- Pricing strategy issues; how to price the product in different markets.
- Counterfeit problems and gray market (occurring in global luxury brands more than in others).

- Cultural and taste differences.
- As businesses usually start locally before going global, the initial strategy is generally tailored to local markets with no provisions to going global. This results in a situation where the company is not ready for such a move, given the culture and resources it has in place.

Therefore, going global requires advance research to prepare for such expansion, such as:

- What are the entry barriers in the foreign markets? These could be legal such as laws and regulations, taxes, market structure, and so on.
- What are the brand's objectives for going overseas? Is it necessary?
- Is there sufficient demand in the new markets?
- How will the brand be positioned overseas? And will the brand be able to extend its value proposition to consumers as successfully overseas as it does locally?
- Who are the competitors, and how are they different form local ones?
- Is there any adaptation necessary? If so, how will this affect the brand proposition and eventually the brand image?
- Are the brand's strengths and differentiators relevant to the foreign market?
- Are the resources needed (financial, human skills, material) available in the foreign country?
- Do managers and employees in the foreign country understand the brand?

Positioning attributes in particular are tested at many levels.

- *Price:* Price is one element that will most likely have to change. We have already mentioned how Zara adopts a policy whereby they calculate different price points for the same product in different countries by simply adding any additional cost incurred to the price. Price policy is an important decision because it has financial and marketing implications on the brand and can affect how the brand is perceived and positioned in different markets, which in return can affect its overall global image.

- *Product:* One major dilemma that arises as a result of globalization is the question of adaptation versus standardization of the product as well as marketing activities in foreign markets. Adaptation to local markets may seem to work against the consistency of the brand's image and offerings, whereas standardization of the products in all markets seems to ignore the realities and characteristics of each market.

Experience has shown that some level of adaptation may be inevitable. Hence, the notion of "think globally, act locally" is a strategy that attempts to avoid adopting a cookie-cutter approach to markets. Adaptation or localization can be cultural or tactical. Cultural localization refers to consumer tastes and behaviors, whereas tactical localization deals with operational adjustments such as pricing or distribution. Adaptation is not always an easy task, and the key to success lies in staying true to the brand and its values.

As mentioned, marketing strategies need to also put cultural and behavioral differences and sensitivities into consideration. Not all approaches are workable in all markets. Issues such as sexuality in advertising, role models, gender roles, and general beliefs of what is appropriate and what is not should be put into consideration. However, although the marketing campaign or approach may differ, the core message may remain the same or at least stay true to the brand. A brand that promotes values of love and social acceptance among people, for instance, may want to promote these same values through images of happy marriages or brotherhood in more conservative societies and stay away from other taboos.

It is important to remember that succeeding locally does not always guarantee global success, even if the resources are available. Thus, although global expansion can be a tempting decision, it needs to be approached after serious assessment of all factors.

Vertical vs. Horizontal Integration

Organizations can also expand operationally by integrating either horizontally or vertically.

Vertical Integration

Vertical integration refers to the organization taking over and controlling various stages of the production or distribution chain. In the apparel industry, a simple chain of events occurs as follows: mills produce fabrics; the fabrics are treated and dyed; they are supplied to manufacturers who make the garments; and then they pass the finished product on to retailers. Each of these events represents a stage in the process or chain that is handled by a separate business such a mill, a manufacturer, a retailer, and so on. A manufacturer may decide to get involved in producing its own fabrics, which is a step behind on the chain, so the move is described as a backward direction of vertical integration. On the other hand, the manufacturer can look ahead into the chain of events and decide to open its own retail operation, which would be a forward form of vertical integration. Of course, in addition to forward and backward vertical integration, a manufacturer may have full integration covering all activities. Companies such as Zara and Benetton, for instance, are forms of vertically integrated companies. Zara is directly involved in all stages, even owning some of its stores. However, both Benetton (which dyes its fabrics as well) and Zara are more backward integrated because they adopt a franchising strategy for most of the stores.

Horizontal Integration

Hortizontal integration refers to expanding at the same level and stage of the production chain, such as a manufacturer or a department store acquiring another similar operation. An example would be when Macy's Inc. (then known as Federated) acquired major department chains around the country, such as May Company, I. Magnin, and Broadway Stores Inc., among others. (See Figure 3.15.)

Both vertical and horizontal integration have a direct effect on the brand. It is through its vertical integration that Zara managed to adopt its quick response policies and control its production cycle to offer new styles in controlled quantities responding to fashion trends and have them available in stores almost on a bi-weekly basis. On the other hand, horizontal integration gave Macy's a larger market share and reach,

as well as a market large enough to sustain its private labels and remain competitive.

Brand Repositioning, Relaunching, and Revitalization

A brand is a long-term investment and is meant to have a long life. Thus, brands being dynamic entities have a life cycle just like people do. As time goes by, a brand may not *click* with its target customer anymore and starts to lose equity, while suffering from what is referred to as personality stagnation. As a result, the brand does not mature or develop any further. Of course, the same problem can be a result of bad management and loss of focus and understanding of what the brand is all about. Brands being organic entities need to develop and stay relevant through innovation and awareness of its external environment, brand personality, and customer needs. The many failures of relaunching Halston as a luxury brand, for instance, are proof that creativity alone is not sufficient.

Therefore, as brands get older, they reach a stage where they may need to revitalize themselves to stay relevant and in tune with their customer. They may need to consider addressing a totally new segment or appeal to a different generation of consumers and redefine their image in the process. Accordingly, brands have three options to consider: to **REPOSITION**, **REVITALIZE**, or **RELAUNCH**. Each of these concepts means something different and requires different strategies to be implemented.

Figure 3.15

San Francicso's
I. Magnin flag-
ship department
store was
purchased by
Macy's in its
effort to gain
horizontal
integration.

(*Courtesy of Macy's*)

- *Reposition:* A plan by which the brand redefines its market position, target customer, and strategy.
- *Relaunch:* A strategy by which the brand is reintroduced after a period of demise or lack of market interest.
- *Revitalization:* An approach whereby the brand is refurbished and modernized yet is meant to stay relevant to its existing customer with the possibility of gaining new groups. For the strategy of revitalization, innovation is a major tool.

Reposition

Why would a brand need to reposition? Sometimes as the brand gets older, so do its customers, and as a result, their needs change. The brand then faces being in a position whereby it is losing its market share, and its sales plummet. Thus, it needs to establish a new relationship and relevance with a new group of customers, but to do so, the brand needs to tailor its message and products to match these new customers.

One solution is repositioning, in many ways a reinvention of the brand. A good example of repositioning is the case of Burberry (formerly Burberry's) under the leadership of Rose Marie Bravo and the creative direction of Philip Bailey.

Relaunch

Many brands eventually die when they fail to remain relevant and updated as this causes them to lose market share and consumer interest. However, one advantage of branding is that even when they do not physically exist in the market, brands may remain in people's minds. There is always a level of awareness of the brand, even if not of the product. Many people still remember and refer to Claude Montana as an innovative designer and brand. Halston is also highly regarded in the history of American fashion, in spite of many years of failures. Thus, brands can outlive their products, and brand awareness may even outlive the brand. Awareness and a sense of nostalgia remain major assets that brands can rely on for a second attempt into a market relaunch. A relaunch is usually combined with a repositioning and reinvention strategy. For example, prior to the Gap years, Banana Republic was a safari-inspired brand. After being bought by the Gap, however, the brand was reinvented, repositioned, and relaunched as a new brand.

Balenciaga had been off the fashion radar since the death of Cristobal Balenciaga and the close of the house in 1968. The brand was later relaunched in 1986 under Jacques Bogart S. A with Josephus Thimister at the helm of design. However, it was with Nicolas Ghesquière as head designer in 1997 and the subsequent purchase by the Gucci Group that the brand was revitalized into a modern, sophisticated, and profitable luxury brand worn by celebrities, such as Madonna and Nicole Kidman (see Figure 3.16).

Revitalization

Revitalization differs in the fact that it does not necessarily include a repositioning strategy and is not meant to appeal to a totally different customer; rather, it focuses on becoming more relevant to its own market with the possibility of attracting more and new customers. Gucci after Tom Ford is a great example of brand revitalization. What Tom Ford did was rejuvenate and revitalize the brand while maintaining its original vision and values. He just made Gucci more relevant to the times and the needs of its customers. Balenciaga under Ghesquière, as mentioned earlier, is another good example of brand revitalization, and it is exactly what Versace was needing after it remained stagnant in its eighties definition of sexiness, while its customers grew and perceived the concepts of "sexy" and "feminine" in a different way twenty years later.

Brand Failure

As we've seen, branding offers manufacturers an effective channel to compete as well as add more meaning and value to their products. However, branding is neither easy nor cheap. In reality, more products fail than succeed. Some sources estimate that about 90 percent of all new products die within five years, and of those over 85 percent fail shortly after their launch. Wrong product, wrong market, wrong time, wrong price are among the many reasons why the failure rate is high and why many brands fail to persist in the market as viable legitimate brands.

So, brands can fail for a number of reasons. In our discussions in chapters 2 and 3 we concluded that the brand-building process goes through four major steps or stages, which can be summed up as:

1. The brand decision (3Cs: customer, company, culture)
2. The positioning strategy (VIP)
3. The communication strategy (promotional activities)

4. The brand audit (growth, repositioning, and so on)

If a brand management team fails at any of these steps or mismanages the process itself, it will have a drastic impact on the brand, making it more vulnerable to failure. Obviously a bad decision at an earlier stage may have a wider impact and a falling-domino effect on all the following stages. For instance, any misinterpretation of market signals and research data at the brand decision stage can result in a brand that does not reflect accurate consumer and market needs, which in return creates an irrelevant and badly positioned brand with an ineffective promotional campaign, and so on. Accordingly, by reviewing the whole branding process, we can conclude various reasons and scenarios that may cause a brand to fail.

- It starts as a bad idea, which is a failure at the decision-making stage. This type of failure can be due to insufficient market research, brand ego, or inability to interpret market signals and consumer needs. For example, Clairol introduced its Touch of Yogurt shampoo in 1979. The new brand and product quickly failed because no one liked the idea of having yogurt in their hair. The idea seemed silly and meaningless. Moreover, there were reported cases of people actually eating the product by mistake. This failure demonstrates an even stronger example of laziness and insufficient market study given that the same company had a similar failure three years earlier with another shampoo called the Look of Buttermilk.

- It misunderstands its true market position and its place compared to competitors, and either underprices or overprices the product, or targets the wrong consumer segment.

These are examples of failure at both stage one (decision) and/or stage two (positioning). In 1990, Tommy Hilfiger thought that it could compete with chic European brands like Gucci and Prada. So it decided to reduce the size and usage of its very American red, blue, and white logo as well as open new stores in locations such as Rodeo Drive, hoping that the trendy people of LA would be shopping there. They never did, and because the average shopper's age was much older than the brand's younger clientele, the move there proved to be a big mistake. In addition, the company decided to introduce the short-lived Red Label, a luxury line with no logo attached and a high price point—a pair of pants once sold for over $6,000. The fact that the line was still attached to the Tommy name and image, however, never attracted enough new high-end customers or current customers wanting to trade up. For a brand initially known for its American preppy look and for being "classic with a twist," as described by Tommy himself, this strategy was a big failure. Overall, the brand was positioned in the wrong markets, at wrong price points, addressing wrong competitors, and targeting wrong customers.

- In spite of being a good idea, there's a flaw in its product proposal. A wrong price, bad design, or lack of functionality can either confuse or alienate the consumer. And in a world of viral marketing and the Internet, a negative consumer experience can be fatal. The same is true for a weak or confusing identity, such as a bad name choice. These cases represent a failure at stage two (the positioning strategy). Such a failure took place when Barbie introduced its Earring

Magic Ken doll in the 1990s in an attempt to create a "cooler," hipper Ken. However, an earring, purple vest, mesh shirts, black jeans, and a necklace made parents dub the new Ken as Gay Ken. No wonder, then, the controversial doll proved to be popular mainly in gay communities.

- It lies about its value or fails to deliver on its hype and promise, causing it to be wrongfully positioned (stage two), misrepresents and communicates (stage three), and above all, risks being untrustworthy. One example is Corfam Fake Leather, introduced by DuPont in the 1960s as a man-made synthetic substitute to real leather, mainly targeting shoe products. Although Corfam did have the look and shine of real leather, in addition to being cheaper, it lacked flexibility, resulting in very uncomfortable products. Moreover, the product triggered leather shoemakers to respond by offering better quality shoes at lower prices, killing any perceived value for Corfam.

- It does not understand cultural sensitivities in its marketing approach or sends confusing messages about the brand and its value, which is an example of failure at stage three (the communication strategy). When Clairol introduced its curling iron known as "Mist Stick," it faced hard times in the German market. As it turned out, the word "mist" refers to "manure" in German slang. On the other hand, a large part of why Levi's Type 1 Jeans failed is attributed to its confusing marketing campaign and TV commercials (such as the one of a man being dragged through the dirt by a seemingly possessed car), which did not resonate with the viewers (see Figure 3.17a).

- A brand is getting old and fails to rejuvenate itself. It can also fail because it misevaluates its brand power or miscalculates its growth strategy by expanding too fast, too soon, in the wrong markets, or with the wrong line extensions. This is an example of failure at stage four (the brand audit) for the current brand and at stage one (the decision level) in the case of a newly created extension. The Harley Davidson perfume mentioned in previous chapters is a good example of an extension that was not relevant to the consumer and did not reflect the brand's image. The negative impact of the over-licensing of the Pierre Cardin brand is also a good example of brand dilution due to over expansion. Two other interesting cases: first, the Cosmopolitan Yogurt, a yogurt product introduced by the world-famous *Cosmopolitan* magazine, demonstrates how brand power may not be enough to salvage an ill-perceived growth idea and how brand ego can blind sensible marketing decisions. The second is Bic's decision to expand its strategy of producing convenient disposable products (such as lighters and razors) into disposable underwear. Consumers were confused; they could not see the link and were left unmotivated and unconvinced to buy the product.

It is also important to remember that although brand rejuvenation may be recommended in many cases for older brands, it can sometimes be deadly if the rejuvenation distorts what the brand is all about (i.e., the promise) or if the brand is already established as a classic iconic brand, such as when Coke introduced the failed New Coke (see Figure 3.17b).

- In addition to the previously mentioned reasons for failure, and in spite of having a well-designed strategy, a brand can still fail because of its inability to manage the process in an effective, orderly, or timely manner. This is a failure at the management and logistic levels. For example, Boo.com was meant to be the fashion equivalent to Amazon.com. Launched in 1999, it failed after only a few months, partly due to a few faults in its business model, but mainly because of bad management of over-expanding and lavish spending at an early stage while attempting to implement all its strategies at once.

Brands can fail due to any of these scenarios, or a combination of them. In all cases, these practices can be fatal and lead to rapid failure. Marketing consultant Matt Haig has, in a way, categorized these practices in the following well-labeled scenarios.

- *Brand amnesia:* When a brand forgets what it is all about. Most common with old brands as they attempt to reinvent themselves in a radical way that may alienate its current consumers and distort its identity and value.
- *Brand ego:* When a brand overestimates its power, thus ignores competitors and new market entrants or believes it can enter any market it desires.
- *Brand megalomania:* As a result of an inflated ego, a brand believes it's powerful enough to expand in every product category it desires.
- *Brand deception:* When a brand lies and sends false messages to consumers.
- *Brand fatigue:* When a brand gets old and loses interest in reinventing itself.
- *Brand paranoia:* When a brand faces tough competition and fails to compete. Or the brand tries too hard to imitate and catch up with its competitors.
- *Brand irrelevance:* When a brand fails to evolve with its market and/or its consumer.

Finally, it is safe to conclude that branding is not a guaranteed path to success, and that a good product or expansive promotional campaigns by themselves may not be sufficient to secure market and consumer acceptance. Branding is a serious business that requires hard work, determination, and dedication. However, if done right, the rewards of branding can be long term and well worth the efforts.

Where Do We Go From Here?

Now that you understand what a brand is and the steps needed to develop one, how would a young designer or entrepreneur about to launch a new brand benefit from this roadmap? A young designer and an entrepreneur will probably have two different starting points. The young designer most likely will start by designing an inspired collection that he or she developed, with no concrete picture of the customer, the market, or the business model. On the other hand, an entrepreneur will be the opposite, starting with a business idea based on a market need that he or she sensed exists, without having a concrete product on hand. Both made a decision to start a new brand, but both lack a clear vision of all this entails. Therefore, the designer needs to determine who will wear these designs, where it will sell, and for how much. One major hurdle that faces young designers is ego. Every young designer dreams of joining the list of famous designers and perceives his or her brand as a designer brand. This does not mean, however, that they all should fall under the same market segment and talk to the same customer. It is essential, therefore, to answer these questions at this stage. One way to do this is by comparing the perceived brand with existing brands in the market. Where will the brand fit in the market scene? And how does it differ from what is already being offered? It is always helpful if the designer has some business background or an understanding of business principles, or is able to find someone to assist on the business front.

As for the entrepreneurs, although they may possess the business sense, they may lack in design creativity and understanding of technical issues. Thus, they will need to either pick an existing collection that needs financial support (such as a struggling new designer) or find the necessary assistance on the creative and technical fronts. After this marriage between design and business is achieved, a clearer picture of the direction of the brand is developed, and the brand's vision is virtually established. The rest of the steps on the roadmap will logically and smoothly follow because every decision about the brand and its products is made in context of its now-clear direction, target market, and place among competitors.

Chapter Summary

- Brand communication communicates the brand's presence, identity, and value through advertising and other channels.

- Communication reflects the positioning strategy as well as plays a role in shaping it.

- A communication strategy built on the VIP concept may be more relevant to branding then the traditional Four Ps.

- Brands are intended to live long. Throughout their life cycles, they may need to grow, be relaunched, or revitalized in order to survive and compete.

Chapter Questions and Issues for Discussion

1. Explain the VIP concept, and compare it to the traditional Four Ps.

2. Explain the concept of co-branding; give examples.

3. How do licensing and brand extensions compare as growth strategies?

KEY TERMS

BRAND AUDIT

BRAND EXTENSION

CO-BRANDING

COMMUNICATION

RELAUNCH

REPOSITION

REVITALIZATION

CASE STUDY: The Rebranding of Burberry

Burberry was founded in 1856 by Thomas Burberry as a draper's shop in Basingstoke, England. Burberry is credited for inventing gabardine, a waterproof and breathable fabric, and during World War I the British army chose Burberry's trench coat as the official army coat (see Figure 3.18). The now-famous Burberry check pattern that eventually became its trademark was introduced in the twenties as a lining. The trench coat gained popularity over the years and was worn by King Edward VIII, Humphrey Bogart and Ingrid Bergman in *Casablanca*, Audrey Hepburn in *Breakfast at Tiffany's,* and even by Peter Sellers in the Pink Panther movies. In 1955, the business was bought by Great Universal stores, a British home shopping network, and in the 1970s, the brand was licensed to the Japanese Mitsui and Sanyo corporations. Through such licensing agreements, Burberrys expanded its categories from apparel to chocolate and a wide range of products that came in a wide range of quality and price as well. With limited control over licensed products, the brand suffered from discrepancies in quality and price as well as from parallel trading, especially in Asia, which by the nineties became the major market for the brand with over 75 percent of its sales. At the time, the brand was mainly popular among older males and Asian tourists and noted mainly for its outerwear products and accessories (such as umbrellas and coats). Indeed, by the mid-nineties the brand's earnings were low, and its image was conservative, noncohesive, and anything but luxury.

The Repositioning Decision

In 1997, Rose Marie Bravo, former president of Saks Fifth Avenue and a respected industry veteran, was appointed as the new CEO. Bravo's main goal was to transform and reposition the brand from the old, unexciting brand it had become into a luxury lifestyle brand that is stylish and innovative. She immediately took a number of measures that included hiring a new team of highly qualified managers experienced in interpreting and analyzing consumer market trends. She also understood the importance of the aesthetic values of the brand's visual identity and therefore decided to change the brand's name from Burberry's to Burberry while introducing a more modern logo and packaging designs. Although the name change might seem purely cosmetic, it was meant to reflect a new and modern attitude, especially as the target of the repositioning strategy was to reintroduce Burberry as a luxury brand and attract younger customers without alienating its core customer base.

Bravo and her new team started by analyzing the luxury market to determine existing gaps where Burberry could step in and establish its niche without compromising its core brand values. Based on their research, they noticed great positioning potential between brands such as Armani and Ralph Lauren in apparel, where they would be neither too classic nor too fashion forward or cutting-edge trendy, and between Gucci and Coach in accessories. Pat Doherty, Senior Vice President of marketing, described the goal of the

Figure 3.18

A vintage
Burberry
magazine
advertisement
from 1931.

(*Image courtesy of The*

Advertising Archives)

- Reevaluating its distribution network, reviewing its partners, and opening new flagship stores in major cities, such as London, Barcelona, and New York.
- Raising prices to reflect the new positioning proposal, increasing the gross margin from 47 percent to 56 percent.

Burberry initially produced three collections:

1. Women's wear, which included outerwear, knitwear, swimwear, tailored garments, and underwear
2. Menswear, which included tailored coats, pants, and shorts
3. Accessories, which included soft items such as scarves and ties, as well as hard items such as handbags and leather goods handbags
Later Burberry introduced children's wear as well.

The Labels

One of the significant decisions was hiring Christopher Bailey as the creative director in 2000. As Bravo put it well, "Our biggest design challenge is to create a consistent brand image. The lifestyle of a teenager is very different from the lifestyle of someone who lives in the English countryside, just as the lifestyle of a banker is very different from the lifestyle of a fashionista. So unless we have a strong vision and speak with a consistent voice, we run the risk of losing our brand credibility."

While Burberry London remained the core brand, Burberry introduced a number of brands within the Burberry portfolio, such as Thomas Burberry, which is a low-priced line available in Spain and Portugal, and Burberry Blue and Black, available in Japan, targeting young men and women. At the higher end, Burberry introduced its Prorsum line to emphasize its new status as a luxury brand. With

brand as being an accessible luxury brand that is aspirational but also functional. Having decided on the repositioning goal and strategy, Bravo and the team began taking certain measures, such as:

- Cutting down the number of existing products from 100,000 SKU to 24,000.
- Ensuring an updated and consistent look across products.
- Redesigning Burberry's traditional products and introducing new products that complement the range. They classified their products as either *continuity* (classics such as the trench coat) or *fashion-oriented* (responding to new fashion trends and introduced on a collection-by-collection basis).
- Exercising tighter control over its licensing agreements where the royalties ranged from 3 to 12 percent of recommended retail value and accounted for 10 percent of Burberry's revenue. Many of the licensing agreements were either cancelled or reexamined to ensure consistency in quality, design, and pricing.

Figure 3.19a, b

(a) In need of
repositioning:
Burberry's
in 1994.

(*Image courtesy of The*

Advertising Archives)

(b) The look of
Burberry today:
a magazine ad
in 2009.

(*Image courtesy of The*

Advertising Archives)

its hand-tailored designs and innovative fabrics, Prorsum is its high-profile, haute-couture-inspired brand that is meant to be seen on runways and communicate the new status symbol of the brand.

Communication

To promote and emphasize the new positioning proposal of Burberry, Bravo and the team needed a new communication strategy and promotional campaign. They hired a world-renowned team of professional photographers including Mario Testino, famous for his work with *Vogue* and *Vanity Fair*. With a budget of more than $14 million, they were given the task to produce a campaign with supermodel Kate Moss that would end the old, tired reputation of the brand and replace it with one that is new and modern without betraying the brand's British heritage (see Figures 3.19a–b).

Success and Challenges

The campaign succeeded and Bravo and her team managed to turn the brand around and successfully reposition it. Photos of celebrities such as Madonna were seen wearing Burberry, and Christopher Bailey was hailed as one of the hottest designers in the industry. The company even received a number of awards, including one from the British fashion council. Bravo attributes part of the success to the brand's British heritage. She believes it is one of the few luxury brands that can be considered classic as well as contemporary. It is clear that Bravo and the team understood the brand very well and what challenges it faced to reach their ultimate goal. Among these challenges was how to treat their infamous checks design, which had been so overused during the early years of uncontrolled licensing. Today the check is approached in a more controlled manner so as not to kill it. It is used more subtly and in less obvious places, such as under a collar or as a lining. The strategy also aims to prove that the brand can offer more than coats and checks.

Angela Ahrendts and Burberry

In 2006, Angela Ahrendts became the new Burberry CEO. With a successful tenure at Liz Claiborne, Donna Karan, Henri Bendel, as well as Burberry,

Ahrendts had the experience and vision to direct the brand toward future growth. One of her first goals was to continue attracting a new generation of customers and emphasize the modern look of the brand through a series of initiatives including a stronger presence online. In 2009, Burberry launched Artofthetrench.com, a Web site whereby customers can buy and learn more about the iconic trench coat. But most important, they can participate and share photos of their trenches through Facebook. It is an attempt to keep the brand relevant and the iconic item "cool and hot" at the same time, as she described it. Burberry is also present on other popular social networks such as YouTube and Twitter.

The newly formed team of Ahrendts and Bailey (see Figure 3.20) managed to keep Burberry growing by introducing more items, taking greater control on pricing, and with two-thirds of revenue derived from clothing, Burberry has focused less on department stores and opened new stores. Ahrendts also emphasized the importance to keep each of Burberry's lines clearly identified.

The Future

After succeeding in repositioning the brand, Burberry faces the challenges of maintaining and defending its position and managing its own growth. Julia Werdigier from the *New York Times* described how Burberry's children's line was so successful that the company ran into production and shipping problems trying to fulfill the high demand. With plans to license beauty and cosmetics lines as well as more men's accessories, challenges of managing growth as well as facing tougher competition, ranging from high-end boutiques to discount stores where the same customer can be seen shopping, become more apparent. Burberry also remains a popular brand among international tourists, which makes it sensitive to exchange rate and international travel fluctuations. Yet Burberry seems to be heading full force toward solidifying its new position as a luxury lifestyle brand.

CASE STUDY Questions

1. Repositioning is a challenging strategy. Based on the case study, what are some of these challenges, and how did Burberry manage to deal with them?

2. Compare Burberry's turnaround under Bravo/Bailey with Gucci's under Ford/de Sole.

SOURCES

"Burberry: History of Burberry." Designer Fashion Trends. http://www.designer-fashion-trends.com/burberry.htm

Moon, Youngme. 2003. *Burberry.* Boston: Harvard Business Press.

Werdigier, Julia. 2009. "Burberry Looks Online for Ways to Gain Customers." *New York Times,* November 9. http://www.nytimes.com/2009/11/10/business/global/10burberry.htm

Figure 3.20

The team of Burberry creative director Christopher Bailey and CEO Angela Ahrendts.
(*WireImage/ Dimitrios Kambouris*)

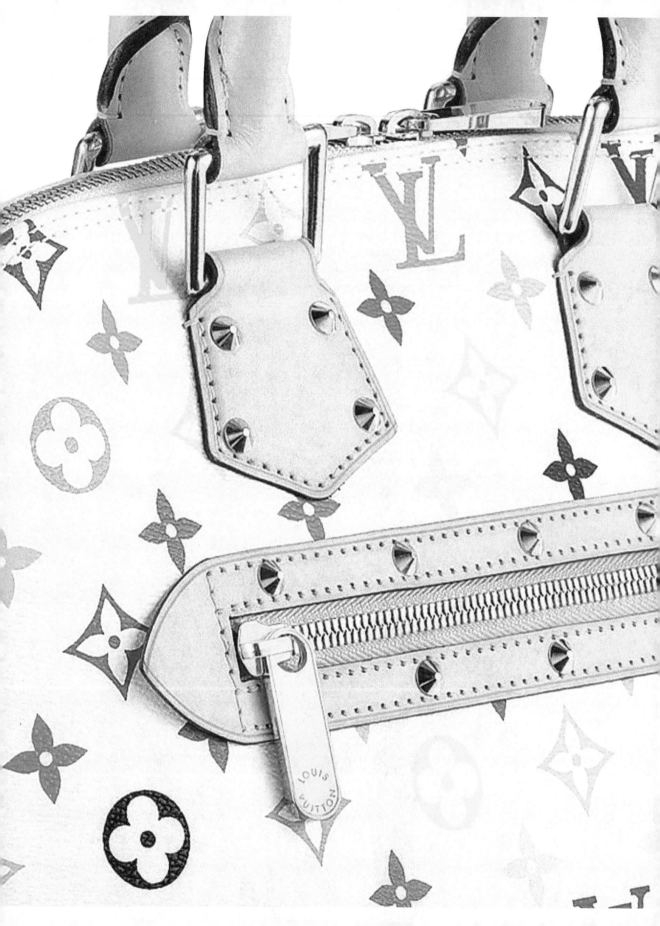

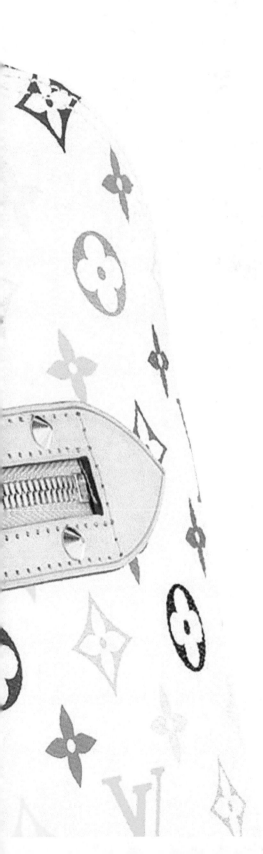

PART 2:

The Fashion Brand

**Successful
brands
are *built*,
not *born*.**

4 Luxury Fashion Brands

The quest for luxury is as old as the early days of civilization. Of all segments, luxury seems to have been a good indicator of social and technological changes. Being so closely driven by quality and craftsmanship, it has been an arena for the manifestation of artistry and innovation. At the social level, it's been a good identifier of social status in almost all societies; it defined aristocracy and royalty and eventually attested to the level of democratization in societies as indicated by how fast wealth spread and how far luxury trickled down.

Until the nineteenth century, much of what was considered luxury was custom made. Clothes, jewelry, shoes, even fragrances were custom made for royalty, the aristocracy, and the wealthy. Craftsmanship was the birthplace of luxury, as it embodied all the associations with luxury, such as artistry, scarcity, and uniqueness. In present times, we can still see custom-made suits and shirts for men, dresses and shoes for women, as well as accessories. But machine-produced luxury is now the common trend, and this causes a significant shrinkage of the crafts industry. Today, instead of small independent crafts shops, we now have major luxury groups such as LVMH, Gucci Group, and Richemont dominating the luxury scene (See Figure 4.1.).

In the second half of the twentieth century, luxury brands grew tremendously into global brands that have expanded and extended not only across borders, but across product categories as well. In addition, they expanded their business model both vertically by adding retailing to their manufacturing activities as well as

CHAPTER
OBJECTIVES

- Define what luxury brands are.

- Understand luxury markets and define profiles of luxury customers.

- Appreciate the role and purpose of luxury brands.

- Identify the branding process for luxury brands.

- Examine the possible luxury positioning strategies.

- Highlight the role of the Internet in the luxury segment.

- Examine the relationship between luxury brands and traditional marketing principles.

LVMH

MOËT HENNESSY ♦ LOUIS VUITTON

horizontally by expanding their range of products to a large range of categories. This growth translated into new marketing strategies and an expansion of the consumers' spectrum, as these brands introduced less expensive standardized products (RTW) as well as accessories and fragrances. As a result, the luxury industry is now estimated to be about a $200 million market.

Why Luxury Brands?

The term **LUXURY** is actually a relative one. What may be luxury to one person or one culture may not be so to another, and what used to be luxury in the past may not be so in the future—in fact, it may even be considered standard. Nevertheless, we all seem to share some common understanding of what luxury ought to be. Just mention the word "luxury" and a mental image is automatically triggered. A few descriptions pop into most people's minds, such as expensive, creative, trendy, exclusive, high quality, and so on. This is how most people envision a luxury brand, and these are their expectations of what the brand promise should be.

Luxury brands have been described as "brands that no one really needs, but everyone desires." If this is so, then what is it about these brands that make them so attractive and coveted? Scholars have concluded a possible set of benefits that motivate us to buy luxury:

- Feel special and stand out in a crowd; feel superior and privileged.
- Demonstrate refinement and connoisseurship.
- Feel of value and importance.
- Exercise ability and freedom ("I can do that").
- Reward ourselves for efforts and achievements; these are symbols of status and success ("I did it," "I can afford that").
- Console oneself and recuperate from a setback or misfortune.
- Command acknowledgement and respect.
- Show feelings of gratitude, love, and affection.
- Feel good, delight the senses, and experience pleasant sensations and feelings.
- Be a part of a certain group and lifestyle; feel a sense of belonging and affiliation.
- Motivate, aspire, and energize.
- Indulge and get pampered.

Luxury brands are designated to fulfill one or more of these aspects. By examining this list, we can conclude some important characteristics of luxury brands and their true relevance to consumers.

- Notions such as feeling special, self-reward, and motivation highlight the strong emotional reward associated with buying a luxury brand and demonstrate how strong a purchase motivator that is. These are brands that highly appeal to the senses.
- Feelings of belonging, admiration, affiliation, even superiority highlight the element of social impact created by luxury brands.

- Feelings of pampering, gratitude, and aspiration imply that these products and services offered under luxury brands are out of normal reach and require an effort to obtain, usually at a premium price.
- Belonging to a group while being apart from the crowd implies elements of elitism and exclusivity.
- Finally, luxury brands seem to have a strong and direct role in defining lifestyles.

These are very important observations that we shall examine in more detail shortly; but with this information on hand, we are now ready to put together a definition that best describes what luxury brands are, a good starting point to our discussion.

Defining Luxury Brands

In chapter 1, we provided the general definition of a brand as an entity with a distinctive idea expressed in a set of functional and experiential features with a promise of a value reward relevant to its end user, and an economic return to its producers (through the building of equity). A successful brand has a strong identity (mentally and physically), is innovative, consistent, competitively positioned, and holds a matching positive image in the consumer's mind.

Being "brands," luxury brands abide by the previously mentioned rules of consistently delivering and adhering to a promise, generating value to their users and (hopefully) profits to their producers, competing through innovation, and establishing a strong and effective identity. As we explore these terms again under the context

of luxury, we will notice how most of these conditions are even more relevant and critical to luxury brands than probably most other categories. However, luxury brands possess further unique characteristics that add the "luxury" dimension to the definition. Given what we have illustrated so far about the nature of luxury brands combined with our general understanding of what a brand is, we are now able to put together a definition that attempts to capture the essence of luxury brands.

A **LUXURY BRAND** can be defined as a brand that consistently delivers a unique emotional value and possesses the capacity of creating a lifestyle experience through a strong identity, a high level of creativity, and closely controlled quality, quantity, and distribution, all of which justifies asking for a premium price. Now let us examine the definition more closely and dissect its key words for a closer understanding. A closer examination highlights the following terms or notions about luxury brands.

- High level of creativity and controlled quality
- Controlled quantity and distribution
- Premium price
- Emotional value
- Strong identity

These notions translate into three major characteristics of the luxury brands.

- Heritage and craftsmanship (based on creativity and exclusivity)
- Social element (based on its strong identity and price)
- Luxury brands as lifestyle brands (based on emotional value and strong identity)

The Elements of Heritage and Craftsmanship

Luxury brands are either *designer* brands (such as Chanel and Dior) or brands that were rooted in craftsmanship (such as Gucci and Louis Vuitton) and eventually have transformed into designer brands. (See Figure 4.2.) Most luxury brands are older brands, and most of the older ones have a historic legacy that is rooted in craftsmanship. (See Table 4.1.) This legacy is usually associated with a country's cultural heritage and image, such as French couture and artistry, Italian romanticism and quality materials, English classicism and tailoring, and so on. This sense of heritage and tradition legitimizes the mystique, superiority, uniqueness, and high standard associated with these brands.

These older brands were produced mostly in small workshops by a team of skilled workers, ensuring exclusivity and quality. Many of these brands have transformed in modern times into designer brands known for their creativity and trendsetting, a trademark of this segment along with its strong association with "star" designers. In all cases, talent and heritage seem to be two strong elements that legitimize luxury brands. And because both need time to develop and be tested, most luxury brands take a longer time to get established and accepted.

TABLE 4.1	MOST LUXURY BRANDS ARE OLD BRANDS

BRANDS	YEAR FOUNDED
Louis Vuitton	1854
Prada	1913
Coco Chanel	1915
Gucci	1921
Pierre Balmain	1945
Christian Dior	1946
Hubert de Givenchy	1952
Yves Saint Laurent	1962
Emanuel Ungaro	1965
Jean-Paul Gaultier	1976
Christian Lacroix	1987

Figure 4.3

Luxury outer-
wear designer
Moncler has
been crafting
high-quality
down jackets
with care since
the 1950s.

(Courtesy of Moncler)

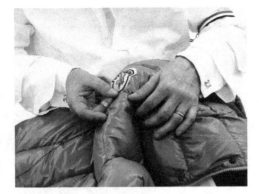

High Quality

Luxury brands' association with high quality is also rooted in their heritage of craftsmanship. Interestingly, it is a level of quality that strives on imperfections. **CRAFTSMANSHIP** is all about handwork and manual labor, which produces a high level of quality that is not really perfect but unique and hard to replicate or reproduce, unlike machine-produced pieces that are standardized and identical. It is this imperfection that gener- ates this one-of-a-kind feel that has become an expected element of luxury. (See Figure 4.3.)

Even apart from couture and hand-made luxury products, the notion of high quality in the world of machine-produced luxury remains of the utmost importance. LVMH, for instance, always bal- ances the need to ensure creative freedom for its designers while maintaining the need to impose a very strict control over the manufacturing process. It surprises people to learn that the manufacturing process of any simple garment or purse can go through around 100 steps (from sample making, color dips, pattern making, manufacturing, and so on). The construction of a LV purse or suitcase may actually go through over 1,000 tasks, including

subjection to torture machines in which it is opened and closed five times per minute for three weeks, then thrown, shaken, and crushed to ensure its resilience and quality. Each of these steps needs to be closely monitored, of course. In the same way, Gucci (and other luxury brands as well) claims to achieve its high level of quality through its selection of the best materials and strict control over production, whether in-house or outside.

Creativity

CREATIVITY assures an ongoing flow of new- ness. (See Figure 4.4.) Fashion houses produce at least two collections every year, highlighting new

Figure 4.4

Haute couture
is both creative
and trend-setting.
Here is a look
from Dior's
Fall/Winter
2009/2010 Paris
runway show.

(© Stephane Cardinale/

People Avenue/Corbis)

a

b

Figure 4.5a, b

(a) Star designer Giorgio Armani embodies the core of the Armani brand identity.
(Getty Images/Bohdan Cap)

(b) Larger-than-life Donatella Versace is another example of a star designer who embodies her brand.
(WireImage/SGranitz)

trends and designs that are meant to surprise, awe, and inspire both customers as well as a trail of factories and manufacturers waiting to copy these trends in every quality and price point possible.

In the world of luxury, designers are usually transformed into superstars and in many ways are seen as *being* the brand themselves. With their talent and character, **STAR DESIGNERS** are a major marketing force behind the brand and in many ways help define the personality of the brand. (See Figures 4.5a–b.) Historically, star luxury designers were the trendsetters and the dictators of what people should wear and when. Today, this power has waned, due to consumers being more informed, empowered, and independent; however, these designers continue to be "celebrities" at the forefront of the brand, and their creativity remains anticipated and influential. It is interesting to see how the industry, consumers, and observers react when a successful star designer leaves a company or retires (such as when Tom Ford left Gucci, Valentino retired, and Alexander McQueen died); questions and speculations are immediately raised about the future of the brand in spite of years of history and tradition behind them. This fact highlights the strong association between luxury and creativity mixed with a strong brand personality. When these masters are gone, it is usually not enough to just bring on board a new creative talent; it has to be someone who is both creative and understands the meaning and personality of the brand. Fresh ideas are always welcomed and surely needed but with a sense of direction, vision, and responsibility.

American Luxury

There is a strong association between luxury brands and heritage, and the fact that most luxury

Figure 4.6

Chairman and
CEO of LVMH,
Bernard Arnault
had proven a
mastermind in
the business
of fashion.

(© Gaudenti Sergio/

Corbis KIPA)

tailor in his youth may use that to imprint that sense of history and craftsmanship on his new brand. For example, while *Bontoni* is a new label[1] (Italian custom-made men's shoes), the family behind the brand has been creating made-to-measure shoes in a small Italian village for years. Owners Franco Gazzani and his cousin Lewis Cutillo use that story to create a sense of history. (See Figure 4.7.)

American luxury brands, such as Ralph Lauren, Donna Karan, Calvin Klein, and others, are comparatively new, and they lack that history and heritage that most European brands possess (see Figure 4.8). This is why these brands are introduced mainly as lifestyle brands that rely on an enormous marketing machine to establish a convincing story and an identity strong enough to overcome the need for any historical references. Timing is another major factor because most of these brands emerged at a time when there were no recognized international American luxury brands; at the same time, American culture and lifestyle were highly admired around the world, so they benefitted greatly from this association.

brands are old brands explains, among many other reasons, why it is hard to establish new luxury brands.

A great example is the Christian Lacroix brand. Lacroix is admired as a true creative genius and probably one of the few remaining couturiers. Yet to the surprise of many, this brand that adorned fashion magazines around the world never generated any profits. It was acquired by Louis Vuitton, only to be sold later, and it finally filed for bankruptcy in 2009. When asked, Bernard Arnault, CEO of Lacroix's former owner LVMH (see Figure 4.6), explained that it is hard to launch a luxury brand from the ground up today, and that a luxury brand must have a heritage to legitimize its existence.

The power of marketing is always used to compensate for the lack of history or heritage. Marketing creates a myth and a story around the brand that provides a sense of history, tradition, or craftsmanship. A designer who was trained as a

Figure 4.7

Luxury shoe
brand Bontoni
plays on a family
heritage of
craftsmanship.

(Courtesy of Bontoni)

The Social Element of Luxury Brands

Another strong element of luxury brands is their strong social reference. All brands respond to their social environments; however, luxury brands seem to have an especially strong social association. Luxury brands are aspiring brands that trigger many social signals, such as success, wealth, sophistication, and so on. The level and breadth of their adoption may also indicate the social structure and level of economic maturity of societies. For instance, more people adopt luxury in economically developed and socially stable societies.

The other social dimension has to do with the fact that luxury brands establish a great part of their legitimacy as aspiring brands from the level of social awareness toward them. For instance, a customer may purchase a luxury brand dress for its design and exclusivity, among other reasons. However, if this is the case, then why not go to a

Thus, timing plus effective and intensive marketing plus new unfulfilled lifestyle aspiration helped make American brands succeed (see Figure 4.9). These combined factors may also explain why great American talents from earlier generations, such as Geoffrey Beene and Bill Blass, never reached the international heights of the newer generation.

In comparison to European luxury brands, American brands have been described as "marketing brands" in that they are clearly consumer based, backed by a powerful marketing machine, and driven by American consumer needs. They define an accessible, relaxed, and casual style.

On the other hand, European brands are clearly creative driven in the sense that the creator or designer seems to have full independent authority over the content and personality of the brand. They value aesthetics and products that appeal to the senses. For them, function is secondary to the emotional value created. See Table 4.2 for a comparison of the characteristics of American versus European brands.

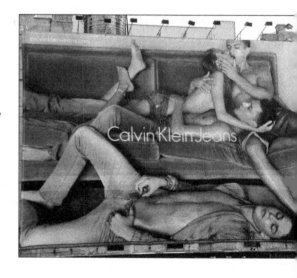

tailor and get a made-to-measure garment that without a doubt will be the most unique and exclusive dress she has?

One of the reasons is that no one will probably know or appreciate the dress the way they would if it was a Dior or a Chanel that they may have seen on the cover of a magazine or on the runway. So part of the significance of acquiring a luxury brand lies in how others perceive and appreciate your purchase. In reality, part of the goals of marketing luxury and its advertising campaigns is to specifically achieve that. Advertising luxury is usually not informative, but rather image focused. It is meant to create awareness and emotional interest. Most regular luxury customers don't really need these advertisements to learn about the brand or where

to buy it. But the image and desire need to stay alive for all to admire and aspire to.

Luxury Brands as Lifestyle Brands

Luxury brands have the potential, more than any other segment, to be lifestyle brands. A **LIFE-STYLE BRAND** successfully identifies itself with a lifestyle and a marketing segment to the point that its name or image is mentally triggered when the segment is mentioned. A brand becomes a lifestyle brand if it succeeds in developing a strong association either through representation or adaptation of a way of life. Thus, a lifestyle brand needs not just to be a part of a lifestyle, but to define that lifestyle. It is common to find almost every manufacturer in the

TABLE 4.2	AMERICAN VS. EUROPEAN LUXURY BRANDS
AMERICAN LUXURY BRANDS	**EUROPEAN LUXURY BRANDS**
MOTIVATIONS: Social	MOTIVATIONS: Individual
· Realization of social dreams and prominence in a group	· Realization of personal dreams
· Fulfill personal ambition	· Fulfill emotional desires
· Perfumes are an external, social accessory; they are about the brand	· Perfumes are about me, my identity, my scent
RELATIONSHIP: Functional	RELATIONSHIP: Emotional
· Practicality, utility, functionality	· Aesthetics, sensory elements, style
· Keywords: wearable, comfortable, informal	· Keywords: emotions, vanity, fantasy
POSITIONING: Customer-driven brands	POSITIONING: Creativity-driven brands
· User friendly, casual, simple	· Eccentric, no constraints
· Practical needs	· Fantasies
· Strong marketing, customer service	· Creativity, imagination, craftsmanship
· Lifestyles, modernity, status	· Culture, heritage, class

Sources: Adapted from Michael Chevalier and Gérald Mazzalovo, *Luxury Brand Management: A World of Privilege* (Singapore: John Wiley & Sons, 2008); and RISC International, *The Luxury Market*, 2003.

Figure 4.10

Harley Davidson
is a classic
example of a
brand directly
linked to a
particular
lifestyle.

(Image Courtesy of the

Advertising Archives)

industry claiming that his or her brand is a lifestyle brand; however, they are confusing this with the fact that every brand belongs to or accommodates some lifestyle but does not necessarily define or represent it in the consumer's mind. A true measure of the brand's capacity to represent and define a lifestyle lies in its ability to extend across a wide range of products such as cosmetics, home furnishings, accessories, and even branching out to services such as restaurants and hotels. A lifestyle brand is a brand you want to see at your home, office, in your car and boat, so that its products become integral to a particular lifestyle. However, such extensions need to remain relevant and consistent in portraying the lifestyle, or it may fail and produce negative results.

Lifestyle brands create a sense of belonging to a desired and sought-after subculture by linking the personality traits associated with the brand to the buyers' own sense of identity. Lifestyle brands are mostly luxury brands, but there are successful examples from other segments such as Harley Davidson, which succeeded in establishing itself as the flagship brand for a certain lifestyle and managed to extend the product range into a wide range tailoring to the needs of that lifestyle and that customer (see Figure 4.10). The association between luxury brands and lifestyles is yet another one that highlights the significant role marketing plays in introducing and eventually establishing the brand as a lifestyle brand.

Branding for Luxury: The Luxury Brand Consumer

As mentioned in previous chapters, buying a luxury brand product is more of an emotional than rational decision. It is a decision where the customer may value aesthetics over economic returns. It is a decision where intangibles such as store atmosphere, image, and sophistication play an important role rather than straightforward value for money.

Luxury brands' customers are affluent, sophisticated, and today they are more confident in making fashion decisions and establishing their own personal styles by mixing brands instead of going for a one-brand look.

The first assumption about a typical luxury customer is that he or she is rich. That may be true for the most part; however, in reality, almost anyone could be a luxury brand customer. Therefore, one way to categorize the luxury customer is through the frequency of their purchases. This breaks down into two levels of customers:

- Regular luxury buyers
- Occasional luxury buyers

Regular Buyers

Regular buyers are those who consistently buy the brand's products. Generally they are wealthy customers, but the origins of their wealth may vary from old money (inherited) to new money accumulated through a self-made fortune. The significance of this distinction lies in the way each group reacts to economic changes. In general, luxury brands' customers are less sensitive to economic and price changes. They demonstrate a highly inelastic demand that is not affected that much by these changes.

On the other hand, research shows that "new money" customers, as well as those who belong to the upper-middle class and whose main source of income is their executive salaries or professions, tend to be more sensitive to economic changes because they have earned their money the hard way.

However, consumer behavior studies and research data reveal an interesting observation about luxury brand customers. Studies show that these passionate customers usually develop a strong emotional link to these products, so much so that these products are not necessarily the first things they drop or give up when the going gets tough. For instance, someone may be willing to sell his car and take public transportation to work in hard times but would still prefer to hold on to his Rolex watch.

Or he might take public transportation and make other sacrifices but keep his Porsche safe and sound in his garage for better times.

Whereas these customers' assets may suffer at times of economic recession, their disposable income generally does not drop

that much. Nevertheless, statistics show that severe global economic recessions, such as that witnessed at end of 2008, usually hit the luxury industry hard. And for the first time in many years, many of these brands were forced to promote their products through discounts and special offers, which is normally highly uncommon in this segment.

Occasional Buyers

Among buyers of luxury products, about 63 percent of respondents in developed countries said they bought a luxury product in the last 24 months.[2] Occasional buyers can be anyone who every now and then may want to treat themselves or someone they love to a special gift for a significant occasion, such as a wedding, graduation, or an anniversary. These groups are referred to by some as the "outsiders."

An important difference between the two groups of customers is their perception of luxury and their approach to the whole shopping experience. *Regulars* usually take many of the characteristics such as quality and exclusivity for granted; their choice boils down to which brand matches their lifestyle and with which one can they identify. On the other hand, for the *outsiders* it is more of a full experience. When they decide to go to Tiffany's to buy *that* ring or to LV to buy *that* bag they anticipate a complete pleasurable experience from the minute they enter the store. They expect ultimate customer service and an experience that is special and different from any shopping experience they have had before. To them, this is both a financial and emotional investment. They take their notion of value for money to a higher level where they expect a high

Figure 4.11

Occasional
buyers of luxury
products want
a particularly
pleasurable
shopping
experience, such
as that enjoyed
by shoppers
here at the chic
new designer
shoe depart-
ment—an entire
floor devoted
to luxury foot-
wear—at Saks
Fifth Ave,
New York.
(AFP/Getty Images)

return for their money yet with the understanding that part of this return will be emotional and experiential. (See Figure 4.11.) Thus, they want the product to be beautiful, unique, and scarce. They are also looking for a special shopping experience that speaks to their senses, and although they know it may not make total economic sense, to them treating your senses is worth it once in a while.

Do Luxury Brands' Customers Differ by Nationalities?

A recent report by RISC International comparing customers' responses in three major luxury markets—the United States, Europe, and Japan—in reference to their top "dream" brands, demonstrated how the three markets are quite different and polarized. For example:[3]

- Most brands on the Japanese list are known for their accessories and leather products.
- The top brands in the United States and Japan are not mainly fashion brands (Rolex, Tiffany, and Hermes), whereas in Europe the top three are Armani, Chanel, and Calvin Klein.

- Calvin Klein and Cartier appeared on the U.S. and Europe list and not Japan.
- Rolex and Gucci were the only brands appearing on all three lists.
- The Japanese list was much shorter, including the six brands of Rolex, Hermes, Bulgari, Gucci, Louis Vuitton, and Tiffany. The United States and Europe had eight.
- The American list of preferences is diverse in terms of fashion image. Although it included Gucci and Armani, it also included more casual brands, such as Tommy Hilfiger.
- The American list also included more fashion brands than the other three regions.
- Finally, preferences had an almost equal weight in Japan and the United States, whereas the disparity was noticeable in Europe. For example, Armani got 21.6 percent of the vote, whereas Gucci got 10 percent and Hugo Boss got 16.5 percent.

In addition, the same study showed that even within a market such as Europe, there are significant differences. For example, in France the list included almost all French brands and in Italy almost all Italian brands. On the other hand, the analysis also showed some similarities among luxury customers in all regions.

- They all seek creativity and innovation.
- They all mix styles and appreciate a variety of brands.
- They all are self-conscious, individualistic, achievers, modern, and trendsetters.
- They all care about feeling good as well as looking good (as demonstrated by the products carried by the brands of preferences).

The relationship between luxury brands and their customers is indeed special and interesting.

In the past, luxury brands and celebrity designers were seen as fashion dictators. Trends were born on the catwalks of Paris and other capitals to dictate how and what people should and should not wear. That influence seems to have waned in last decades as customers, especially women, became more socially independent and empowered by career opportunities, education, and new technologies such as the Internet. Customers are more willing to define their own styles and mix and match trends and brands as they please. However, this does not mean that luxury brands have totally lost control. Luxury brands are still trendsetters but not in the old "my way or else" attitude. Indeed luxury brands had always established this interesting relationship with their customers whereby they are not expected to follow their customers all the time (as marketing theories recommends) as much as they are expected to educate them; after all, this is what trendsetting is all about. This idea is a major departure from marketing principles where brands are supposed to respond to customer needs. Make no mistake, a luxury brand still needs to understand its customers, their habits, and their aspirations to stay focused. However, they also need to be innovative and manage to surprise their customers. They are supposed to be the reference to good taste and new trends and not vice versa.

LVMH conducted a focus study before it launched the Kenzo perfume, Flower (see Figure 4.12). The consensus among respondents and potential buyers was generally negative toward the scent and bottle design. However, the Kenzo team believed that the perfume delivered something new and that it had good potential. They went through with the launch, and the result was an increase in Kenzo's sales of more than 75 percent. The Kenzo team was not just a group of stubborn, egocentric marketers; they were a group who probably understood the potential of their product, its market niche and competitive advantage, and, above all, the role of their brand in the lives of its customers. Luxury is not always meant to offer what people expect. It needs to surprise and innovate.

The Luxury Brand Decision: The Brand Vision

As mentioned in earlier chapters, any new brand idea starts in the mind and imagination of a visionary who sees an opportunity for something new and exciting that will please and satisfy the needs and aspirations of new customers and

Figure 4.13

Legendary
Coco Chanel,
in her signature
multiple strands
of pearls,
photographed
by Cecil Beaton
in 1938.

(Condé Nast Archive/
CORBIS)

has the potential to strive and grow. In the case of luxury brands, that visionary has historically been the creative designer or the craftsman who possesses the skill, talent, and imagination that made his or her offering unique and special. These visionaries include Coco Chanel (see Figure 4.13), Guccio Gucci, Calvin Klein, Christian Dior, Cristobal Balenciaga (see Figure 4.14), as well as other legendary figures.

However, as these brands grow and transform from being a craftsman's workshop- (or atelier-) based brand into a designer brand and a complex and extended operation, the business confronts new market realities and challenges. Thus, it becomes clear that with the creative vision there is a need for an entrepreneurial one as well as strong business acumen. For that reason, the responsibilities of stirring the business are usually delegated

Figure 4.14

Visionary
Spanish designer
Cristobal
Balenciaga
brought his
House of
Balenciaga to
Paris in the
1930s, where he
became known
as the "couturier
of couturiers."

(© Lipnitzki/Roger-
Viollet/The Image
Works)

to business managers and CEOs or a business partner. All successful luxury brands have this mix of talents. After all, fashion is serious business. Bernard Arnault once said

> true artists . . . do not want the process to end there (referring to creating new designs), they want people to wear their dresses, or spray their perfume, or carry the luggage they have designed. . . . If you ask them they would say they don't actually care one way or another if people buy their products. But they do care, it's just buried in their DNA, and as a manager you have to be able to see it there.

This indeed is the responsibility of the manager or the business partner. It is no surprise, therefore, that most successful launches, re-launches, and repositioning of luxury brands in recent history have been either orchestrated by a visionary CEO or businesses managers who teamed up with creative designers to achieve the transformation. Good examples are the teams of Domenico de Sole and Tom Ford for Gucci and Bravo and Bailey for Burberry. Both these cases demonstrate that the brand decision is not just a creative decision, but a marriage between true creativity and a sound business proposal.

LVMH pinpoints five priorities that reflect the fundamental values shared by all group stakeholders.[4]

1. Be creative and innovate.
2. Aim for product excellence.
3. Bolster the image of their brands with passionate determination.
4. Act as entrepreneurs.
5. Strive to be the best in all they do.

are meant to be trendsetters, aggressively bold, and, to borrow from the TV show *Star Trek*, go places where none have gone before. It is through continuous innovation that luxury brands are expected to maintain technical superiority and technological advancement.

Luxury brands do not need just innovation, but leadership in innovation, which some have tagged as "radical innovation," meaning innovation that surprises and awes. This level of innovation is highly expected by luxury customers who traditionally fall into the innovation category on the customer adoption curve. (See Figure 4.15.)

However, whereas innovation can have a strong and positive impact on the functionality of the product and deliver a rational justification for buying it, it is creativity and artistry that delivers the emotional impact that is highly associated with this

The Product Mix

We have determined in previous chapters that a product in its essence is a sum of its features and attributes that we referred to collectively as the product mix, which include: the product itself with its tangible features, the price, the distribution choice, and the relevant service (such as customer service, warranties, etc.). Together this "mix" defines the product.

Product

Luxury brands are driven by high quality, technical superiority, technological advancement, and unique craftsmanship. Creativity and innovation are key factors to the survival of any brand in any category, but it is more so with luxury brands because they

Figure 4.15

Dutch designers Victor & Rolf are masters of innovation who consistently push the boundaries. Here, a look from the Paris runway of their Spring/ Summer 2010 ready-to-wear collection.

(WireImage/ Dominique Charriau)

category. As B. Arnault once said, "a new product is not creative if it does not shock. Our whole business is based on giving our artists and designers complete freedom to invent without limits." Thus, it is an essential marriage between innovation and artistry that forms the DNA of luxury brands and their status as trendsetters. (See Figure 4.16.)

Luxury products range from haute couture to RTW. They include various segments such as garments, fur, leather, even jeans, and extend to cosmetics, jewelry, watches, and perfumes. Probably the biggest difference between luxury in today's world and luxury in the past is the relative disappearance of custom or bespoke products.

Another important element of luxury fashion is the concept of the *collection*. A collection is a coherent group of pieces that tell a story. It may sound like a given concept, but in reality it is a common problem among new businesses and young designers who have the tendency to produce beautifully designed *pieces* that do not necessarily work together to form a true collection. The collection concept is important in defining the story and theme behind the designs and highlighting the trends. In collections, individual pieces make more sense than on their own because they are appreciated in relevance to other pieces and a larger concept.

Price

Choosing the right price is still of the utmost importance. Price is a function of many elements, such as cost, competition, and so on. Luxury brands are known for their **PREMIUM PRICES,** in part because a premium price contributes to the exclusivity factor. So in deciding upon price, there is a psychological and marketing element to consider. But obviously there is a financial necessity as well. Luxury brands are expensive to produce, manage, and market. By definition, luxury brands use the best of materials and talents available and are produced in small quantities

They have high costs, and the price needs to cover expenses and generate maximum profit and return on investment while maintaining a healthy cash flow, if possible. As a matter of fact, luxury brands have a lot of limitations and constraints that contribute to their high costs and margins, such as the need to open retail stores in only the best and most expensive locations in every city they enter. (See Figure 4.17.) Their flagship stores, normally

located in the city of their headquarters, are usually extravagant in order to better showcase the brand and its image. (See Figure 4.18.)

Extensive marketing is another major cost factor; in the case of fashion, luxury brands rely on producing at least two fashion shows annually. Fashion shows cost a lot, with no direct financial return; and many of the couture clothes showcased are meant for publicity and media coverage rather than for sales. So from a financial perspective, fashion shows seem to be a losing venture; however, it is through these fashion shows and the buzz they generate that the brand is able to sell and market its more saleable items, such as RTW, cosmetics, and perfumes.

From an economic perspective, price is always a function of supply and demand (scarcity), among other factors such as the elasticity of the price in relation to these two elements. By looking at luxury brands, we notice that they are usually in short supply, in high demand, and are price inelastic (demand is not highly affected by price changes), all of which contribute to the premium price strategy.

It is important to remember that just raising the price does not by itself transform the brand into a luxury one. Just as being rich does not make you an aristocrat, so it is with brands: a higher price by itself does not make a brand a luxury brand. There is still the need for some point of reference, such as a heritage or a legacy, to make it legitimate and believable.

One major constraint that luxury brands face with their price strategies is their inability or unwillingness to drastically reduce prices as demanded by economic changes. As a matter of fact, many brands would rather kill the product than offer it at a discount price and harm the brand's image.

Given the high costs and constraints, luxury brands actually take much longer to break even, let alone make profit. However, successful brands have the potential for very high profits due to their big margins, product extensions, and global reach. The example of Christian Lacroix given earlier in this chapter is a good demonstration of how a talented designer and a brand that dominated the fashion scene for some time never made a profit and ended up filing for bankruptcy. On the other hand, the Alexander McQueen brand only started to be profitable in 2007 in spite of the celebrated ingenuity of the late designer.

Why do luxury brands take a long time to make money, and why do they still exist if they are losing money?

Figure 4.18

The Louis
Vuitton Paris
flagship store
covered in
a display of
giant luggage.
(*Bloomberg via Getty
Images*)

First, the high costs of distribution, quantity, and production restriction result in luxury brands taking much longer to financially break-even compared to mass-produced brands, which also means that they need higher investment up front in order to start the business. Paired with a long production lead time that is a characteristic of the fashion industry in general, the financial strain on luxury brands is stronger.

Second, although the luxury brand's customer is generally less vulnerable to economic changes, luxury brands may still be forced to deal with unsold merchandise due to severe economic downturns and weakening economies. They have to discount merchandise (a highly unpopular option due to potential negative impact on the brand's image); move the merchandise to their outlets; sell to their employees; or sell to other discount stores that agree to conceal the brand's name and label. In all cases, any unsold amount will represent a higher percentage of total merchandise compared to other mass-produced brands that produce a larger amount of merchandise.

Finally, many investors may shy away from the high cost and long-term financial commitment of developing luxury brands, which could be one of the many reasons why most luxury brands start as family or private operations.

Luxury goods, although sometimes having a utilitarian function such as clothes or shoes, usually do not carry a price tag that reflects their intrinsic cost or the added value they provide, certainly not in comparison to an ordinary pair of shoes or an inexpensive handbag. The markups on some luxury products is sometimes eight to ten fold. Luxury goods are typically of exceptional quality, but the prices charged to consumers are at a huge premium over cost. The price is irrational and justified on the exclusivity and creativity of the products. In recent years, luxury brands have witnessed a dramatic increase in production and occasional reduction in price due to moving many production activities to the Far East. However, the combination of greater availability, affordability, and in some cases diminished quality threatens the luxury status of many brands. If the notion of being extremely expensive is a defining component of being a luxury product, then affordability becomes a measure of reduced luxury. If a brand becomes affordable to a larger market, it brings into questioning its status as a luxury brand.

Whereas these pricing principles may be shared by all luxury brands, pricing strategies may differ from one company to the other. Louis Vuitton, for example, used to adopt a simple strategy of multiplying cost by a fixed gross-margin rate. This strategy is rooted in the old days when LV was made to order, like most luxury crafts-based brands, making one trunk at a time. However, as the company grew and expanded its product range, they kept that policy in place for a long time. Prices were determined simply by multiplying the cost by the fixed margin and then comparing it to the market; if the final price turned out to be too high, they started examining measures to lower cost without compromising quality in order to maintain the desired fixed gross margin. If it could not be achieved, then the product could be easily cancelled. The idea behind this policy was to maintain a certain level of profitability across all products without the need to compromise for the sake of adapting to the market. This attitude is not the norm, and it demonstrates that the craftsman's mentality and artisan attitude somehow remain built in the DNA of many luxury brands no matter how the business model may change.

Distribution

Luxury brands are said to achieve part of their status by being a dream that is only affordable by a few. They are meant to be *exclusive brands* that require some effort to obtain. The exclusivity factor of luxury brands is achieved in part by a low volume of production and a tightly controlled distribution channel.

Luxury brands are generally smaller operations compared to other segments. Even large luxury groups such as LVMH usually operate through a portfolio of smaller operations (over 50 for LVMH). However, because they are trendsetting brands and at the forefront of innovation and creativity, they possess high awareness, status, and respect that may be much larger than their actual size as a company. This great interest and high exposure does create the illusion that these brands are larger than life.

Exclusivity and the high level of control associated with luxury brands result in mini-mizing the middleman and franchising arms, while tightly controlling licensing in order to retain control of how and where the products are made and sold. As a matter of fact, this attitude was one of the first strategic decisions adopted by Burberry in the process of reposi-tioning the brand as a luxury one.

In terms of luxury brands' distribution, retailing remains the main channel of distribution. These brands are usually distributed and sold through exclusive or tightly controlled channels: such as:

- *Free-standing or fully owned chains of boutiques:* LV and Hermes sell only in their stores around the world (except for perfumes, which are sold through various chains). For the most part, all the stores are fully owned and controlled from headquarters that enable many activities to be coordinated. In addition, inventory systems are usually very well organized. For instance, classic items are shipped directly to stores, while store managers can selectively decide on seasonal or specific items. It is a highly controlled and efficient system. LV has over 1,000 directly operated stores whereas Bottega Veneta has a network of 83 directly operated stores, which generated 87 percent of the brand's 2005 revenue.[5] These chains usually include a flagship store that is usually the largest of all their stores and the ultimate storefront for displaying the range of products and experiencing the brand's personality. It is the ultimate place to live and experience the brand as it was envisioned. The Ralph Lauren flagship store on Madison Avenue is a great example of an ultimate brand store that reflects the brand's spirit and personality in every detail and product. Flagship stores are usually located in the city of their headquarters and possibly other major fashion capitals of the world such as New York, Paris, Milan, or Tokyo.

- *Exclusive franchise stores:* There are stores that are not owned by the brand, but look and feel like fully owned stores, carrying the brand exclusively and operating under tight guidelines.
- *In-store boutiques:* These are unique areas inside of the world's prestigious department stores (such as Neiman Marcus, Bloomingdale's, and Takashimaya). In most cases, these areas are rented and managed independently from the host store.
- *Catalogs or the Internet:* These are other retailing options that might be employed.

It is possible to have a mixed system of a few exclusive stores headed with a flagship, department store corners or shop-in-shops, as well as counters in case of perfumes and accessories. Cartier and Bulgari are good examples of this mixed system whereby they maintain their own exclusive stores but also sell watches and selected fine jewelry at individual jewelers.

In general, the system must take into consideration the brand's specific strengths and weaknesses in determining the best channels. In some cases, the nature of the market dictates the nature of the distribution channel. Japan, which is one of the top markets for luxury brands, is very hard to penetrate independently due to a tightly closed and complicated retail and distribution system. Because of this, most foreign luxury brands such as LV and Gucci have entered the market through some form of partnership or alliance with a local player.

Location Challenges

The options for luxury brand store locations are much more strictly limited than those of mass-market brands. It is customary to locate luxury brand stores in exclusive neighborhoods and high-end streets around the world to reinforce the brand's image and status. (See Figures 4.19a–b.)

Some of the famous locations where luxury brands are commonly found are:

- Rue du Faubourg Saint-Honoré in Paris
- Via Montenapoleone and Via della Spiga in Milan
- Fifth Avenue and Madison Avenue in New York
- Rodeo Drive in Los Angeles
- Ginza district in Tokyo

Even within these limited choices, more limitations apply. For example, the most desirable part

Figure 4.19a, b
(a) The Christian
Lacroix boutique
on Paris' tony
Foubourg St.
Honoré.
(BIM/ARNAUD
MONNIER/MAXPPP/
Newscom)
(b) Tokyo's
Ginza district,
home to luxury
boutiques like
Chanel and
Bulgari.
(AFP/Getty Images/
YOSHIKAZU TSUNO)

of Fifth Avenue is a small section roughly between 54th Street and 57th Street.

The choices are also limited for distribution through hi-end department or specialty stores, which may include Bloomingdale's, Saks, Nordstorm, Neiman Marcus, Bergdorf Goodman, Barneys (United States), Galeries Lafayette, Le Bon Marché (France), Selfridges, Harvey Nichols (England), Seibu, Matsuzakaya (Japan), Grand Palace and Luxury Village (Russia), and Daslu (Brazil). This shallow breadth of choices creates a major challenge for future expansion within the same city. With such limitations, the options for opening a stand-alone store may be minimal, and eventually other options such as in-store boutiques in luxury department stores will be viable.

Luxury Brands on the Internet

Most luxury brands have a presence on the Internet. However, most luxury brand Web sites are designed to offer information, news, and brand updates. For other luxury brands, online shopping options are usually available for standard and lower-priced items. This limited and conservative approach adopted by luxury brands toward the Internet may be due to many factors, such as:

- Shopping luxury products in brick-and-mortar stores and boutiques is an exciting and integral part of the whole experience for many luxury shoppers. The Internet simply can't offer that experience. Shopping in luxury boutiques allows the customer to experience the brand from the moment they enter the door and get pampered by the well-trained sales personnel. This is in addition to fulfilling the obvious need to examine, touch, or feel the product before buying. Also, for many customers, the act of buying a luxury product is an experience in itself. Understandably, all these factors cannot be fully emulated online.

- There is a common belief by luxury brands that the luxury customer is not the typical online shopper; not only because of missing the shopping experience, but because of their lifestyle and working habits.

- The high price tag of most luxury products makes it riskier and less conventional for online shopping.

- The Internet overexposes the brand and denies it one if its main characteristics—exclusivity.

- There are concerns that online customer services may never match the service level and personal factor the customer experiences in stores.

Another factor that may hurt the brand's image if made available online is the tendency for online shoppers to use price comparison sites and software such as kelkoo.com, Net-A-Porter, and so on. The price discrepancies these sites deliver is believed to hurt the brand's image and again limit its exclusivity.

On the other side of the argument:

- Statistics show that wealthy online shoppers spent more per year on luxury goods: $114,632, compared with $23,000 for in-store shoppers, which may indicate that luxury customers are spending more time and money online than believed.[6]
- Fear of lessened exclusivity may be a factor only if the products are sold through various channels, which is usually not the case with luxury brands.
- It is true that the in-store shopping experience is unique; however, research shows that it

may be more relevant for first-time luxury shoppers rather than regular customers who would appreciate an online alternative given their busy schedules. It has also become a common practice for many shoppers to first visit the stores to see and feel the products, then make the actual purchase online at their convenience. Thus, the online experience may actually complement the shopping experience and not necessarily compete with or replace it.

In spite of this cautious attitude toward the Internet by luxury brands, most do have an electronic presence of some form, as discussed in the following sections.

DESIGNER'S ONLINE STORES

A few luxury brands, such as Louis Vuitton, Gucci, Stella McCartney, and Tiffany's, allow customers to shop online. However, most of these Web sites do not offer the complete range of items in their collections, especially high-priced items. (See Figure 4.20.)

SHOPPING PORTERS

These are Web sites that sell different brands and are not exclusively owned by any one brand. Examples are Net-A-Porter and Zappos Couture. They are a one-stop shop for many brands. Their products range from fashion to accessories and shoes. They specifically offer good exposure and marketing opportunities for newer brands and young designers. These sites could offer other services as well. For instance, Net-A-Porter offers an editorial magazine section that covers latest trends and fashion news (see Figure 4.21). These online shopping porters also include discount

Figure 4.20

Oscar de la Renta's Web site allows one to view collections, learn about the house, find retail locations, and make limited purchases.

(Courtesy WWD/ Fairchild Publications)

outlets such as TheOutnet.com, which offers
original designer handbags and apparels with discounts that range from 40 percent to 60 percent.
Ideeli.com is a members-only shopping portal/
blog that offers limited-time discount prices on
sought-after brands. Every day a few brands are
featured for almost 80 percent discounts as a
limited-time event.

INFORMATION AND EDITORIAL WEB SITES

These Web sites do not have shopping options;
rather, they offer the latest industry trends and
information, including runway videos, photos; and
designers' profiles. Examples are Style.com and
Fashion TV.

LUXURY RENTALS

An interesting group of stores that offer luxury
products for rent on a weekly or monthly basis
(usually with a purchase option). These sites are
seen as yet another step toward the democratization of luxury through the Internet. Examples
are Frombagstoriches.com and Avelle (a.k.a.
bag borrow or steal), which offer customers
a chance to rent expensive designer bags and
accessories at reasonable prices. The bags are
delivered with free shipping within two days and
are to be returned on a specific day in a postage-
prepaid carton provided with the product. They
offer a large selection of brands, such as Betsy
Johnson, Louis Vuitton, Burberry, Fendi, and
others.

With so many options, at the time of this
book's publication, a customer looking for a Louis
Vuitton Totally MM handbag has at least four
online purchase alternatives (see Figure 4.22).

1. *From Louis Vuitton.com:* Around $970
2. *BagBorroworSteal:* For members, $30/week, $90/month; nonmembers, $45/week, $115/month; plus $9.95 shipping, $10 insurance, $5-$9.95 monthly membership fee
3. *FromBagstoRiches:* Small bag: $139.95/month
4. *eBay:* Lightly used bag was recently sold with a Buy Now option for $800

Replicas

The luxury segment is the hardest hit by the counterfeit industry. Fake luxury bags are produced in massive quantities in Asia, making copies available of seemingly every brand (see Figure 4.23). With most of the counterfeit products coming from Asia, the Internet has created a new and convenient outlet for these manufacturers and their replicas or fake products to reach a wider market. What is interesting is that many of these sites do not lie about their products. They clearly state that these are almost identical replicas. The same Louis Vuitton $970 handbag can be bought for a fraction of the price (less than $200) together with easy payment and delivery options, and even a lifetime warranty.

Here is how one site openly describes its services:

> Nnbag is dedicated to providing the best and newest designer handbags at a fraction of the cost. We start by purchasing original designer handbags and shipping them to our factories in China. We then inspect every nook and cranny and purchase the same materials to ensure that the products we manufacture are virtually indistinguishable from the designer originals in every way.[7]

Rolex watches, one of the most replicated luxury items, come in about four grades and three major categories, each with its standard of quality and service:

- Chinese manufactured replicas: Watches in the Chinese grade replicas can cost up to $120.
- Japanese manufactured replicas: Watches in the Japanese grade replicas can cost up to $240.
- Swiss manufactured replicas: Watches in the Swiss grade replicas can cost up to $1,000. They claim to be exact matches in material and mechanism to the original style to the point that most people cannot tell the difference.

Parallel Markets (a.k.a. Grey Markets)

Parallel or gray market products are not replicas. They are genuine products that are bought from one market to be sold in another for which it was not intended and usually at higher prices. Parallel markets are common with perfumes, where they are bought at wholesale prices from locations such as Panama and sold at much higher prices in other countries like Japan. The gray market in luxury fashion is a bit limited due to limited quantities of product and short life cycles, but it has more success with accessories. Gray markets also exist because they offer some official distributors a channel (albeit illegal) to get rid of old inventory.

There have been many efforts and legal measures to overcome and counterattack the growth of gray markets. Such efforts include adding laser numbers or barcodes on each perfume box to trace where it is sold. A few luxury brands like Louis Vuitton and Fendi have started stitching holograms into the lining of many of their products, such as handbags, clothes, scarves, and shoes. The holograms are rectangular, colored stamps with encrypted codes visible only with a special magnifying device. They have a wireless tracking device that is deactivated when the item is sold, allowing the company to track their bags and determine if they have been sold in an unauthorized store.

Service

Luxury customers are known to be among the most loyal group of buyers. However, their loyalty level is in a direct relationship with the level of service they receive. They expect the highest degree of service and an experience that does not just start and end with the purchase of the product. Accordingly, luxury brands are built to pamper their customers in many ways. (See Figure 4.24.)

Four principles are common to nearly all top-performing luxury brand companies[8].

1. *They create a customer-centered culture* that identifies, nurtures, and reinforces service as a primary value.
2. *They use a rigorous selection process* to populate the organization with superior sales and support staff. The impulse to care about accommodating customers cannot be taught to people who are not predisposed to it.
3. *They constantly retrain employees* to perpetuate organizational values and to help them attain greater mastery of products and procedures.
4. *They systematically measure and reward customer-centric behavior* and excellence in sales and service to enforce high standards and reinforce expectations.

Life warranties, flexible return policies, free adjustments and alterations, free delivery, personalization of products, customization, VIP loyalty

Figure 4.24

You can sign up for Nordstom's personal stylist service directly on its Web site.

(Courtesy of Nordstrom)

programs, personal shopping assistance in stores, special collection viewing and updates, not to mention special in-stores services are but a few examples of the level of service expected from luxury brands. The bottom line is not to just meet customers' expectations, but to exceed them. It's the *Wow* factor.

The tremendous growth and expansion of the luxury market over the past 20 years, however, has diluted the allure of these brands' exclusivity as well as the level of customer service expected. The rise in number of outlet stores where the product is discounted is an indication of these changes. Thus, it seems that luxury brands need to re-examine these traditional strategies, especially in situations similar to the recent economic recession. Still, a high level of customer service will continue to remain a key factor to the success of luxury brands in such conditions. This is something the luxury customer is not willing to compromise, so more luxury brands need to introduce new special programs and services that reward and retain their very best customers. Developing new programs that can be executed in the manner of old-fashioned services is an important differentiating factor between luxury brands.

Brand Identity

The process of creating a brand identity is about developing a personality reinforced by a set of attributes and visual symbols, such as a shape,

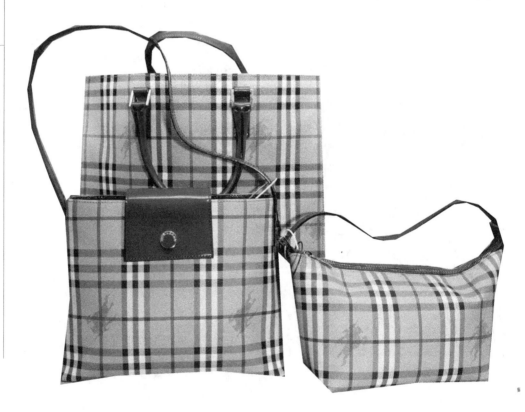

a color, a logo, a package, and so on. (See Figure 4.25.) The personality is developed through the accumulation of activities, decisions, and stories, as well as its products' features and attributes. It's both a process and the development of a culture. Visual symbols play an important role in this process and have great significance for luxury brands because of the strong relevance of their identity to the purchase decision.

When Burberry planned to reposition its brand and relaunch it to a new generation of customers, their goal was to reinforce its status as a luxury brand. In the process, they realized that their biggest asset was their strong visual identity; however, their weakness was a diluted personality that weakened the image and the value perceived by the customers. Thus, in the process of repositioning the brand, they highlighted their signature trench coat with its infamous plaid placed in a new context and modernized the name. Identity symbols are discussed in the following sections.

Iconic Items

These items represent design concepts and signature looks that became iconic for the brand. Usually, it is after the brands establish themselves in these areas that they gain the credibility, status, and stamina needed to extend into other areas such as fashion. Even then, they may choose an iconic product to symbolically identify the brand, such as:

- A Louis Vuitton leather bag
- A Fendi fur coat
- A Hermès silk scarf
- A Kelly bag
- The Burberry tartan
- A Diane von Furstenberg wrap dress

Name

The most visible aspect of a luxury brand's concept is the brand name. Traditionally, luxury fashion brands' names adopted those of their founders or creative designers, whose names in return may reference their country of origin and thus evoke specific mental references about style, craftsmanship, qualities, uniqueness, and so on. Some examples are:

- Gucci, Salvatore Ferragamo (Italy)
- YSL, Dior (France)
- Yamamoto (Japan)

The power of the name is also evident in brands that use a fake name that might indicate different origins but still evokes associations with certain images and cultural references that the creators see appropriate. Examples of this strategy are:

- Comme des Garçons (Japanese brand with a French name)
- Paul & Joe (French brand with English name)
- Jimmy Choo (British brand with Asian name)

In the world of luxury, unlike with mass-marketed brands, there are very few cases of brands with general descriptive names, such as Bottega Veneta (Venetian Workshop), or purely made-up names such as Rolex.

The brand name is the first point of contact between the consumer and the brand, so choosing the right name is very important. No matter which naming strategy is used, the name should evoke positive and relevant associations about the brand. Consumers should be able to decipher some brand connotations from its name, even without necessarily being in contact with its products or advertisements. Thus, it was not a coincidence that designer Rei Kawakubo picked a

French rather than a Japanese name for her brand (Comme des Garçons) in order to associate the brand with a French heritage and generate a specific luxury appeal that is not otherwise achieved with a Japanese name on the label. In the case of luxury brands, which are usually developed with the intentions of global distribution, choosing the name becomes even more challenging, as the name needs to be appreciated in different markets and cultures. The name, therefore, needs to posses an international appeal, be easy to pronounce, and not have any negative connotations in other countries and languages. In addition, it is common with luxury brands to give names to individual products, such as the Kelly bag, the Daytona Rolex watch, and so on. This demonstrates the possible iconic status individual luxury products can acquire.

Initials and/or Logos

In addition to their name, many brands have a logo that could be a word, a graphic symbol, or both (Polo, Lacoste alligator), or letter initials (LV, YSL). (See Figure 4.26.)

Figure 4.26

Logos can be monograms, graphic symbols, or initials.

More than names, logos are easier to modify and develop as times change and the brand grows. Christian Dior has evolved to simply Dior and Burberry's to just Burberry. Initials and logos are particularly relevant for luxury brands, given that they are mostly lifestyles that people are keen to identify with and flaunt.

The use and selection of fonts, typeface style, and colors, as described in chapter 2, is another significant identity choice for luxury brands that can be the design focus of the logo and the vehicle to convey the identity connotation needed. Examples are the signature-like style of Ferragamo, or the whimsical pink typeface of Betsey Johnson. Finally, we can find a logo that is a combination of name and design, such as in the case of Hermes (name + horse carriage).

Slogans

Slogans are another identifiable attribute meant to differentiate one brand from the other and attract the consumer's attention to a specific message and what the brand signifies. However, it is interesting to notice that luxury brands rarely have slogans or tag lines, probably because the message is strongly embedded in the name. In addition, the luxury consumer is usually familiar with the brand prior to purchase.

Personality

A brand's personality is the sum of its culture, vision, and behavior. It translates what the brand is all about and defines the brand promise. A personality also humanizes the brand and allows us to describe it in certain ways such as being hip, sexy, sincere, extravagant, and so on. Luxury brands that are trendy and aspirational as well as lifestyle brands convey, for the most part, personalities

Figure 4.27

Lifestyle brands
such as Ralph
Lauren possess
strong brand
personality.
(*Image Courtesy of the
Advertising Archives*)

specific area, which it can use later as a launch pad for other extensions and endeavors. With a set of benefits and values to transfer to the consumer, plus a strong matching identity, the brand is ready and bound for market positioning. It is important to remember that positioning is merely a strategic proposition by the brand, whereas the true position achieved will be decided upon by customers based on the way they interpret and experience the brand.

Luxury brands generally have a very clear positioning strategy in terms of price, market seg-mentations, and demographics. Yet their biggest differentiator and comparative advantage remains their level of creativity, the creative juices of the celebrity designer that are meant to be unique and trendsetting. This level of creative distinctive-ness associated with every luxury brand raises the following question: If, by definition, every luxury brand is creatively different and unique, do they really still need a positioning strategy?

Is Positioning Relevant to Luxury Brands?

Some may believe that the concept of positioning is not relevant to the luxury brands segment, based on the premise that (by definition) a luxury brand is born creatively different and in many ways pre-positioned. This would imply there is no point in comparing it to competition. However, this view is based on the principle that positioning is highly product-based, ignoring the value added by the branding process and its ability to alter the decision outcome. We concluded in chapter 2 that positioning a brand can take place at two levels: at the product level, through any element of the product mix, such as features (creativity), price, distribution, or service; and at the brand

reflecting excitement, sophistication, and sensu-ality in addition to honesty and sincerity.

Although positioning is heavily built around the product—and in case of luxury, around its creativity—positioning at the brand level is still very relevant because it reflects the emotional core value of the brand translated in its personality. We as consumers are attracted and consumed by the brand's personality. (See Figure 4.27.)

Positioning Strategy

A brand cannot be all things for everyone. It needs to be known and associated with perfection in a

level, through the brand's identity (especially personality). It is true that luxury brands are unique as products, that every collection is unique and reflects a vision and design philosophy that is different from one designer to the other. However, what might happen if the same garment is offered to the customer with the label concealed or replaced by a label of a different brand? Is there a chance the buying decision might be affected and altered? The answer is probably *yes*. It is the same garment with the same aesthetics, but it is not the same brand anymore. If a potential buyer changes his or her decision because, under a different label, the garment is now perceived differently, then the garment as a product was not positioned convincingly enough to compete on its own aesthetic values. If the decision was altered because of the label and in spite of the design, then the value produced by the branding process has to be appreciated as a positioning force and a positioning tool. Thus, even a luxury brand may need to draw from the power of a stronger positioning message.

Luxury Brand Communication

Marketing for luxury has always been seen as more reliant on *pull* marketing strategies—strategies meant to entice the potential buyer to seek (and pull) the brand's products and generate sales accordingly.

Being emotionally motivated and lifestyle driven, luxury brands are highly reliant on communication through heavy advertising and marketing campaigns to create and emphasize this aspirational world.

Marketing communication is meant to achieve for luxury brands the following:

- Demonstrate and establish the lifestyle status and proposed image of the brand.
- Compensate for lack of history and heritage in the case of new brands.
- Create social awareness, which makes owning of luxury more meaningful.
- Combat economic downturns.

Communication strategies for luxury brands utilize different media and channels, such as advertising, personal selling, promotions, sponsorships, celebrity endorsements, and PR events (such as fashion shows).

Advertising

Harvard economist John Kenneth Galbraith made the argument that society as a whole has become affluent, enjoying modern conveniences and previously unknown luxuries. As a result, businesses must create consumer wants through advertising to generate an artificial demand for products beyond the individual's basic needs. This theory is particularly relevant in light of the common perception that luxury brands are not necessary or essential brands. One of the interesting realities of marketing luxury goods seems to be the relative ease luxury brands have in convincing consumers to spend vast sums of money on things they simply don't need. No matter how high the price, luxury consumers are typically very happy with their purchases, even though they are completely aware that the cost of the item is usually far too high for its utilitarian worth. Advertising and promotional hype plays a significant role in motivating demand or wants for these products. Thus, advertising becomes essential to creating

Figure 4.28

Some luxury brands have moved beyond traditional channels of advertising and promotion: one can watch an entire Dolce & Gabbana runway show on an iPhone.

(Courtesy WWD/ Fairchild Publications)

the dream and evoking the necessary interest. Indeed, luxury brands rely heavily on fantasy and lifestyle building. Accordingly, luxury brands allocate a comparatively large budget for advertising. The average budget is between $14 million and $50 million, representing about 5 to 15 percent of revenue, which increases to 25 percent with the inclusion of other aspects such as PR events and sponsorship.[9]

Luxury brands' advertisements can be seen in top fashion magazines, such as *Vogue* and *Harpers Bazaar*, business publications, and airline in-flight magazines. Unconventional locations such as on buses and public transportation can be seen in some markets such as Paris, London, and New York but are otherwise not very common. The Internet, iPhones, and other electronic devices and platforms are new channels that have been tapped by luxury brands as well. (See Figure 4.28.)

Choice of advertising options depends on the target market and its size, the circulation and coverage reach of each media, the frequency of exposure needed, cost, and the message and its degree of urgency. One problem with many advertising options such as TV, magazines, and even radio is clutter. These media are so overly crowded with advertising messages that it is very hard for receivers and watchers to recall them long after they are exposed to the ad. Accordingly, many other options have gained a lot of ground, such as PR events (like fashion shows), the Internet, and special promotions (such as VIP previews for loyal customers).

Celebrity Sponsorship

Luxury brands have traditionally had a strong association with celebrities and socialites. Movie and music superstars, top athletes, media personnel, and even politicians are in the public eye at all times. They are trendsetters and the "innovators" among consumer groups. They have a significant influence on their fans and pop culture in general. In addition, celebrities, being brands in their own rights, have various successful collaborations with luxury fashion brands that are effective co-branding efforts. Such collaboration helps both partners draw from the star power of the other brand and emphasize a certain status or image. Another benefit is the global appeal of celebrities, which is extremely essential for luxury brands. Association with celebrities can also be instrumental in repositioning or revamping a brand and appealing to a new generation of customers.

Collaborating with celebrities as part of a communication strategy can take various forms.

- Appearance in TV and printed advertisements
- Endorsement at events, for example, celebrities wearing designer gowns on the red carpet of major events like the Oscars

Figure 4.29

Uma Thurman is the type of A-list movie star with beauty and international recognition a luxury brand seeks to feature in its advertising. (*Image Courtesy of the Advertising Archives*)

Sold exclusively in Louis Vuitton stores. 866.VUITTON www.louisvuitton.com

LOUIS VUITTON

- Product placement in movies or video clips
- Associating a luxury item with a celebrity (Kelly bag by Hermès)
- Using celebrities as spokespersons of a brand, particularly common in the cosmetics and beauty industry

All of these are good examples, not to mention celebrities using their star status to launch fashion brands of their own (L.A.M.B by Gwen Stefani or Sweet Face by Jennifer Lopez). Luxury brands' expert Uche Okonkwo has identified five rules of celebrity endorsement for luxury brands.[10]

1. *Credibility:* The celebrity must be credible and have a high level of expertise and talent in his or her field; he or she must be a star. It is through this star status that they bring credibility and add value to the brand.
2. *Global appeal:* The celebrity must have international recognition to ensure global appeal. (See Figure 4.29.)
3. *Personality:* The celebrity's personality must match the brand's personality. The association with the celebrity should not just be based on the star's popularity but on his or her relevance to the brand. Ms. Okonkwo highlights the appropriate collaboration between Chanel and Nicole Kidman and between Uma Thurman and Vuitton as good examples.
4. *Uniform power:* The celebrity must not overshadow the brand—especially important for new and up-and-coming luxury brands.
5. *Constancy:* The celebrity must have constancy and lasting appeal.

Okonkwo goes on to add some of the challenges of working with celebrities:

- The image of celebrities can be damaged as a result of professional or personal circumstances, automatically transferring this to the brands they currently represent.
- Celebrities can get into public controversies that can harm the brands they endorse. (Remember

the controversy over Tiger Woods and the speculation over its effect on his relationship with Nike.)

- Celebrities can disappear from the spotlight before or after the advertising campaign is over.
- Celebrities can become overexposed and lose their star appeal as a result of endorsing multiple brands.
- Celebrities can also decide to change their image, which might sometimes be contradictory to the image of the brands they currently endorse.
- Celebrities can decide to intentionally damage a brand that they feel didn't meet their extraneous demands or did not give them the star treatment they desired.

As a result, it is clear that although celebrity endorsement can be a rewarding collaboration, it is a strategy that needs to be well planned, implemented, and monitored in order to succeed.

PR and Fashion Shows

PR stands for public relations, or as it is sometimes called, press relations. It includes activities and events carried out by the organization to boost the brand's image both in the industry as well as in the community. Many of such activities target influential journalists who in return can offer positive publicity and editorial coverage of the brand and its activities. Private PR agencies can play a role in assisting brands with such activities around the world. Fashion shows can be considered a major PR event; they are costly with no direct financial return but are necessary to showcase the brand and its new ideas and trends. In spite of the fact that the fashion

arm of operations for many luxury brands is a losing one, it remains the one that is the most exciting and creates the necessary buzz to grant media coverage and generate interest in its other products. This is one of the reasons why fashion shows usually include impractical, over-the-top designs that are provocative and shocking. It is this eccentricity that gets the coverage and attention needed. A few seasons ago, for example, John Galliano showed dresses made of newspapers in one of his Dior shows. Understandably, this provoked the necessary attention and interest. When it was time to sell the clothes in the stores, B. Arnault was smart enough to reproduce the garments in real fabrics with newspaper prints on them.

Other events of great importance are product launches (such as perfumes) and store openings. All of these events are treated with significant fanfare and media frenzy. Celebrities are invited, lavish parties are held, and every possible member of the media is invited as well.

Sponsorship

Luxury brands have a tradition of sponsoring events of high status and interest in various fields and areas such as art, sports, and movies. Louis Vuitton sponsors the prestigious America's Cup sailing race (see Figure 4.30), whereas Hugo Boss sponsors Formula One. Another example of such a level of collaboration is when designers offer their garments to movie stars to wear at highly visible awards events.

Product Placement

Product placement refers to placing products in productions such as movies and video clips so

Figure 4.30

The winning team of the Louis Vuitton-sponsored America's cup celebrates victory as a crew member drinks from the trophy cup itself.

(Getty Images/ Kos Picture Source)

that they appear as part of the scripted scenes. James Bond's character wearing Omega watches or riding BMW cars are good examples of product placements where the brand's name and logo are deliberately mentioned or seen on the big screen. Designing for movie characters has also seen a lot of success, as we mentioned in chapter 2 with the example of Giorgio Armani and Richard Gere's *American Gigolo*.

Co-Marketing

Co-marketing can take place in the form of collaboration between a luxury brand manufacturer and a retailer. Announcing exclusive distribution arrangements and/or availability of luxury brands at certain boutiques or specialty stores are good examples of this strategy.

Promotions

Promotional activities are not as common or diverse for luxury brands as they are in the mass-market segment. Luxury brands do not often offer discounts, nor do they compete on such basis. However, luxury brands are extremely keen on customer service and relationship. Their level of service is usually so high that it becomes very personal. Accordingly,

these brands usually work on personalizing the shopping experience for their customers and rewarding their loyalty in different ways. That may include birthday cards or gifts, VIP treatment, catalogs, loyalty programs, invitations to special events, collection previews, and complementary gifts. All of these activities aim to build a stronger and longer-lasting relationship with the consumer rather than a one-time purchase incentive.

Internet and New Media

The relationship between luxury brands and the Internet was discussed earlier in this chapter. And it is clear that the Internet has been more adopted by luxury as a communication channel than as a distribution one. Luxury brands have Web sites that are well designed with exciting media material and information to promote the brand and highlight its products. In addition to corporate Web sites, many luxury brands have ventured into popular social media options such as Facebook and Twitter in order to stay relevant and in touch with fashion enthusiasts. Diane von Furstenberg, Annu Sui, and Karl Lagerfeld are a few examples of this trend. Other attempts include utilizing mobile technology and creating special apps for iPhone whereby users can get the latest news and video clips from fashion shows—this has been used by Chanel and Ralph Lauren, among others. Updates, store locators, and even shopping options are now available on these devices. It is an effective medium for real-time communication, highly personalized content, offers, and news. These new technologies will be examined later in more detail in chapter 7.

The Brand Evaluation and Audit

Any branding strategy needs to be evaluated as it is implemented. A brand's true position is determined by the customer. The customer positions the brand based on the mental image he or she creates as a result of personal experiences with the brand, as well as other external factors such as competitors' behavior. Accordingly, how effective the branding process and positioning strategy has been matching the perceived image with the proposed one is an essential issue to evaluate and measure. The result of the evaluation process may be a decision to continue with the strategy, tweak it, or reconsider it completely. Moreover, most luxury brands are old brands, and in the span of their life cycles, the need may arise to revamp or reposition it to target a different and younger market. In the process, the brand may need to be re-launched and re-introduced in a new form and manner. As a matter of fact, some believe that to prolong a luxury brand's life, it is a marketing necessity to approach it as a series of shorter life cycles during which the brand is continuously re-launched and re-vamped. This seems necessary because of the brand's need to continuously respond to social and other external changes it incurs throughout its lifetime. However, this can be a necessity and a dilemma at the same time. If the brand ignores these changes, it will be out of touch, irrelevant, and may lose its customer's interest; on the other hand, if it responds to every new trend, it will lose focus and identity. Thus, a certain balance needs to be struck that takes into consideration a few important points:

- It is critical to not lose focus of the customer and the brand's core value. Brands should respond only to relevant trends that make sense to their customers. Revamping or revitalizing the brand is a good strategy and may be necessary at times; however, it should not be at the expense of what the brand stands for and means to the customer. Revitalizing the brand is a stage of the brand's evolution, but evolution is not always meant to be a revolution.

- If a brand decides to approach a different customer or focus on a different core value, then it has decided to shift the strategy from revitalizing the brand to repositioning it. Repositioning may be necessary, as mentioned earlier, when the brand ages and its image fades out, or if it has lost focus of its meaning in the process. Repositioning is a serious strategy that needs to be carefully approached and backed with intensive marketing.

- Repositioning a luxury brand is usually more difficult than repositioning a mass-market one. Repositioning mass-market brands upwards such as H&M, Coach) will always be regarded as an improvement and a brand upgrade, which should generally improve the brand's image. However, in the case of luxury brands, it is harder to convince customers of the necessity or rationale behind the shift without raising questions.

In recent years, Gucci and Burberry have been great examples of brands that were re-launched either as part of a revitalizing or repositioning strategy.

Gucci

Gucci's turnaround under the collaboration between Tom Ford and Domenico de Sole is a good example of brand revitalization rather than repositioning. What Tom Ford and his team did was in essence catch up with their customer. Ford managed to re-align the brand's existing image and value as a sensual Italian luxury brand to how these values were defined and perceived in the nineties. He simply met the expectations of the brand's customers and gained new ones in the process. He did not redefine Gucci as much as make it more relevant and modern, while keeping it true to its heritage in an updated way.

We can compare this situation to the recent downturn of the Versace brand. Versace had been known in the eighties and nineties as the ultimate sexy, risqué, luxury brand. It embodied how "sexy" was perceived in the eighties: flamboyant, glamorous, and even what some saw as a bit vulgar. But that was how sexy was perceived then; lately the definition seems to have changed. Today "sexy" has become more subdued and subtle, so when Versace's designs continued to maintain the same attitude as before, they became less relevant, a bit outdated, and out of touch. As a brand, Versace was trying to stay true to its niche and image, but what they did not realize was that they needed to stick to the core value of the brand while innovating and revitalizing the product and its aesthetics. They needed to interpret the new definition of "sexy" into their designs, to remain the sexy brand in a modern and relevant way. They needed to understand the new needs of their customers and find ways to surprise them, something Versace had failed to achieve in recent years. However, in the past few seasons, the House of Versace seems to have realized this conflict and has presented new collections that were calmer and less provocative in an attempt to regain some of their lost market share. Although initial feedback is positive, time will tell how this will work, but unless the move remains true to the core value and the brand's personality in a way that is relevant to our times, the odds are not in their favor, and it may end up distorting the brand's image and confusing the customers instead.

Burberry

Burberry, on the other hand, had slipped through the cracks for some time and was not perceived as a luxury brand. With a lack of originality and control over its trademark tartan design, the brand lost its cachet. When Rose Bravo took over and teamed up with Christopher Bailey, the goal was clear—to move Burberry upwards again and reposition it as a luxury brand. They knew they would alienate many of their current customers, but that was a calculated move toward targeting a new customer and regaining the confidence of some lost ones. This was a clear example of repositioning the brand and not just revitalization.

It is acceptable, therefore, for a brand to revisit its strategies and market positioning throughout its lifetime. However, there is a difference between deciding to polish the image through reinterpreting its values and to completely redefine them.

Brand Growth

Luxury brands can adopt different strategies of growth. Brand extension, licensing, and global expansion are the three common growth strategies discussed in the following sections.

Brand Extension

Brand extension is a common strategy in the luxury brand segment, especially for lifestyle brands. It is through extensions that the brand manages to create a coherent identity that touches every aspect of the customer's life. In general, there are two options for extensions:

- *Product or line extension:* This approach means the extension of products through addition of more items under existing brand categories, offering a wider range of options (more sizes, colors, styles, and so on).
- *Brand extension:* Another approach is extending the brand by introducing a new category of product under the same brand. This approach allows brands to portray themselves as lifestyle brands offering a variety of products with a single coherent and relevant message (for example, extending into perfumes and cosmetics, or when Armani introduced Armani Casa, Armani Jeans, and boutique hotels).

Luxury brands can also expand their operations through brand creation, which is basically the creation of a new sub-brand that allows the mother brand to expand into new markets and segments based on the power of its name and previous successes. Examples are ck by Calvin Klein, DKNY by Donna Karan, and Purple Label by Ralph Lauren.

It is obvious that brand extensions have lucrative financial and marketing potential. In addition to being new sources of revenue, they also solidify the brand's image as a lifestyle brand and attract new customers in the process. However, as with any strategy for brand extensions, there are many challenges as well. The main challenge is achieving a lucrative level of diversification without diluting the brand. Brand dilution occurs when the brand is overextended to products and areas that make no sense to the brand personality and values and thus are irrelevant to the core customer of the brand. Therefore, brand extension is a diversification strategy that may support and boost the brand's performance, but brand dilution can diminish its relevance, erode its image, alienate the customer, and eventually kill the brand.

Brand extension is a growth strategy that should be considered after the brand has established itself with a clear position and identity in the consumer's mind. The more loyal the consumer, the more he or she is willing to adopt other offerings from the brand. This is true even for nonluxury brands, although it is usually harder to achieve this level of loyalty in the mass-market segment because of the fact that the bond between consumers and luxury brands is, for the most part, an emotional one.

We need to remember that if a luxury brand is widely available, it is no longer rare, which is one of the defining components of a luxury brand. In other words, the tremendous success and expansion of some luxury brands may threaten their own luxury status if not handled diligently. Pierre Cardin's case of uncontrolled over-expansion and exposure is always a good example.

Licensing

Licensing is one of the most common channels for product and brand extensions. Subcontracting or giving other manufacturers the right to produce under a specific label is an economically efficient growth strategy. However, if licensing results in diluting the brand with a range of irrelevant products, styles, or low quality merchandise, the customer, no matter how loyal, will feel betrayed and lose interest in the brand. In the past, licensing was not a common strategy in the luxury segment; however, times have changed, and most of the accessories now produced under luxury labels, such as watches, glasses, and, of course, perfumes, are licensed products. Yet there are still many brands (especially smaller ones) that do not rely on licensing to introduce new products or new categories (such as Louis Vuitton and Hermes); this way they can exercise better control on quality and styles, which helps to maintain a stronger image.

For those brands that must turn to an outside manufacturer to produce new lines, choosing the right licensing partner (the licensee) is of the utmost importance. A brand (the licensor) needs to partner with a licensee that has the expertise and financial means to go through the long testing and production process and deliver the desired quality.

In the world of luxury licensing, the licensors receive a royalty fee of around 10 percent on sales (and around 5 percent from perfumes' wholesale volume). "Products that are difficult to develop and to sell like men's and women's ready to wear, for example, can command royalties of 6 to 8 percent. On the other hand, products that are quite far removed from the licensor's usual universe can sometimes justify royalties of up to 12 percent. In addition, brands may impose minimum sales (or at least minimum royalties) and minimum communication budgets per year."[11] It is essential for the sake of the brand's image to impose strong control over its licensing agreements, as was previously mentioned. After all, for most licensees this may be only perceived as an investment venture without appreciation of the branding process or the other concepts of heritage, value, and emotional investment.

Timing is another essential element of licensing. Introducing new products under licensing is important to be done at the right time and in the right markets. M. Chevalier and G. Mazzalovo highlighted two examples that demonstrate this point:

- When Louis Feraud signed a perfume license agreement with Avon cosmetics for the United States, it turned out to be a mismatch due to Avon's door-to-door distribution strategy.
- Christian Lacroix introduced his "C'est La Vie" too soon in 1990, when his name was not yet known outside of Paris and New York where the perfume was to be sold, so the results were unsuccessful.

Global Expansion

We have mentioned several times that luxury brands, for the most part, are meant to be global brands. It is more of a necessity for survival than a marketing scheme. Their selective distribution, quality standards, and limited quantities make it financially sound to expand geographically. In addition, lifestyles adopted by these brands are understood and appreciated in all cultures and societies. The luxury customer is generally an international, sophisticated citizen who needs to be able to find the product he or she bought in Paris the next time he or she is in Tokyo or New York.

There are various cases of small, one-store luxury brand operations that exist in certain cities, producing limited quantities and made-to-order products. These luxury brands are more focused on the crafts, workshop, and tailoring side of operations and are not meant to be global lifestyle brands.

It is generally easier to go global with ready-to-wear brands for logistic and practical reasons. In addition, it is ready-to-wear brands that are usually covered in magazines and generate the buzz that fuels the sale of other products such as accessories and perfumes.

Modes of Entry

Luxury brands can expand geographically in global markets in different manners:

1. *Owned subsidiaries:* Luxury brands have the options of opening their own stores and boutiques in exclusive areas of major cities in the world. Although it is an option that delivers the highest level of control on distribution as well as boosts the brand's image, it is also a very expensive alternative. And given the restrictions of location choices imposed by luxury brands, it may not be easy to find the right place and space. In addition, there may be the hurdle of laws and regulations in some countries that do not allow a 100 percent store ownership by foreign entities.

2. *Local distributors:* Local distributors such as specialty or department stores can be an appropriate vehicle for expansion. In many cases, they can be granted exclusive distribution rights. It is a cheaper alternative with less risk; however, it also entails less control over the merchandise choice and reduces the opportunity to showcase the full range of products in one place. In some cases, choosing local distributors can be a first option until sales reach a certain level to justify owning a subsidiary.

3. *Joint ventures:* These are necessary in markets where it is not easy for brands to get into by themselves. One example is in the intricate and tight market in Japan; to overcome the multileveled retail and distribution network, it is always a better option to work with a local Japanese partner. Louis Vuitton and Giorgio Armani are two examples of luxury brands that took this approach. Giorgio Armani, for instance, opened Giorgio Armani Japan in 1987 through a joint venture with Japanese Itochu Corporation and the Seibu department store.

4. *Other options:* Potential options include duty-free operations and airport boutiques (see Figure 4.31). A good example is DFS (duty-free shoppers), a division of LVMH, with its chains of Galleria stores. These channels are important to certain products, such as perfumes, and account for about 30 percent of perfume sales volume.

Global brands face the challenges of competing and surviving in foreign markets under various market and economic conditions, such as exchange rates, inflation, and different taxation systems and labor laws. Fluctuation in exchange rates, for instance, can have either a positive or a negative impact on the profit margin of the brand and its pricing policies in respective markets. For example, the growing strength of the Euro in the past few years has inflated the price of a luxury bag from a typical $800 in 2003 to as much as $2,400 in 2006.[12]

On the other hand, any hikes in exchange rates can also affect prices of material and production, resulting in even higher price increases. Luxury brands are generally priced at a premium, and the fluctuation in exchange rates, in addition to other factors such as local taxes and costs, may create a discrepancy in prices from one market to the other. This discrepancy occurs, for example, in Japan, where prices tend to be much higher compared with other markets. This situation is not necessarily problematic, but it can create a good opportunity for parallel markets to exist and flourish, as described earlier.

Luxury Brands and Economic Downturns

The economic downturn that started in 2008 has spotlighted the effect of economic recession on the luxury segment. In spite of being generally less sensitive to economic downturns, the recent dip was so severe and global in nature that its impact on luxury brands and their customers has been clear and significant. Under such severe circumstances, the rules of the game changed and a decrease in demand was inevitable. Brands attempted to counterattack with an increase in promotional activities and adopting strategies of lowering prices, which are traditionally unusual for this segment, in an attempt to turn inventory into cash in every possible way. For the first time in a long period, customers have seen brands such as Gucci and Bottega Veneta being discounted at luxury retail stores. Luxury stores such as Saks Fifth Avenue and Neiman Marcus, among others, offered various promotions such as "friends and family" discounts of 40 percent or more.[13] Hard times did call for drastic measures indeed.

In the recent years of economic prosperity before this downturn, the base of luxury customers (as well as premium ones) had increased more than ever before, which also meant that a higher number of luxury customers became more sensitive to these economic changes than traditionally perceived. Another outcome is a decline in travel and the number of tourists who have been traditionally significant buyers of certain luxury items

Figure 4.31

The Versace boutique in the Kuala Lumpur Airport, Malaysia.

(© Manfred Bail/age fotostock)

in major tourist destinations and airports. To many people, luxury goods are unnecessary, and for those nontraditional luxury buyers, luxury goods are easier to give up in hard times.

Luxury and Traditional Marketing Principles

By examining our discussion of luxury brands in this chapter, it is easy to understand why luxury brands seem to defy every known marketing principle. It is an observation that we share with other scholars such as J. N. Kapferer and V. Bastien. Many of the points we raised in this chapter seem to support this point of view, which we can summarize in the following points:

- As mentioned earlier, luxury brands are built on high quality, but not perfect quality. In other words, the level of craftsmanship and handwork expected from every luxury product is one of a kind and uniquely flawed, like most handmade products are. Nothing can beat a machine level of perfection and consistency. However, these imperfections are sought after and admired in luxury brands and guarantee its uniqueness.

- Traditionally, luxury brands possessed a level of arrogance, and designers were meant to dictate trends, not follow them. Even today, although luxury designer brands have lost part of that influence, the segment is meant to surprise and awe customers and not respond to their wishes and demands as much as try to shape them. After all, flair of arrogance and elitism is still linked to this segment. Thus, this attitude defies the basic marketing principle of totally responding to and following your customer.

- Luxury brands do not spend a lot of effort changing who they are in order to be more relevant to new customers. The elitism and exclusivity of the brand makes wider availability be perceived as a sign of brand dilution. This is a totally different mentality from a mass-market brand that would be happy to claim relevance to as many market segments as possible.

- If marketing strategies are meant to increase sales volume and market shares and allow for maximization of profit through smaller margins but higher volumes, this is totally the opposite with luxury brands. Luxury brands are keen on deliberate limited production and exclusive distribution, in spite of any rise in demand. Luxury brands are expected (and accepted) to be harder to acquire. Customers understand and appreciate that the product is rare and may require being placed on a waiting list to obtain it. The fact that luxury brands are anti-volume is in itself opposite to simple marketing principles as well.

- Again, luxury brands' rarity and exclusivity mean that they are not easy to access. As we mentioned, it's a brand that customers are expected to exert some effort to obtain, which in a world of mass-market brands can be a call for the brand's demise.

- The role of advertising is totally different. There is usually no sales proposal in luxury advertising. It is usually minimalist with a photo and logo and not much to say. Even more interesting, most of the ads may not be really targeting the luxury customer who is already aware of the brand, its products, and where to find it. In many ways, these ads target the "others" who are meant to be aware of the brand—even if they cannot afford it. This level of awareness is necessary, as was explained in the discussion of the social dimension and the social status of the brand. Customers need to know about the brand and desire it. If it is currently out of their price range, they should aspire to have it—and the brand will be ready for them if and when they can afford it in future. Moreover, this emotional buildup helps weave the social status and allure of the brand.

- Price for these brands is mostly a function of perceived luxury. Thus, price is determined more by the strength of the brand's identity than actual costs. In mass-market brands, on the other hand, products are created based on possible acceptable prices.
- Another major difference related to price is how luxury defies the simple law of demand. In the case of mass-market products, the lower the price, the higher the demand for it. In the case of luxury, price is not usually an issue nor the basis of positioning; on the contrary, rising prices maintain the brand's prestige status, and while it may lose some of the not so serious luxury customers, it becomes more relevant and attractive to the die-hard ones.

How to Create a "Star" Luxury Brand

Highly profitable luxury brands possess one of the most important credentials to become "star" brands. Of course all luxury brands would love to turn into "star" brands but, according to B. Arnault, a **STAR BRAND** needs to possess four characteristics: timelessness, modernity, fast growth, and high profitability.

Timeless and modernity refer to whether a brand is created with the aim of being around for a long time while staying relevant, current, and desired. In other words, it should have the ability to stay modern and reinvent itself without losing its identity—an interesting mix of being old and new at the same time. Growth is also essential because it confirms the timelessness and relevance of the brand. Growth is achieved through continuous interest in the brand as manifested in its expansion into new products and new markets. As for profitability, the Christian Lacroix example shows that although luxury brands are expected to take longer to generate profits, they cannot survive without sound financial basis. It is very expensive to develop and maintain luxury brands.

Chapter Summary

- Luxury brands have the greatest potential to be lifestyle brands.

- Although there are many reasons for buying luxury, the emotional reward remains the strongest.

- There is a strong social relevance to luxury buying.
- Luxury brands are rooted in craftsmanship, for the most part.

- American luxury brands are relatively new and empowered by powerful marketing.

- Luxury brands can be star brands

- Luxury brands seem to defy traditional marketing principles.

Chapter Questions and Issues for Discussion

1. Explain the social element of luxury brands, and explore how this concept relates to some of the challenges facing luxury brands, such as counterfeiting and parallel markets.

2. What is the meaning of a lifestyle brand? Why are most luxury brands described as such?

3. Explain how luxury brands seem to defy traditional marketing principles.

KEY TERMS

CRAFTSMANSHIP

CREATIVITY

LIFESTYLE
BRANDS

LUXURY

LUXURY BRAND

PREMIUM PRICE

STAR BRANDS

STAR DESIGNERS

CASE STUDY: Louis Vuitton in Japan

The Japanese Market

Often described as a confusing jigsaw puzzle, the Japanese distribution system has been notoriously complicated and complex. Characterized by extended channels, large numbers and sizes of retailers, as well as domination of manufacturers, the system created a major barrier for market entry. And in spite of some gradual deregulation and liberalization of capital in the retail industry, the changes were not permissive enough for foreign brands to break into the market independently. Thus, most luxury brands such as Gucci and Hermès had to enter the market either through a partner, such as a department store chain that would act as an agent, or through establishing a joint venture with wholesalers, such as in the case of Loewe.

In 1978, Louis Vuitton assigned Japanese consultant Kyojiro Hata to examine the best ways for the brand to enter the Japanese market. Mr. Hata realized at the time that LV did not have the staff nor the funds necessary to enter the market in the traditional ways, so he proposed a new and different strategy that would be based on a two-contract model:

1. A distribution contract between retailers, mainly department stores and Louis Vuitton, whereby department stores would pick up the merchandise directly from the LV warehouse through their Paris offices and ship it themselves to Japan.

2. A management service contract between the LV Japan branch and these department stores, whereby LV would have the right to oversee and take all the necessary measures to maintain the brand's proposed image through quality control, advertising, and management, in addition to charging a franchise and management service fees. In this way, LV managed to build a controlled system with little financial and human resources.

Examples of measures covered in these contracts:

- Department stores would set up in-store LV boutiques at their expense. Eventually LV demanded that these corners would be enclosed spaces and be moved to ground floors, which was a highly uncommon move at the time. As a matter of fact, the idea was initially met with resistance, and it took LV 10 years to completely relocate in department stores.
- Everything from store furnishing, staff uniforms, and supplies such as wrapping paper was to be determined by LV.
- LV controlled advertising and split costs with department stores.
- LV products were not to be sold through discounts for members' loyalty programs, gift catalogs, at events outside the store, nor through the direct marketing practice known in Japan as "Gaisho," which refers to direct sales catered to important customers.

reconsider its distribution strategy. According to the new strategy, LV Japan imported products directly from LV France and distributed them to all other stores. The previously adopted two-contract system was replaced by a one-contract system in which LVJ owned the inventory it had in its stores as well as other departments stores They worked with six department stores at the time, and the move was followed by a leasing system in which LV leased its in-store boutiques in department stores as well as oversaw the staff in order to fully control operations.

After relocating their flagship global store in Paris to the Champs-Elysées, LV started opening a series of what became known as the "global stores." The global store concept meant that customers were to find all the brand offerings under one roof. There were watches, jewelry, leather goods, eyewear, fashion, and shoes for men and women. The Osaka global store opened in 1998. In all its stores, LV always gave special attention to architecture and design, working with world renowned architects to develop modern and original designs.

In a market known for the substantial influence and power of department stores, it was initially challenging to get them to agree to such conditions.

Expansion

In 1982, the LV branch office in Japan was converted into a corporation, and they opened LV's first standalone store in the Ginza district. At the time, Tokyo had no major street known for its luxury brands such as Foubourg Saint-Honoré in Paris or Fifth Avenue in New York, so they picked Namiki Avenue, known for its well-established stores. With the opening of the new store, LV Japan had to

Pricing

LVJ reviewed and adjusted its prices at least once a year, putting into consideration fluctuations in exchange rate. It adopted a simple strategy that was rooted in its early years as a made-to-order business. The price was basically determined by multiplying cost by a fixed gross margin rate. If the price seemed too high to compete, it worked on lowering cost without compromising quality; if it wasn't feasible, the product could be cancelled. That way LV ensured a sustainable level of profitability without venturing into areas where products could be unsuitable or of lower profitability. This strategy, although too simplistic in modern terms, seemed to work well for LV at the time because its business model and products had not dramatically changed through the years. LV also had a strategy for making sure that it offered the same price to all consumers; through contract agreements with retailers, LV products were not included as part of store special promotions or loyalty program rewards as mentioned earlier.

Promotion

In general, LV did not rely heavily on advertising but rather decided to focus on events, such as the LV exhibition that highlighted the brand's heritage and long history. However, LVJ made a strategic decision to target the male consumer in an attempt to change the established image of LV as a woman's brand. It ran a series of interviews and articles in men's lifestyle magazines where they selected famous Japanese men in various fields to share their views about LV products and how these fit in their lifestyles. Eventually, LVJ decided to run advertisements that were produced locally rather than using their universal ad campaigns since brand recognition in Japan was still limited and largely based on its bags.

Figure 4.33

A view of the store's interior.

(*Courtesy of UNStudio.*)

LVMH

When LV became part of LVMH, more men's products were introduced, including watches, scarves, bags, and pens. The merger meant transforming LV from a brand with traditional luxury products to a fashion company offering a ready-to-wear collection. After the appointment of Marc Jacobs, the company witnessed an increase in sales of almost 300 percent. The company also maintained its tradition of quality in establishing a local product repair system and a customer information service. LVMH had plans to open an impressive new flagship store in Japan's Ginza district in 2010, but since being hit by the global economic downturn in 2008, it announced that it is abandoning the plan. (See Figures 4.32 and 4.33.)

CASE STUDY Questions

1. How do LVJ's strategies in Japan demonstrate the challenges of global expansion?

2. LVJ and Mr. Hata have attempted to maintain the integrity of the LV brand in the new market. Discuss some of the measures they adopted.

SOURCE

Hata, Kyojiro. 2004. *Louis Vuitton Japan: The Building of Luxury.* New York: Assouline Publishing.

http://www.gmtmag.com/en/14_atm_vuitton.php

ENDNOTES

1. Lauren Sherman, How and How Not To Sell Luxury. http://www.forbes.com/2009/04/16/luxury-strategy- marketing-opinions-book-review-vuitton-hermes-fendi.html

2. Michael Chevalier and Gerald Mazzalovo, *Luxury Brand Management: A world of Privilege* (Singapore: John Wiley & Sons, 2008), 152.

3. Ibid., 168.

4. http://www.lvmh.com/

5. PPR-Reference Document (2005), 6.

6. http://www.forbes.com/2009/04/16/luxury-strategy-marketing-opinions-book-review-vuitton-hermes-fendi.html

7. http://www.nnbag.com/

8. http://www.strategy-business.com/enews/enewsarticle/enews040307

9. Uche Okonkwo, *Luxury Fashion Branding* (New York: Palgrave Macmillan, 2007), 145.

10. http://www.brandchannel.com/papers_review.asp?sp_id=1234

11. Michael Chevalier and Gerald Mazzalovo, *Luxury Brand Management: A world of Privilege* (Singapore: John Wiley & Sons, 2008), 363.

12. http://www.reuters.com/article/pressRelease/idUS137779+10-Feb-2009+MW20090210

13. Ibid.

5

Mass-Market Fashion Brands

Mass-market brands follow the general guidelines of branding discussed in chapters 2 and 3. Thus, in this chapter, we shall focus on how this broad segment is unique and differs from luxury brands. In the process, we will highlight two categories of significant importance in today's market: premium (or new luxury) brands and private labels.

CHAPTER
OBJECTIVES

- Learn how mass-market brands differ from luxury brands.

- Identify the characteristics of mass-market brands.

- Define private and premium brands.

- Examine positioning and branding strategies for private and premium brands.

Mass-Market vs. Luxury Brands

MASS-MARKET brands are ones that are mass produced. They range in price from low-priced budget brands to high-priced premium brands with mid-priced consumer brands in between. Mass-market fashion brands are generally fashion followers and not trendsetters. They may suffer from sameness, indistinguishable differences, or lack of creativity compared to luxury brands; thus, they are rarely positioned on creativity but on values derived from price, and convenience. Accordingly, these brands' values usually stem from price, functionality, and their value for money.

In the first instance, mass-market brands may seem to be anti-luxury in every element we discussed earlier. However, as brands, they still share some common principles, such as the need to generate values and to possess a strong identity. The main difference may be that the core value for most mass-market brands is rational in nature, while for luxury brands, it is emotional.

157

Figure 5.1

Mass-market retail shops are sometimes located on small-town main streets like this one in Middleburg, Virginia.

(© Jeff Greenberg/age fotostock)

Because mass-market brands are not usually trendsetters, or at the forefront of creativity, the design and creative process is usually different. There is no real purpose for the superstar designer, and designing is usually done by teams of young designers unknown to the public, who in many cases take the role of product developers that are expected to follow and adapt trends rather than create new ones. Accordingly, most design decisions are business and merchandising decisions taken at the executive level and made with price and fashion constraints in mind rather than in partnership with designers—a very different process from the luxury segment. Thus, in the mass-market segment, decision making is highly driven by cost and volume rather than originality and margins.

Price

Mass-market products are highly price driven. At the budget range, for instance, they are quantitative and based on the concept of more for less, so in most cases these brands are positioned primarily based on price. A mass-market brand can adopt any of the pricing strategies mentioned in chapter 2 such as odd pricing, price penetration, price lining, and so on. However, we can identify a couple of major differences between luxury and mass-market brands in relation to price.

- *Attitude toward price premiums:* Mass-market brands do not adopt a premium price strategy.
- *Re-pricing strategies:* Mass-market brands are more susceptible to re-pricing adjustment strategies, such as promotional sales and clearance markdowns, than luxury brands are. Markdowns and price reductions are caused by many factors that can be either internal, such as overbuying of merchandise, broken assortments, or errors in the initial pricing of the product, or external such as an economic slowdown or competition. In all cases, markdowns are meant to stimulate sales, face competition, and entice customers to buy more under the premise of offering a "bargain." Luxury brands have a totally different attitude toward repricing and bargain hunting, of course. They rarely mark down products, and some totally refrain from adopting this strategy, relying on a more controlled production strategy and limited quantities. As an alternative, luxury brands may sell excess merchandise through their own outlets and/or discount stores after taking some measure to conceal the brand, such as removing their labels.

Location

For the mass-market segment, the options are not as limited as they are with luxury brands. (See Figure 5.1.) The options regarding locations may include:

- Central locations, usually downtown where business and shopping activities are mainly centered.
- Main street areas in smaller towns.
- Shopping centers and malls where a cluster of stores are located under one roof or area with an adjacent parking lot and possible food courts.

The choice is made among various options based on accessibility, traffic flow, ease of parking, place and visibility of slot, nearby stores, and competition. (See Figure 5.2.) All these are factors that play a role in the customer's decision-making process. A lot of data are used and analyzed to assist managers in determining the best locations where their target customers are clustered and within easy reach. For example, data obtained from credit card records and mailing lists can be used for creating a demographic profile of certain neighborhoods and areas. Even casual observation of shopping patterns and stores' traffic can produce a lot of information on the activity of the location, such as hours of heavy traffic, ease of parking, customers' profiles, and so on. Stores can also benefit from locating close to competitors because they already attract the same targeted customer. When Steve & Barry was in business, they managed to maintain low prices by lowering their costs through a series of measures, such as operating in underperforming malls where they could get low rents, in addition to manufacturing overseas in countries like China and India. Such a strategy worked for a while; however, it would not have worked as an option for any luxury brand, even if small in size.

Unlike luxury brands, most mass-market brands have a strong presence online. They seem to have utilized the Internet in more effective and innovative ways than luxury brands that are taken aback by the idea of selling their products online for fear of hurting their image by hindering their exclusive appeal, or out of the belief that it is not a suitable environment for their customers.

Service

The difference between luxury and mass-market brands on the level of service is clear. Luxury brands are expected to take extra measures to pamper and please the customer, whereas mass-market brands may only offer the most basic level of services. The level of service within the mass-market spectrum may still differ according to segment and price range. Bargain brands will usually offer the minimum when it comes to complementary services such as extended warranties—and sometimes offer none at all. On the other hand, premium brands' services may be closer to the level of luxury. However, with strong competition at all levels, customer service in general (together with

Figure 5.2

Malls similar to this one in Honolulu, Hawaii, offer the convenience of visiting many stores in one place.

(© Jon Hicks/Corbis)

innovation) has become a major competitive tool in today's markets, especially with the plethora of choices available to the consumer. As a result, levels of service have generally improved and should continue to improve even at the mass-market level in order for brands to compete and survive.

Identity

All brands need to establish a strong visual and emotional identity. After all, this is what branding is all about. However the approach may vary for different segments. Visual symbols such as logos, names, and colors adopted by mass-market brands have fewer restrictions than with luxury brands. They range from made-up names to ones with specific insinuations such as Urban Outfitters or Nautica (see Figure 5.3a). Other mass-market brands like to emulate a luxury attitude toward naming by adopting made-up names that imply the existence of a designer or country heritage (Alfani or Massimo Dutti, for example) behind the brand. By assuming such names, they imply messages of quality, creative legitimacy, and innovation that are generally attributed to luxury brands. (See Figure 5.3b.)

Personality

As always, an identity is a reflection of the brand's vision and of the five personality groups mentioned in chapter 2. Mass-market brands will most likely build their identities around personality traits that reflect:

- Friendliness, warmth, excitement through being cool, young, outgoing, and contemporary
- Competence through being hard working and efficient

Communication and Promotion

Mass-market brands utilize the full spectrum of media options: TV, radio, Internet, and printed media. These brands need all these channels in order to compete with the tough competition they face as a result of their level of sameness and lower level of creativity. As a result, the major differences between luxury and mass-market brands lie in the focus of their promotional messages and content.

- Mass-market brands usually compete and position themselves on the basis of functionality and product features rather than experience, emotions, or lifestyles. They use various communication channels to inform potential customers of these benefits as well as announce any reduction in prices or special sales that would motivate them to seek the brand and make a purchase.
- Their reliance on promotional activities, such as sales and discounts, require more frequent and regular announcements.
- Because mass-market brands differentiate themselves on the basis of convenience, they have a stronger presence in catalogs and infomercials where ease of shopping and access to special products prevail.

Growth Strategies

Although mass-market brands adopt similar growth strategies to luxury brands, such as brand extensions and globalization, they may adopt different implementation strategies.

- Brand extensions are used as a way to upgrade into higher segments by introducing brands that appeal to higher market segments (such as Gap into Banana Republic or H&M to COS).

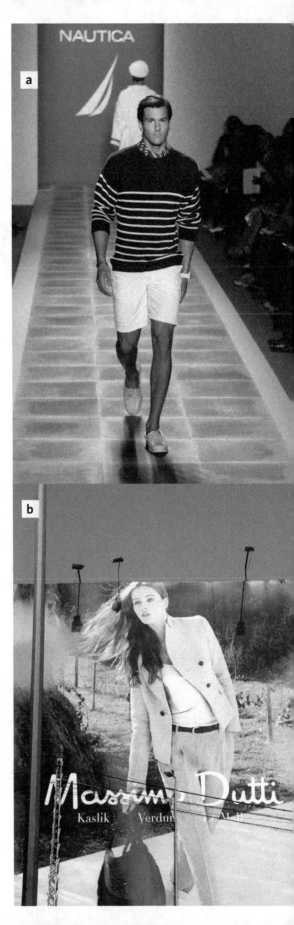

- Licensing is also a more common mode for global expansion in this segment.
- Franchising is a common distribution strategy, especially as a mode of entry into foreign markets. (See Figure 5.4.) On the other hand, many luxury brands prefer full store ownerships whenever possible.
- Mass-market brands rely heavily on outsourcing for cheaper material and factors of production. Over 60 percent of the world's apparel production is exported from developing countries where cheap labor and low costs of production prevail. On the other hand, many luxury brands still manufacture in workshops or factories located in European fashion capitals.
- Mass-market brands are prone to product adaptations or localization in foreign markets in terms of design, sizing, and marketing. Some level of adaptation can be acceptable for luxury brands, although they are largely built on the universality of their image and products.
- Being cost and price inelastic, mass-market brands face a major pricing challenge as they enter different markets. Transportation costs, taxes, and standards of living may force the brand to change pricing strategies in different markets, causing the brand to be positioned and segmented in a different way. Zara's price in Europe, the United States, or Japan differs greatly from in Spain, where Zara fashions are produced.
- The luxury customer is in general more globally homogeneous than the mass-market customer. Being mainly lifestyle brands, luxury brands represent common values and cultures that are appreciated by their customers everywhere. Many mass-market brands, on the other hand,

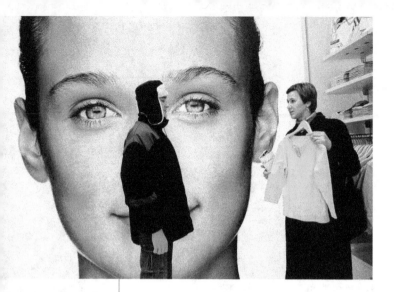

Figure 5.4

Benetton's franchising strategy has proven highly successful for entering foreign markets. In 1992, this 21,000-square-foot United Colors of Benetton megastore opened in Moscow, Russia.

(© Gerd Ludwig/Corbis)

failed to attract or identify similar segments in foreign markets (such as Gap in Europe).

Premium Brands: The New Luxury or New Luxe

In recent years, the premium segment of brands has emerged with tremendous growth. **PREMIUM BRANDS** are also referred to as "aspirational" or "new luxe" brands and include brands such as Coach, Victoria's Secret, and most RTW labels introduced by luxury brands (see Figure 5.5). By definition, this segment stands at the highest spectrum of mass-market brands; placed just below luxury brands, it shares a few characteristics with them. Some of these characteristics are as follows.

- Whereas premium brands may not be built on exclusivity, they are based on emotions, and consumers have a much stronger emotional engagement with them than with other goods in the mass-market segment.
- Premium brands possess better quality, benefits, and functionality based on a higher level of innovation and creativity. Although

most premium products still rely on following trends introduced by luxury brands, it is important to remember that premium brands are not created by simply improving existing products or attempting to reposition them through marketing and advertising. Consumers are sophisticated enough to understand this, and there must be a genuine added value in these products.

- The decision to create a premium brand is primarily a business strategy and as such must be developed and executed by CEOs and divisional leaders of large companies as well as entrepreneurs and innovators of small companies. A premium brand is product centered and also requires keen understanding of consumer motivation and buying behavior.
- Premium brands may have elements of craftsmanship but are not completely handmade or artisan in nature.
- Premium brands are not promoted as elite, the way luxury brands are. Rather, they appeal to a set of values that may be shared by people of many income levels, in many walks of life. As a matter of fact, premium brands are a major culprit in what has been referred to as the democratization of luxury.

In recent decades, the luxury brands segment has witnessed major changes in terms of organizational structure and type of ownership. For instance, this can be seen with the creation of large multibrand luxury groups. Yet it is important to remember that premium brands are more than a marketing exercise or cheap copies of luxury brands. They are legitimate brands created through a strong collaboration of all organizational functions.

Customer

This segment appeals to a category of customers that has grown in number and relevance in recent years as a result of an increase in wealth gained from economic prosperity in many societies such as China. As a result, these customers aspire to trade up to premium brands, motivated by the following:

- Discretionary income has increased among many households due to both parents working. Higher incomes have been matched by an increase in home ownership and equity. In addition, these customers manage to save on basic items through frequently patronizing discount stores.
- Relevant to the previous point, many women have joined the work force and are earning top salaries as well.
- On the other hand, there has been an increase in the number of independent singles with more money to spend on themselves and their desires.
- Demographic profiles have changed; the middle class is better educated, more sophisticated, and better traveled than before.
- The media and celebrities have contributed to the increase in desire for obtaining such brands and other pleasures in life.
- The increased number and spread-out design of shopping centers and malls created opportunities for the new premium group of brands and stores such as Victoria's Secret and Guess to exist and expand through mall-based chains of stores. The rise of these specialty retailers has helped make premium goods more geographically available, while still offering a limited selection of goods and categories at close to premium prices.
- Rapid changes in technology and communications have made it easier to democratize fashion in general and thus made it easier and cheaper to access information and generate interest in these trends.

As for their profile and shopping habits, the premium or new luxury customer has a few notable characteristics, such as:

- Premium-brand customers are generally price and economic sensitive and are willing to trade down if necessary.
- They are very selective and have a tendency to mix brands from different segments. For instance, they might carry a Coach handbag and wear a pair of Levi's jeans at the same time.
- Their selectivity is also motivated by their decision-making process, which can be both rational (involving technical and functional considerations) as well as emotional (aspirational).

Price

Premium brands demand high-end prices that are at the higher end of the mass-market spectrum yet still lower than luxury brands. However, one

Figure 5.5

Coach is considered a premium brand, just below the luxury segment. (© Qi yunfeng— Imaginechina/AP Images)

163

challenge these brands face is their limited ability to reduce pricing without highly eroding their margins. The fact that they are mass produced in larger quantities than luxury means that they have already received and benefitted from supplier discounts, so they usually have little opportunity to manipulate prices. As a result, where luxury brands are forced to discount their prices in tough times, premium brands may find it even harder to respond and keep their products attractive to their customer. For a premium-brand shopper who may have the choice of purchasing a Coach handbag for around $700 or a Prada on sale for around $900, buying the Prada handbag will most likely make more sense.

Product

New luxury goods cover a wide range of products that can be categorized in three main categories:[1]

1. *Super-premiums:* Products that are priced at or near the top of their category and at a considerable premium to conventional offerings.
2. *Old luxury brand extensions:* Lower-priced versions of products created by companies whose brands have traditionally been affordable only for the rich.
3. *MASSTIGE brands (mass prestige):* Neither at the top of their category in price nor related to other brands. They occupy a sweet spot in the market between mass and class, commanding a premium price over conventional products but priced well below super-premium or old luxury goods (such as Bath & Body Works).

Premium products are more responsive to trends than conventional goods. They may still not be trendsetters but are faster in responding to high-end trends where innovation generally appears first. Therefore, they are able to interpret these trends within a few weeks in less expensive versions. A good example is Zara, which manages through a vertically integrated system to reduce the production cycle, control quantity produced, and minimize inventory so that they can offer new styles in their stores almost every week. However, whereas this system of controlled quantities and shorter cycles allows these brands to respond quickly to trends trickling down from the luxury segment, it also makes it harder to increase their volume of production fast enough if a larger quantity is needed.

Distribution

Many premium brands such as Zara adopt a *fast response* concept of production and distribution. This concept allows them to have better control over the production and development stages as well as better management of inventory by adopting *just-in-time* concepts in operations. (Just-in-time is a strategy whereby raw materials are ordered and delivered only when needed and thus saves in cost and space of warehousing.) As a result, it allows customers to find something fresh and new almost every time they visit the store, raising their level of interest and surprise and motivating them to visit the store more often. However, this also means that most products are produced in small quantities to minimize stock and reduce the need to discount their prices.

Some of the measures these brands take to enhance the distribution process are as follows.

- They use local distribution centers.
- They have real-time communication with stores to respond to each store's need of inventory in a short period of time.

- Whereas these brands, unlike luxury brands, rely on outsourcing in cheaper markets such as Asia, production in some cases may have to be done domestically to ensure a quick response.
- Many of these brands may also rely on workshops or dedicated factories to ensure better control and response.

Premium brands are distributed through a range of distribution channels. In addition to company-owned, stand-alone stores, they can be distributed in other specialty and department stores as well. Premium brands also adopt franchising as a viable channel of expansion, and they are more flexible in being present in locations such as suburban malls and shopping centers than most luxury brands would be.

Communication

The premium brand's communication strategies are similar to the luxury brand's strategies in focusing on high advertisement expenditure in magazine and editorial coverage. As a matter of fact, many believe that the luxury-style communication of premium brands contributed to the changing perceptions that consumers generally have today about mass-market fashion brands versus luxury brands.

Examples of the communication strategies they adopt are:
- Celebrity endorsements.
- Prestige retail locations, though they have a stronger presence outside major cities than luxury brands do.
- Co-branding. H&M for example, has a track record of cooperating with celebrity designers such as Karl Lagerfeld and Roberto Cavalli,

and celebrities such as Madonna, in producing specially designed limited-edition collections with great success. Due to this strategy, they may be regarded in some areas as a premium brand.

Growth

Premium brands borrow their global appeal and potential from luxury brands. Aided by their greater flexibility in adopting different modes of entry, such as franchising and through local distributors, premium brands tend to be true global brands. Their fashion appeal and comparative affordability make them more attractive and accessible in different markets while maintaining a certain class status that they may even lack in their home markets (again, H&M is a good example).

Premium brands still face a major challenge of where to go next. They appear to be in a better position than other mass-market brands to enter the luxury market through brand creation; however, they may still suffer from lack of heritage and history. On the other hand, they do have the necessary infrastructure and logistics should they consider downgrading to a lower-priced offering in the mass-market segment.

Private Labels

PRIVATE LABELS are brands owned by a retailer and not a manufacturer. Retailers usually contract these products and have them produced under their own labels.

The definition of private labels has expanded to refer to both private labels sold next to manufacturers brands in multibranded stores (such as Club

Room at Macy's or Target's Isaac Mizrahi collection) as well as private brands sold solely in their exclusive stores (such as Gap and Esprit), which would also fall under the specialty stores category. (See Figure 5.6.)

To avoid confusion in this chapter, we shall focus on the first kind of private labels: those that are produced by retailers such as Macy's and Nordstrom to be exclusively sold side by side with other manufacturers' brands.

Private labels have come a long way since 20 years ago when many consumers preferred national brands because they recognized the names and trusted their reputations. In the past, private labels were generally seen as cheaper products with inferior quality. National brands had the means and legitimacy to attract creative talents as well as the need and capacity to advertise and expand. Today the apparel industry is one of the largest sectors for private labels, which currently account for an estimated 45 percent of sales in the United States, whereas in some categories such as women's wear, skirts, and children's clothing, the share is more than 65 percent.[2] Now these brands compete with established national brands, not just on the basis of price, but of quality and style as well, especially considering that they use the services of the same contractors as national brands. The rise in the transformation of many stores into chain stores and their expansion into global brands have also created the need to be different and compete on the basis of product and service, and not just price.

Today these brands are well positioned as proper brands that possess the same emotional elements generally associated with manufacturers' brands. This is a big transformation from the pure functional role these brands played in earlier years.

One of private labels' core values is creating a sense of "smart shopping" for the customers. Customers feel they are making smarter decisions buying a "designer" creation at Target, JCPenney, Macy's, or H&M, yet at a much more reasonable price. (See Figure 5.7.) This is one of the many reasons why these brands usually become more popular during economic downturns. An interesting research outcome shows how these brands manage to maintain a longer relationship with customers even after economic hard times, demonstrating that these brands have more to offer in values than just price. As a matter of fact, there are some indications that buyers are increasingly shifting their loyalty from manufacturing brands to retailers' private labels.

The rivalry between retailer and manufacturers' brands is also evident in their fight over in-store space and locations dedicated to each brand. Retailers will normally give priority to their own brands.

Figure 5.6

Macy's private label Alfani has become one of the fastest-growing segments of their business. (Associated Press/ZAK BRIAN/SIPA)

Private labels are generally not trendsetters. They tend to imitate creative and technological innovations of manufacturers' brands and offer their versions at competitive prices. These brands are thus a major source of differentiation and competitiveness for these retailers. Melissa Hopkes, vice president and divisional merchandise manager of INC, Macy's largest private label, said once that "INC has been vital to Macy's success in differentiating the store from its competition. If private labels didn't exist, there would be no reason to shop at Macy's rather than Nordstrom's."[3] As a result INC is given prominent display in the store, where it is usually placed to be seen by customers as they first enter the store.

Product

Private labels are generally created by a team of young designers or product developers, except for those instances where stores decide to work with famous celebrity designers to create exclusive collections. This form of co-branding is seen in collaboration between Target and Isaac Mizrahi, JCPenney and Nicole Miller, and Kmart and Martha Stewart. Target's slogan "Expect more, Pay less" is a good reflection of this strategy.

Categories

In the world of private labels, there are four main categories: generics, copycats, premium store brands, and value innovators.[4]

GENERICS

A dying breed and not very relevant to the fashion industry, **GENERICS** refer to no-name products such as shampoos and soaps that were sold at large discounts next to branded products in supermarkets.

COPYCATS

This used to be the initial rationale behind private labels. In the fashion industry, it is common to find **COPYCAT** private labels that basically imitate the styles, color stories, and details of an established manufacturer brand and offer their alternative at a competitive price. Usually these brands are positioned and marketed on the premise that they offer equal quality and styling with a lower price that they achieve due to their ability to eliminate the middle man from the developing process. Retailers benefit in many ways from such a strategy. By copying trends and styles of manufacturing brands, they indirectly benefit from those brands' proven creative resources and investment. Also, retailers can gain bargaining leverage with manufacturers by competing with their brands, so they can secure better margins and deals with these manufacturers. Finally, they benefit from in-store traffic created by manufacturers' brands to promote their own competing private labels. No wonder that these private labels are usually placed in-store close to the manufacturers brands they imitate.

PREMIUM STORE BRANDS

Retailers began to realize that although the copycat branding strategy helps to generate traffic and compete against manufacturer brands, it may not help differentiate the store from other specialty stores. The alternative was to introduce private labels that offer superior quality at lower prices and high creativity. It's the retailers' way of participating in the premium brand segment that has been gaining an increasing popularity in recent years.

Macy's, JCPenney, Target, and Nordstrom are among the many department and specialty stores that offer a range of private labels that have been successful and instrumental in positioning their store brand. Indeed Macy's has a wide range of private labels with proven successes and history. Terry Lundgren, CEO of Macy's Inc. (formerly known as Federated), said that the "objective is to have more merchandise that is unique to our stores," acknowledging the fact that most department stores sell almost the same manufacturing brands and range of products. Macy's private labels, most notably INC and Alfani, have proven to be the fastest-growing part of their business. Other brands include Style & Co, Charter Club, Tahari by Elie Tahari, and an exclusive collection for the home by Martha Stewart, among others. Lundgren expressed hopes that this strategy will attract the customers' attention away from sales and coupon promotions. As a matter of fact, in recent years, Macy's has reduced the number of promotions by about 20 percent and focused on fewer but better sales.[5] It is interesting to note that at Macy's, sales of private-label apparel, accessories, and other items have outperformed other merchandise categories for years, accounting for 19 percent of Macy's sales in fiscal 2007. In fact, Macy's derives 35 percent of its annual sales from its private-label goods and designer items exclusive to Macy's by celebrities, such as Martha Stewart and Tommy Hilfiger.[6]

VALUE INNOVATORS

The value innovators are an interesting group of retailers that manage to balance low-priced value-driven private labels with a high level of innovation and style. Examples could be Target's collaboration with big name designers like Isaac Mizrahi as well as H&M with Lagerfeld, McCartney, and Cavalli. These brands offer fashion at attractive prices through a series of efforts that focus on consistently lowering and controlling costs, such as:

- Sourcing from low-cost developing countries, mainly in Asia
- Having fewer middlemen
- Buying in large volumes
- Controlling costs at every level and stage
- Using an efficient distribution system that secures quick delivery
- Employing effective marketing campaigns that are in tune with their target market (mainly hip and young) and successfully create the necessary buzz around these collections

Accordingly, these brands differentiate and position themselves on the basis of delivering good quality and design at a very reasonable and competitive price. It is a successful mix of value for money and innovation that has been traditionally hard to achieve.

However, one challenge these brands face is that they obviously cannot rely on price to achieve growth or higher margins. They rely heavily on volume, which means that they either need to target new segments or expand globally. Each option is lucrative but also challenging. Targeting new segments might risk alienating customers of existing ones and thus repositioning the brand, whereas international expansions incur other cost and logistic challenges, requiring extra effort and time to succeed. Nevertheless, these labels' success with shoppers will definitely attract more bands to follow suit.

The strategy seems to also have a positive impact on the store's image. Target has been repositioned as more hip than it used to be in the past and has been nicknamed by many of its customers "Tar-jay," a French-flavored pronunciation to reflect its new trendy fashionable image. However, time will tell if this strategy will backfire in times of economic turndowns if Target chooses to remain positioned as a low-priced discount store.

Price

Most of the previously mentioned private label categories demonstrate that pricing is a major factor in their success. Offering equal or better quality than their competitors' manufacturer brands at a lower price has been instrumental to their positioning strategy and success. One strategy some retailers adopt in promoting their private labels is to inflate the price gap between the retailer's private label and the competing manufacturer brand. The big difference in price makes customers feel that the extra money they pay for manufacturer brands is not proportionate to the perceived extra benefit they may receive. As a result, retail labels make more economic sense to them and appear to be more attractive. Although effective, this strategy may be counterproductive if mishandled. Too much of a difference may reduce the retailers' margin and revenue. Thus, in deciding on this price gap, retailers need to put into consideration the nature of the product and the price sensitivity and elasticity for both competing brands. Elasticity simply measures how strongly customers respond to these changes and how it would affect their demand for the brand. The other challenge is that if customers focus on the lower-priced private labels and totally ignore the manufacturers' brands, the result may be a decrease in the store's total dollar revenue.

In the case of premium private labels, they usually adopt a different strategy. These brands are not necessarily significantly cheaper than their manufacturers' competitors and in some instances may even be more expensive. Thus, their profitability is driven by other factors such as their exclusivity, lower costs creating higher margins by as much as 25 to 30 percent, and an increase in brand loyalty as a result of private labels in general. In addition, they benefit financially from the leverage bargaining power they gain in negotiating with manufacturers as a result of the threat their private labels impose on the manufacturers' brands.

From an economic perspective, consumers will switch if the benefit they perceive in quality or image is less than the price they pay. Thus, private labels must be able to compete not just on the basis of price but on quality and creativity as well in order to create the right incentive for the consumer. However, these elements do come with their own challenges.

- Measures such as dollar/square foot cannot be ignored. These can be in favor of manufacturers' brands because of their higher prices and turnover. Also, manufacturers offer many services that stores are now forced to provide themselves, such as transportation or warehousing, therefore imposing an added cost burden.

- Manufacturers, in many cases, share costs of promotion and marketing activities, which will be totally handled by the stores in case of private labels.
- Although private labels give retailers a negotiation leverage with manufacturers, they can also alienate manufacturers and force them to take their brands somewhere else. The result is a narrow and less diverse merchandise mix.
- Retailers are selective of what they offer in their stores, and they never buy the full collection of a manufacturer. As a result, many designers have decided to open their own boutiques to showcase their full lines in a space and atmosphere that reflects the image and lifestyle they represent. An increasing tension between retailers and manufacturers has therefore surfaced, and retailers have decided to fight back with various measures including more private labels.
- One other major challenge is that private labels will never be able to compete at the same level of innovation with manufacturers because they do not have the dedicated resources. And the more manufacturers' brands hit the market, the less the share of private labels will be.
- Private labels' success is dependent in a way on the power of the retailer brand, even if they have different names, especially those that are sold exclusively at these stores.
- They also suffer from a general lack of advertising, at least at a level below that of manufacturers' brands.

Communication

Private labels generally advertise less than manufacturers do. However, private labels rely heavily on in-store and point of sales communication. It is an effective and cost-efficient strategy. Products strategically placed in-store where they are visible and can effectively compete with manufacturer brands, signs, sales promotions, and discounts are other examples of how the brands are internally marketed.

Stores also use catalogs and direct marketing to promote their brands. New media such as the Internet and digital devices have allowed retailers to personalize their messages and special offers at a fast rate and in a cost-effective manner.

Global Private Labels

Private labels are global phenomena. Their success is evident in many markets around the world. The United Kingdom, for instance, is generally considered a pioneer in private labels and in various industries: Marks and Spencer, the leading British retailer, launched its highly popular apparel brand St. Michael in 1928. In this chapter, we decided to focus on private labels manufactured by retailers and sold alongside other manufacturers' brands they carry, as opposed to private brands sold solely in exclusive stores, such as H&M and Gap. The latter group's expansion into the global scene is evident through a mix of store ownership and franchises. As for the former group (our focus), their geographic expansion is evidently highly reliant on the retailer's own expansion. However, the Internet and online shopping have opened the doors for global reach to these brands. In addition, private labels have a strong connection with global markets through overseas manufacturing and outsourcing.

Chapter Summary

- Mass-market brands are not usually trendsetters or at the forefront of creativity.

- Buying a mass-market brand is a rational decision for the most part.

- Mass-market brands are still expected to deliver value.

- Compared to luxury brands, mass-market brands generally adopt different distribution and pricing strategies.

- Premium brands gained big growth recently as they respond to new socioeconomic changes.

- Private labels have come a long way and play an important and competitive role in the face of manufacturers' brands.

Chapter Questions and Issues for Discussion

1. How do mass-market brands compare to luxury brands in terms of brand value, pricing attitude, and location choices?

2. Briefly compare premium brands to luxury brands.

3. Name a few of the challenges private labels face to compete with manufacturing brands.

KEY TERMS

COPYCATS

GENERICS

MASS-MARKET

MASSTIGE

PREMIUM
BRANDS

PRIVATE LABELS

CASE STUDY: Zara

Zara opened its first store 1975 in La Coruña, Spain, as a store selling medium-quality fashion apparel at affordable prices. By the end of the eighties, the brand was located in most major Spanish cities including Madrid, and in the nineties it began to expand overseas as well. Since 2002, Inditex, the parent company of Zara, now comprises several brands: Massimo Dutti (sophisticated urban fashion), Pull and Bear (casual laid-back fashion), Bershka (street fashion), Stradivarius (young cutting-edge fashion), Oysho (lingerie), Zara Home, and Uterqüe (accessories), with Zara still the largest of its brands.

Inditex

Inditex is a vertically integrated company where most products, especially fashion-sensitive items, are designed and manufactured internally, then distributed to stores. Its design strategy is not to be a trendsetter but rather a fashion follower, responding to customers' preferences and new trends seen on fashion runways, trade shows, and magazines. Zara's competitive edge lies in how fast and efficiently it is able to transform these ideas and trends into quality products that are available in its stores with a short lead time. As a result, both internal and external production channels direct to a central distribution center from where merchandise is shipped directly to stores twice a week. The system is based on the concepts of quick response, a set of policies meant to improve coordination between retailing and manufacturing to ensure more flexibility and better response to market changes such as just-in-time manufacturing (a strategy based on orders, not inventory built-up) and the use of bar codes and electronic devices to share information, thus eliminating the need for warehousing by keeping inventory as low as possible. This system allows the company to shorten its cycle from design to store placement to about five weeks for new designs and almost two weeks for modifications or restocked products. Compared to an industry standard of an average six-month cycle, it manages to beat the system and stay fresh and competitive. The shorter cycle also means reduced working capital and the ability to continue supplying the stores with new merchandise, as well as having the capacity to commit resources to new seasons' merchandise later than most competitors.

Merchandise

Zara produces three lines—women's, men's, and children's—through a team of designers who follow fashion trends and base their new collections on them. Zara has adopted a philosophy of quick response rather than prediction of trends. Fabrics and trims are picked, samples prepared, and prices are determined, followed by production. Zara's designers produce two basic collections each year for Fall/Winter and Spring/Summer. The whole process of product development is done with close consideration for and link to the stores. On many occasions, they will produce limited quantities of new items and place them in a few stores for testing. The brand produces large quantities based only on consumers' reaction. In general, 89 to 90 percent of basic designs are common in all stores, while 10 to 15 percent vary according to country. Items that are slow are swiftly cancelled, and returns are either shipped to and sold at other Zara stores or disposed of through a small, separate chain of close-out stores near their distribution center. The target is to minimize the inventory that has to be sold at marked-down prices in stores during the sales period that usually ends each season.

Retailing and Distribution

The company designed a centralized distribution system based in Arteixo, Spain, with a network of satellite centers in other countries. Warehouses are regarded as centers of distribution for moving merchandise to stores rather than storing it as inventory for a long time, and shipments are generally made twice a week to their stores. Zara owns and operates many of its own stores. In 2001, it operated over 200 stores in 18 countries other than Spain. Its vertical integration is more backward oriented, focusing on responding to fashion trends quickly, so in retailing, they also rely on franchising as well as joint ventures in areas where there are market barriers to direct entries, such as in Japan.

The vertically integrated model built on the concept of quick response has generally proven to be effective and profitable for Inditex by reducing merchandising cycles and errors as well as inventory risks.

Promotion

The stores play a major role in promoting the brand because Zara spends very little on traditional media advertising—approximately 0.3 percent of its revenue compared with 3 to 4 percent for most other specialty retailers. Its advertising is generally limited to the start of the sales period at the end of the season. Accordingly, the brand relies heavily on its store front to market the brand (see Figure 5.8). As a result, their stores are usually large in size and located in central locations. The company always prefers to enter a market with a flagship store and considers expansion based on results after they gain local experience. Thus, compared to H&M, for instance, it will usually be running fewer stores in countries where both these brands exist. It also historically has preferred new markets that resembled the Spanish one with a lower level of economic development and easier entry. Store windows are also of great importance because they are meant to showcase the brand. Store window prototypes are usually set up at headquarters to indicate design themes and direction, which are later carried to stores around the world through a team of visual merchandisers and window designers with some allowance for adaptation. In-store music and employees' uniforms are also determined to achieve a consistent look and atmosphere throughout the stores. Store managers decide on which merchandise to carry, then transmit their orders electronically to headquarters, and manufacturing is planned accordingly.

Pricing

A major aspect of Zara's global expansion is its pricing strategy. It adopts a strategy whereby it passes the extra cost of distributing overseas to its customers. This creates a large price discrepancy compared to prices in Spain. For example, prices would be 70 percent higher in the United States and 100 percent higher in Japan than in Spain due to this policy. As a result, the brand is positioned differently in each of these markets. (See Figure 5.9.) In Latin America, for instance, it is positioned with a high-end status emphasizing its "Made in Europe" image (as opposed to being made in Spain), while it is still positioned and priced at the middle market in Spain. Such discrepancies may be among the reasons why the company was late in offering online shopping at their Web site.

Recent Growth

In recent years, Inditex celebrated a few growth milestones, for example:

- In 2009, Inditex signed a joint venture to open stores in India starting in early 2010. Massimo Dutti, Bershka, and Pull and Bear have opened for the first time in China.
- In 2008, Inditex launched Uterqüe, a retailer specializing in accessories. Inditex achieved a new milestone by reaching 4,000 stores in 73 countries.
- In 2007, Zara Home introduced Inditex's first online store. Zara also celebrated the launch of shop number 1,000 in Florence, Italy.

CASE STUDY Questions

1. What are the main challenges in the business model adopted by Zara?

2. Evaluate Zara's marketing and distribution strategies, and compare them to those of another brand you are familiar with. Decide how these strategies would work if Zara decided to enter your local market.

Figure 5.9

With stores in so many countries, Zara prints its hang tags with international sizes.
(*Bloomberg via Getty Images/ Markel Redondo*)

Figure 5.10

This diagram takes us through the stages of the design, production, distribution, and retailing cycle that represent the Zara model.

(Illustration by Andrea Lau)

THE ZARA MODEL

The Zara team researches new fashion trends in fashion shows, magazines, university campuses, dance clubs, etc.

Research results sent to Zara's headquarters. Commercial team analyzes research results and shares them with design team to decide together on the new line's look, materials, price points, etc.

Similar meetings are held to analyze store feedback and decide the fate of current products.

Stores use their computer systems and handheld devices to send sales results and reorders to headquarters.

Once the line is decided, fabric is prepared, dyed, and finished as needed. Accessories are allocated, and production starts.

Finished garments are sent from manufacturing centers to the automated distribution center. Using computers and a system of bar codes similar to mail distribution, garments are boxed and sent to stores based on their orders and locations.

SOURCES

Dutta, Devangshu. 2002. *Retail @ The Speed of Fashion.* Gurgaon, India: Third Eyesight.

Ghemawat, Pankaj, and Nueno, Jose Luis. 2003. *Zara: Fast Fast.* Boston: Harvard Business School Press.

www.inditex.es

www.Zara.com

ENDNOTES

1. Michael Silverstein and Neil Fiske, *Trading Up: The New American Luxury* (New York: The Penguin Group), 7.

2. Nirmalya Kumar and Jan-Benedict Streenkamp, *Private Label Strategy* (Boston: Harvard Business School Press), 7.

3. Pia Sarkar, "Stores Boost Sales with Own Labels," SF Gate, May 5, 2006, http://www.sfgate.com/cgi-bin/article.cgi?f=/c/a/2006/05/05/BUG82IL0QR1.DTL#ixzz0NWTSoWSg

4. Kumar and Streenkamp, *Private Label Strategy*, 26.

5. Jayne O'Donnell, "Beloved Stores Get a Lot More than a New Name," *USA Today*, June 8, 2006, http://www.usatoday.com/money/industries/retail/2006-06-08-macys-shopping_x.htm

6. Kathryn Kroll, "Low-cost Private Label Brands Growing More Popular with Stores, Customers," Cleveland.com, January 20, 2009, http://blog.cleveland.com/business/2009/01/lowcost_private_label_brands_g.html

6 Retail Brands

RETAILING is the major service side of fashion. In general, products and services follow the same principles and rules of marketing and branding. However, there are some obvious differences, such as the intangibility of a service and the human element, where individuals delivering the service, such as sales personnel, are at the core of the brand.

The twentieth century witnessed how stores have grown in number, size, shape, and specialization. Unlike in the past, where shoppers had limited choices of outlets to buy their necessary goods, stores today cater to every need and lifestyle. And in order to compete, a store needs to be more than just a space with a collection of merchandise. It needs to be an experience that is unique, engaging, and fulfilling—both emotionally and functionally. Thus, just as with products, stores need to be branded in order to stand out and simplify the choices for their customers, while ensuring a higher level of emotional satisfaction as well. After all, shopping is indeed an emotional experience.

According to freedictionary.com, a retail store is simply defined as "A place where merchandise is offered for sale."[1] As simple as this definition may seem, it actually highlights the three major components or attributes of any store. They are:

1. *Place:* The need for a space and a location.
2. *Merchandise:* The need for a product to be transacted and sold at a suitable price.
3. *A platform:* The need for a business model or a selling concept that makes this transaction possible.

CHAPTER
OBJECTIVES

- Differentiate between a product and a service.

- Examine the concept of fashion retail branding.

- Identify the positioning strategies for a retail operation.

- Determine the components of the retail concept.

- Highlight the importance of the store experience and the role of sales personnel in shaping the store identity.

- Examine the role of internal and external communication in retailing.

- Explore the significance and challenges of e-tailing.

- Identify retail growth options.

These three elements formulate the base core of any retailer, which combined with a strong identity and store experience, transform the store into a brand with a unique experiential proposal and **PERSONALITY**.

Adopting the same branding roadmap we used earlier for product brands, our adapted steps for fashion retail branding will be as illustrated in Figure 6.1.

Product vs. Service

In spite of the common grounds among them, there are a few important differences between a product and a service that should impact the branding decisions and process:

- The obvious difference is that products, for the most part, are a sum of tangible features meant to satisfy a functional purpose and need,

Figure 6.1

The retail branding process.

(*Illustration by Andrea Lau*)

RETAIL BRANDING PROCESS

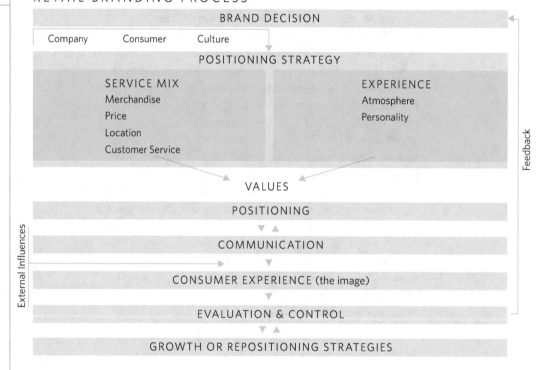

BRAND DECISION

Company   Consumer   Culture

POSITIONING STRATEGY

SERVICE MIX
Merchandise
Price
Location
Customer Service

EXPERIENCE
Atmosphere
Personality

VALUES

POSITIONING

COMMUNICATION

CONSUMER EXPERIENCE (the image)

EVALUATION & CONTROL

GROWTH OR REPOSITIONING STRATEGIES

External Influences

Feedback

whereas a service, though meant to satisfy a need as well, is intangible, emotional, and generally experiential.

- A product is usually fully experienced by the consumer after the purchase decision has been made; in the case of retail shopping, a major part of the experience is consumed and evaluated before the purchase decision is made.
- Same products are expected to be identical and perform the same way for all users. They may not be appreciated equally yet are expected to be functionally identical. This is hard to achieve with services. The human element and experiential nature of services makes it difficult to duplicate the same experience and circumstances for all customers.

Accordingly, many believe that a service possesses a higher level of risk than a product, so branding becomes even more relevant. Therefore, in this chapter, we shall approach the retail store as a brand in its own right and not just as the distribution component of the product mix.

The Retail Brand Decision

Like any other brand, retailers need to have a clear vision that drives the branding strategy and all other activities. A retail store plays various roles in the life of any product brand. Retailing is the core of any distribution channel; it is also a communication tool. In addition, it is instrumental in monitoring consumer trends and behavior as well as gathering market data. There are many types of stores, each with a different market focus and strategy, so it is essential for every retail venture to

determine the suitable retail concept and business model that fits its philosophy and strategic goals. However, all models share the basic principle of creating the right experience with the right merchandise and service, at the right price, and for the right consumer.

Fashion retailers can be categorized based on different criteria. For example, as a distribution channel, fashion retailing can take various forms:

- **FREE-STANDING STORES**: Available in major streets, malls, or shopping centers.
- **FLAGSHIP STORES**: Usually the biggest and most impressive of the chain and mainly located at the brand's headquarters or in major centers of the world.
- **IN-STORE BOUTIQUES** (shops-in-shops): Fully individualized stores located inside department stores; can be either a space rented by the brand or run and managed by the department store itself while employees are picked and trained by the brand.
- **STORE CORNERS**: More open spaces or boutiques within a department store, compared to in-stores boutiques where the space is enclosed and the brand is the focus of display.
- **DEPARTMENT STORES**: Brands and their products are ordered and managed by the store and are among other brands displayed.
- **CHAINS** of specialty stores: These may sell one or multiple brands, yet the focus is on a segment or a category such as women's ready to wear, lingerie, and so on.
- *Online shopping:* E-tailing offers various models and formats that either complement the physical store's operations or stand on its own.

The Retail Consumer

Similar to products, retailers fall into the three major segments—luxury, mass-market, and premium. Within these categories are various business models that exist in response to the characteristics and shopping habits of each segment's customers.

To satisfy customers, it is essential to understand their shopping habits. In general, shoppers' shopping habits could be categorized as:

- *Routine shopping for basic and daily purchases:* These items usually do not require major decisions and are expected to be conveniently available and affordable. It is a shopping situation where either the product and brand choices are familiar or not very critical. It is a situation where clothing is just a utilitarian commodity and not necessarily "fashion."
- *Shopping to fulfill lifestyle needs:* This is where shopping gets more specific and more about satisfying emotional rather than functional needs. Products sought are usually fashion items where the brand choice is relevant and the decision requires more searching with a willingness to pay higher prices.
- *Shopping on an impulse:* This is where the decision is made in response to external factors and influences that directly appeal to the senses, not necessarily based on recurring or urgent needs.
- *Shopping for solutions rather than for specific products:* This is where the shopper's decision is based on specific items, such as the right gear for their next skiing vacation. Customers may not necessarily be aware of this segment

nor have a previous experience with such products, so they mainly look for brands providing confidence and assurance.

These habits are clearly affected by needs as well as the socioeconomic environment that influence them. Accordingly, retailers have always attempted to monitor such social, demographic, psychographic, technological, and economic trends in order to have a better understanding of their customer's behavior and segment their markets accordingly. Examples of such relevant trends are as follows.

- *Population growth:* As population growth slows down, retailers consider shifting their strategies from expansion through opening new stores, to increasing productivity of existing stores, or complementing their operation with online services. Generational differences are also important. The aging baby boomers are at an age where they would prefer saving for retirement than shopping. A decline in the number of child births and the smaller size of new generations, such as generations X, Y, Z (also known as the Google Generation), respectively, who also have different needs and aspirations, has a strong impact on every decision made. In addition, a rise in the number of single professionals and women in higher job ranks all promise a wave of new shopping trends.
- *Economic environment:* Changes in income levels, disposable income, credit, and personal savings level are all examples of economic factors that directly affect the purchasing power of buyers and redefine their priorities. In times of economic downturns, for instance, buyers look for bargains and greater values for their

money as opposed to leisure spending in times of prosperity.

- *Lifestyle trends:* Recent decades have witnessed many changes in lifestyles as a result of the economic and social changes. Moving out to the suburbs, interest in exercising and healthy living, and ease of travel costs have transformed how many people live or spend their leisure time. And with the changes in lifestyles come changes in buying habits and interests. Accordingly, retailers must respond to these new factors and work on fulfilling them when and where needed.

The Retail Concept

The **RETAIL CONCEPT** is the business model and retail philosophy adopted by the brand. The **SERVICE MIX** is the mix of attributes that formulate the concept or define the business model, including:

- The **MERCHANDISE**: The product mix that is offered for sale.
- The **PRICE RANGE**: The price range that defines the segment of focus.
- The **LOCATION**: The retail location signifies the level of shopping convenience and availability.
- The **SERVICE**: Mainly customer service policies that are adopted both at the time of purchase and after.

In many ways, this is similar to what is sometimes referred to as the retailing mix, or the Seven Ps of retailing: place, product, price, promotion, people, process, and physical environment. However, in our model, we prefer to separate them based on their role and stage in the branding process. Any of these attributes (or a mix of them) can be the base of a retail-positioning strategy, just like the product is for a product-based brand.

Retail brands face similar challenges to those faced by product brands. For instance, the service mix is at the core of the retail brand and faces the same challenge of being easily copied and imitated by other stores competing in the same segment and adopting a similar business model. Therefore, like any brand, a retail brand needs to compete by establishing an emotional value for its customers built on a strong identity (or experience) so that although two stores may have a similar business model or concept and carry similar merchandise, they may not necessarily create the same level of experience and value to the same customer.

Retail Channels

The different types of **RETAIL CHANNELS** mentioned earlier in this chapter can exist under various retail concepts or business models. The range of concepts or business models is designed to target various segments, incomes, and shopping habits. These concepts may include:

- *Specialty stores:* Specialty stores are retailers that focus on one category of products, such as men's sportswear, lingerie, and so on. Although these stores carry a narrow range, they are usually deep in color and size options. Specialty stores range from one of a kind, independent, stand-alone stores or boutiques to a chain of stores (such as Ann Taylor, Talbots, Hollister, Banana Republic).

Figure 6.2

Guess is a brand
with a chain of
specialty stores,
this one in
Venice, Italy.
(© Jeff Greenberg/
Alamy)

(See Figure 6.2.) In all cases, they tend to be trendier and fashion oriented, carrying designer brands and/or exclusive lines. Some specialty stores are superspecialized (such as Tie Rack), with an even narrower but deeper line of products; others, such as boutiques, are usually small stores with a niche market clientele and a trendy, avant-garde image and merchandise. Whether in the mass-market or luxury segments, specialty stores tend to complement their trendy merchandise with a higher level of service and price range. Their generally smaller size and focused merchandise allows them to be more specialized and knowledgeable, as

well as capable of offering a more personal and attentive service to their clients. In return, they are usually in the higher price range of their segment.

This concept of an exclusive retail space with a trendy image has paved the way for the creation of in-store boutiques (shop in shop) in department stores by many designer brands, such as Ralph Lauren, Tommy Hilfiger, and Tommy Bahama, among many others. Apart from in-store boutiques, many branded specialty stores grow and expand through a franchising network. The growth has also been attributed to the rise of suburban malls and shopping centers where most of them exist and expand.

• *Department stores:* Technically, a department store is a retailer that sells both soft goods (such as apparel) and hard goods (such as appliances and furniture). Thus, whereas Macy's is a department store, Neiman Marcus would be classified as a specialty store. However, there has been a tendency to refer to any large store with many departments and large number of employees as a department store, so Neiman Marcus or Nordstrom can be commonly referred to as specialty department stores. Most department stores are chain stores: they all offer a wide range of products, yet compete on the segment focus. For example, JCPenny and Sears are known for their moderate prices, whereas Macy's offers value through trendier merchandise at a mid to high price range (see Figure 6.3).

Department stores have played a major role in the American retailing scene since the late nineteenth century. In the 1980s, a major wave of mergers and consolidation took place that made

Federated acquire some of the nation's prominent department stores such as Marshall Field's and Rich's, among many others. Today Federated is known as Macy's Inc., and it operates Macy's and Bloomingdale's. Recently, there has been a lot of cynicism about the future of department stores. In the past few years, department stores seem to have continuously lost a lot of ground to both higher- and lower-price-range competitors. Lower-price discounters such as Walmart and Target have had much better performance, as have luxury chain specialty stores such as Nordstrom and Neiman Marcus. On the other hand, mid-price department stores like Sears and JCPenney have demonstrated less comparable gains. One major factor is that department stores do not carry many of the categories they did in the past (from fashion to stationary); and when they do, it is never as wide and deep a range as customers now find at category killers, outlets, and specialty stores. Actually, some experts believe that the main factor that may have kept department stores going is Christmas gift shopping. Another factor is the decline in the status of the mall, which has been rapid and dramatic. Mall-based stores' share of retail sales has been halved since 1995, accounting for only 19 percent of total retail sales in recent years. Many of these malls have witnessed a wave of acquisitions and consolidations led by weak sales and low interest rates. In addition, most of these locations have been redeveloped into different retail formats, such as upscale shopping centers with specialty stores, category killers, or discounters like Walmart. Those sectors now command some 80 percent of total retail sales.[2] Indeed, specialty stores have increased their size and scope in cities and suburbs; on the other hand, some believe that the day may come when the majority of currently existing department stores will be acquired by none other than Walmart!

Experts believe that the survival of department stores lies in their ability to provide exceptional customer service, including loyalty programs that are customizable and truly rewarding. Distinctive products and new initiatives are also necessary. In 2002, Sears purchased Lands' End for $1.9 billion; with Lands' End's established customer base, the integration of its merchandise into Sears stores along with the introduction of the new private label, Covington, seem to have helped Sears revive its sales numbers. Another initiative taken by stores such as Nordstrom and Kohl's is to open outside

traditional malls. In the case of Macy's, internal restructuring and operational streamlining, as well as its strategy to tailor its merchandise to local markets, seem to have helped the company as well.

- *Category killers:* Another form of specialty stores that offers the largest range of a specific category and at competitive prices. These offer both breadth and depth of merchandise assortment, including stores such as Bed, Bath & Beyond and The Home Depot (see Figure 6.4). Category killers manage to dominate their segment through a number of factors.

  1. *Price:* Both category killers and discounters are able to compete on the basis of price. They consistently adopt the adage of "everyday low price," which they are able to deliver through volume of merchandise, expanding their sourcing origins to places such as China and other parts of the globe, and a very efficient and sophisticated system of inventory management and logistics. Although these stores offer a higher level of customer service than discounters do, they still rely on centralized checkout points and a self-service environment (including self-service check-outs as well). Similar to many other retailers, several category killers have also introduced private labels, which helps them to achieve a few objectives: a wider selection of products to fill their usually large-sized stores and extended chains; a competitive price with a higher profit margin due to the elimination of the middle man; and an exclusive product range that differentiates them from their competitors and attracts potential shoppers.

  2. *Competition:* In terms of size, volume, and merchandise range, the closest concept to category killers are department stores. However, as we mentioned, there has been a noticeable decline in the role of department stores in recent years. Many department stores have stopped being the one-stop shop they used to be, and with negligible differences in merchandise and the fact that many have transformed from being true department stores into merely large specialty stores, category killers are facing much less competition.

  3. *Location:* On the other hand, their flexibility in terms of location gives them an edge over department stores, which are still stuck for the most part in the "mall anchor" format in terms of growth and expansion.

- **DISCOUNT STORES**: These are stores that sell known brands at discounted, below-market prices. These no-frills stores offer minimal services and in-store experiences in return for cutting their costs and passing part of these savings on to

Figure 6.4

Bed, Bath & Beyond, a nationwide category killer.

(© James Houck/ Alamy)

customers by adopting a low-margin/high-volume policy. (See Figure 6.5a.) Discount stores, in return, come in different formats.

1. *Off-price discounters:* Such as Ross, T.J. Maxx, and Marshalls (see Figure 6.5b).
2. *Factory outlets:* Owned and managed by specialty retailers and used as an alternative to selling off-season and broken sizes merchandise at a discount. On some occasions, the retailer may purchase merchandise especially for their outlets. These outlets are usually located in suburban areas where they offer great bargains to shoppers. Examples include: Nordstrom Rack, Off-Saks, Fossil, and Lacoste outlets. (See Figure 6.6.)
3. *Membership clubs:* Examples such as Sam's and Costco offer merchandise at close to wholesale prices for member customers. Popular for large quantity purchases of household merchandise at great discounts, many of these chains offer their own brands as well.
4. *Mass merchants and hyper-stores:* The major distinction between these stores and other department stores is that in addition to a mix of hard and soft merchandise, they sell groceries as well. Too, they are value oriented with a wide range of inexpensive product, centralized checkout points, and self-service.

As mentioned earlier in this chapter, discount stores, especially Target and Walmart, seem to have been performing much better than other department stores. They obviously become even more attractive at times of economic downturns because they attract newer customers with their range of products (including groceries) and low prices. It is important to remember, however, that a store model or format in itself is no guarantee for success or failure.

Positioning Based on a Retail Concept

Can a store position itself based on a retail concept or a business model? After all, these concepts mentioned earlier in this chapter are conceptually common to all retailers adopting that specific model or strategy. How they differ will most likely be in their execution, which is reflected in what we have called the *concept mix*, such as the merchandise selection, price strategy,

Figure 6.6

Another type of
discounter is a
factory outlet.
Several outlets
can be found in
the Las Vegas
Premium Outlets
Shopping Center,
shown above.

(© PCL/Alamy)

location, or service level. In today's environment
where technological advances have created
new tools and unconventional opportunities for
businesses of all natures, especially retailers,
POSITIONING based on a concept is possible
and refreshingly common. It is the same principle of disruptive positioning that we explored
in chapter 2 whereby a business positions itself
not against a group of traditional competitors
but against the whole segment. In chapter 7, we
shall examine many new business models that
have developed as a result of new technological
advances. All of these models are stepping out of
the ring of competitors and challenging the retail
environment's status quo by offering new experiences to consumers. Even older retailers such as
Nike or Sony have transformed their stores from
being purely functional to being entertaining
and interactive as well. At a Niketown store,
shoppers are intrigued by the interactive displays,
sports memorabilia, and images of sports icons,
all displayed in a large multifloored space of pure
entertainment. In the store, visitors do not just
shop, but play and learn as well. They experience

the brand and its philosophy (and personality)
hands-on. What Nike did (in addition to others
such as Sony) was introduce a new store concept
that redefined the role of the retail store in
our lives.

Thus, positioning based on a concept, if
possible, can be highly effective because of its
disruptive nature, which allows the business
to carve out a niche and be a market leader.
However, it is important to remember that a
concept is built on its elements or attributes, any
of which can be instrumental in a new concept's
creation. For example, what has Victoria's Secret
really accomplished? Apart from introducing a
specialty store with a rich assortment of lingerie,
it actually redefined the segment. It took lingerie
to a new frontier, from a basic clothing item
bought out of necessity, to a fashionable item
that might be purchased any time for various reasons and occasions. Having created a new niche
and established a new concept, the rest of the
attributes followed to shape the model, such as a
new distribution channel (a chain of specialized
stores) as well as a pricing strategy that reflects
the brand's fashion status, and so on.

The Merchandise

As the object of revenue transaction, merchandise is at the core of retailing activity. Selection
of merchandise is obviously based on the store
concept, which in return responds to the needs of
a targeted customer. (See Figure 6.7.) Choosing
the right merchandising mix, therefore, is of
the utmost importance. It is not just a question of fashion and trends but investment and

operations as well. Hence, merchandise management is a series of activities that involve analysis, planning, acquisition, handling, and control of merchandise. Merchandise planning starts with a budget, a sales target, and, accordingly, an inventory forecast. The sales target depends on the pulling power of the brand, the size of the store, and breadth of merchandise offered. Store buyers put together a dollar merchandising plan, which is a six-month or one-year budget that reflects the projected dollar value of the merchandise needed. The dollar merchandise plan is only the starting point. When the retailer has decided how many dollars can be invested in inventory, other decisions need to be made, such as the assortment of merchandise within each category (menswear, ready-to-wear, accessories, and so on). Choosing the right assortment (or merchandise mix) is influenced by the following elements:

- *Variety:* The number of lines carried in a store.
- *Breadth:* The assortment or the number of brands in a line.
- *Depth:* The number of styles, sizes, and colors within each brand, or what is referred to as the SKUs (stock-keeping units).

These elements in return are affected by other factors, such as:

- *Budget constraints and money available:* By definition a budget is a constraint on spending, so retailers need to control their spending and make decisions that maximize the return on their investment. One measure of control is achieved through the concept known as *open to buy* or *OTB*. OTB represents the dollar amount a store buyer can spend on merchandise without exceeding the planned dollar stock.
- *Store space:* The manner of utilizing store space is important because it affects in-store traffic, merchandise exposure, and return on investment. *Sales per square foot* is a tool used to measure the productivity of each department or even section and its contribution to sales.
- *Inventory and turnover consideration;* A deep merchandise mix means more items needed to be stocked and managed, which in turn requires more space and money. In general, managing inventory is equally as important as choosing the inventory. No matter what kind of merchandise you carry, it needs to be available when needed. A customer who is consistently unable to find the item, size, or color he or she needs will be discouraged and eventually take his or her business somewhere else. Obviously customer expectations differ from one business model to the other. A customer shopping at an off-price or a factory outlet store shops with the pre-understanding that not all items or sizes will be available. Actually, the adventure and element of surprise (and possible frustration) becomes part of what defines the bargain-hunting experience at these stores. On the other hand, expectations while shopping at Macy's are totally different: the customer expects to find all offerings available at all times.

Positioning Based on the Merchandise

Using merchandise as a base for positioning is equivalent to using product features in a product brand. Thus, it is an essential positioning tool. Here are few guidelines to consider when positioning on the basis of merchandise.

- Build a merchandise mix that is hard to emulate by competitors. This can be achieved by carrying exclusive lines. H&M's collaboration with designers such as Cavalli and Lagerfeld and celebrities like Madonna produced exclusive and limited collections that proved to be a great success, giving the store's brand an image boost and a competitive edge.
- Distinguish merchandise by its depth as much as its breadth, meaning a store can offer a wider range of sizes (such as full women's sizes) to distinguish itself among competitors. An example of this point is the deep specialization in a specific item or range such as demonstrated by Tie Rack and Victoria's Secret (see Figure 6.8).
- Carry merchandise that caters to a social trend (such as going green and organic), ethnic groups, or specific religious needs. (See Figure 6.9.)

Figure 6.8

Tie Rack is an example of deep specialization in a particular category of product.

(© uk retail Alan King/ Alamy)

Figure 6.9

This hijab store in Indonesia offers merchandise that caters to religious needs—another type of specialization.

(© dbimages/Alamy)

- Determine your brand mix. Carrying a unique mix or exclusive brands is a great differentiator, so choosing your merchandise sources is essential. Barneys New York built its legacy on being the pioneer in introducing new European designers, such as Giorgio Armani who was virtually unknown in the United States at the time.
- Examine your merchandise cycle because this can be an effective differentiator as well. Zara's competitive edge lies in its ability to put merchandise in its stores fast and frequently. The Zara strategy is to have something new in their stores almost every week. This requires smaller quantities, less or no stock, and more flexibility in responding to market demands. It is effective in increasing customers' interest by catering to their anticipation for new products every time they visit.

The Price

Determining the right price is crucial. Too high, and your customers are alienated; too low than expected, and they may doubt the quality of the product offered. Pricing strategies fall into the following categories.

Competitive Pricing Strategies

- *Pricing below competition:* Also known as competition-based pricing, it refers to setting prices based upon prices of similar competitor products.
- *Pricing above competition:* Also known as prestige pricing.
- *Price skimming:* Selling initially at a high price before lowering the price to competitive levels.

- *Price penetration:* Starting with a low price to gain market share and customer base.

Psychological Pricing Strategies

- *Odd pricing:* Setting at a price point implied to be lower than the real price (for example, $1.99, which is perceived as cheaper than $2).
- *Bait and switch pricing:* The practice of advertising the low price of a product to lure shoppers into a store, then attempting to convince them to purchase a higher-priced model. This practice is Illegal if the advertised low-priced model is actually unavailable.

Discount Pricing Strategies

- *Multiple pricing:* Selling more than one unit of the same item at a discount for one price, such as three items for $1.00.
- *Bundle pricing:* Here the items bundled are distinctly different.
- *Any other discounts and promotions:* This includes seasonal and occasional discounts such as sales, clearance, or promotions such as buy 1 get one free, and so on.

Other Pricing Strategies

- *Price lining:* Establishing certain price points for a particular merchandise group, such as the case of a $1.00 store.

- *Flexible pricing:* Offering the same products and quantities to different customers at different prices; this occurs in markets dominated by bargaining or personal selling.

Pricing Strategies' Objectives

It is important to remember that any pricing strategy is meant to achieve one or more of the following objectives.

- *Maximize profit:* Targeting as much profit as possible. Suitable policies can include prestige pricing, price skimming, and price penetration (based on volume).
- *Sales and market share:* The economic goal for every business is to maximize profit; however, sometimes the business realizes that its strategic goal at a certain time (as in the case of new businesses) is to increase market share and solidify its market presence, even if it is temporarily at the expense of profit maximization. Thus, achieving a certain level of sales or percentage of market share becomes the goal.
- *Status quo:* Maintaining the current market share or profit levels in the face of strong competition.

Positioning Based on Price

A price is obviously a major differentiator among stores, especially in the mass-market sector. A store will usually offer a range of retail prices that suit their proposed retail concept. However, this price range is bounded by the pricing strategy adopted by the store. In return, the strategy identifies the stores and reflects on its positioning.

Choosing the price as a positioning strategy depends on the retail model, the target market,

and type of merchandise. "Offering the lowest price" strategy, for instance, is more suitable for price sensitive items that have marginal differences and are readily available among competitors. Generally speaking, as we move higher on the pricing ladder, quality and fashion become the focal concerns for the shopper. Accordingly, retailers can also be categorized on the basis of their price range, for example:

- *Designer signature price:* The highest price points available at designer boutiques.
- *Bridge price points:* Between designer and better price points, as demonstrated with premium brands.
- *Contemporary price points:* Appealing to a younger fashion-forward market. This mass-market category targets a wide segment of young customers looking for trendy looks at a reasonable price.
- *Better price points:* Aimed at the middle-class market. Many private labels fall into this category.
- *Moderate price points:* Appealing to the less fashion-conscious customers who seek reasonable prices and value for money. JCPenney would be a good example.
- *Budget price points:* Fashion followers and price conscious, these copy fashion trends and offer them at lower quality and prices.

Any of these policies can be adopted as a positioning strategy; however, it is important to remember that offering the lowest price in the market and basing your gains on volume is not an easy strategy. Unless you have the capacity and ability to withstand the pricing war, the time will come when you cannot outbid your competitors or raise your prices to original levels again. Thus, it is usually operations with the size and capabilities of Walmart and Target that can afford such a strategy. Walmart, for instance, is known for its EDLP (everyday low price) policy and adopts the strategy of consistently beating competitors' prices. It even announces that it is willing to offer refunds to customers to maintain that promise. Interestingly, research shows that low-price shoppers are usually not loyal customers. Discounts do attract price-motivated customers, but when they see a lower price somewhere else, they quickly switch.

On the other hand, premium pricing is a strategy common in the luxury segment, whereby a low price might actually raise the suspicion of the consumer regarding the quality and functionality of the merchandise. Premium prices imply high levels of quality and style. In the same manner, by shopping at exclusive boutiques selling exclusive and luxury brands, customers expect a high level of service and quality merchandise. Overall, they expect a shopping experience that is pampering, sensual, and unique.

Most stores fall between these two extremes and compete in their category on the basis of combining a pricing strategy that includes occasional price cuts and promotions with other features such as in-store experience, customer service, or location to offer a unique value to the consumer.

Unconventional pricing strategies, such as allowing shoppers to bid on an item or offer a "best offer" option as seen on ebay.com, attract customers through another form of psychological pricing that totally responds to the market forces of supply and demand. Swoopo.com is an online electronics retailer that adopts an interesting model that may soon find its way to fashion e-tailers. It's a new model that is somewhere between eBay auctions and gambling. Basically, shoppers pay for every bid they make. Every bid increases the price by small increments as well as delays the auction's countdown. The winning bidder pays the winning price, shipping costs, and the cost of the number of bids he made. In the end the shopper still gets a bargain price compared to the item's original retail price, and the retailer, Swoopo, ends up collecting close to the original price from the sum of what the winning shopper has paid on bids and shipping, plus the amount all other bidders paid for their bids on the same item. A win-win situation for all— except the losing bidders, of course.

Location

In previous chapters we established differences in location choices made by luxury and mass-market brands. Luxury brands have limited options because they are usually located in major city centers and fashion capitals, whereas mass-market brands are more flexible and can be easily located in urban and suburban areas, small towns, malls, resorts, and shopping centers, so their options are certainly wider. However, no matter the choice, choosing a store location remains to be a process that includes the following steps:

1. Identify a target market.
2. Analyze the site.
3. Select the site.

Identifying a Target Market

The retailer must identify the most attractive markets in which to operate. To make that decision, the selected market segment must be:

- *Measurable:* The market can be qualified in terms of objective measures for available data, such as age, gender, income, education, ethnic group, and religion.
- *Accessible:* This is the degree to which the retailer can target its promotional or distribution efforts to a particular market segment.
- *Substantial:* Successful target marketing requires that the segment be significant enough to be profitable for the retailer.

Analyzing the Site

Retailers must evaluate the density of demand and supply within each market and identify the most attractive sites that are available in terms of the buying power index (BPI). BPI is an indicator of a market's overall retail potential and is composed of weighted measures of effective buying income (personal income, including all non-tax payments such as social security, minus all taxes), retail sales, and population size. Other factors include consumers' mobility, size of the trading area (which also has an impact on the merchandise because the more people you attract, the larger the assortment needed), competition, and so on.

Selecting the Site

When the best available sites within each market have been identified, the retailer needs to make the final location decision and select the best site (or sites). When reviewing a site, a retailer must consider:

- nature of site
- traffic characteristics
- types of neighbors

- terms of purchase or lease
- expected profitability

Positioning Based on Location

Positioning based on location ultimately refers to the level of convenience. Earlier in this chapter, we mentioned that luxury brands' customers may be more willing to spend some effort to obtain the brand. However, in all cases a brand should be located where it is expected and needed. Just as price may be a major factor in the decision by the consumer to pick a store, so is the time factor. Easier shopping, including more available parking, less traffic, and longer operating hours are all issues relevant to shopping convenience and are always welcomed, no matter which segment. After all, convenience remains the major differentiator and competitive advantage behind the success of the Internet and online shopping.

Service

Every retail concept comes with certain expectations regarding the level of service it will offer. However, customer service is still important and relevant at every price level because it is a major driver for customer loyalty, which in return is a reasonable measure of success. Customer service and store policies such as operating hours, return policies, alterations, and special services are highly regarded by customers of any segment. Budget and low-price stores generally compete on the basis of convenience and are among the best in offering longer operating hours. They understand that what they offer is easily attainable at other places and that shoppers can easily look for alternatives somewhere else if they don't have easy access to the store. On the other hand, premium and luxury brand stores have more restrictions on location and operating hours. But they offer a greater range of services and benefits. Nordstrom, for instance, is known for its leadership in service and its efforts to please and accommodate customers as much as possible. In addition to free alterations, personal shopper assistance, and relaxed return policy, Nordstrom employees are willing to take unconventional measures to satisfy the customer and gain their loyalty. The following is a true story that took place at a Nordstrom store.

> In Portland, Oregon, a man walked into Nordstrom asking for an Armani tuxedo to wear to his daughter's wedding. The sales representative took his measurements but said she'd need time to work on his request. She called later to say that the tuxedo would be ready the next day. As it turned out, Nordstrom did not carry Armani tuxedos at the time. The sales representative had found the tux through a distributor in New York, then had it rushed to Portland and altered to fit the customer in time for the wedding.[3]

This level of service needs to be deeply embedded in the culture of the store. Retailers are unique in being at the forefront of interactivity with the final consumer. Where there is personal interaction with the customer, the employee turns into a brand champion and, just like designers who end up embodying the brand, store employees become the brand in many ways as well. Greg Holland, Nordstrom's midwest assistant regional manager, once said, "Great

customer service is not an initiative. It is not the thing of the day. It is part of our culture."

As we've seen so far, one component of what we called *the concept mix* complements the other components, and together they define the type of store and the concept behind the model. The same is true for the level of service expected within the store. The level and mix of services offered is dependent on:

- *The store's physical characteristics:* Customer service can be affected by physical factors, such as location and size.
- *The store concept or business model:* A store outlet by definition will not offer the same level of service as, for example, a full-priced boutique.
- *Competition:* Service is an integral source of differentiation. As a matter of fact, with so many stores offering very similar merchandise, customer service may become the main competitive advantage.
- *Type of merchandise:* This also has an influence because some products may require complementary services such as alterations for suits or for wedding dresses.
- *Price and level of service:* These are directly proportionate: a higher level of service means higher cost, which will reflect on retail price.

All of these points also reflect on the shopper's expectations of service. Stores that exceed expectations and not just meet them achieve a higher level of customer loyalty. The case of Nordstrom and the Giorgio Armani tuxedo is a good example.

Examples of types of customer service are:

- Operating hours; in determining the working hours, many factors need to be considered, such as customers' needs as well as cost and safety.

- Payment and credit options.
- Alterations, gift wrapping, and packing.
- Personal shopping, more common in
  high-end retailers.
- After-purchase support.
- Return policies.
- Shipping and delivery.
- Layaway services.
- Loyalty programs that reward loyal customers
  and entice new customers to join and share
  some real benefits.

It is important to remember the significance
of after-purchase service, which is the focus of
what has been known as *relationship marketing*.
It is cheaper and probably more rewarding to
maintain older customers than new ones. New
customers cost more because they need to
be lured with promotions and advertising. Old
customers, on the other hand, are more familiar
with the store and its services and are financially
more rewarding in the long run through repeat
purchases. Turning every customer into a loyal
customer is the ultimate goal. It may not be easy,
but is worth trying because loyalty is probably
one of the best measures of a brand's success.
(See Figures 6.10a–b.)

Positioning Based on Service

With so many stores offering almost the same
merchandise, customer service becomes an essential differentiator and competitive advantage. As a
matter of fact, many experts believe that innovation and customer service are the two forces of
success in the twenty-first century. Customers
have many choices and options nowadays, and it
is easier to move and commute than ever before,
not to mention the impact of the Internet in terms

of choices as well as extended customer service. Accordingly, customers' expectations and
demands for service have gotten higher. They need
to be impressed. Thus, retailers need to compete
by exceeding customers' expectations through:

- *Personalized service programs:* The Internet and many existing technologies, such as mobile technologies, allow businesses to communicate with customers on a much more personal and customized level and at a very low cost. A few of these technologies will be discussed in chapter 7, but consider how special promotions, updates, and news can be tailored to each customer's interests and needs and then e-mailed to their computers or mobile phones. Companies that learn how to integrate all these technologies and channels have a better opportunity to attract the customer's attention for a longer time and keep him or her more interested and engaged. One new technology they might consider allows customers to check store inventory availability from a magic screen in the dressing room, make a purchase, or check other customer's review. Customers can use the same screen to take a snapshot of themselves wearing the garment and then upload it to their e-mail or even Facebook to get feedback from friends in real time.
- *Level of convenience:* The more convenient it is to make a purchase transaction or return a garment, the more satisfied the customers are. At a Nordstrom store, you can return any item you purchased online or from a Nordstrom Rack to a regular Nordstrom store, no questions asked.
- *Promise of value:* Remember that like all other brands, retail brands are built on a promise of value to the customer. The aim of the process is to increase the level of loyalty. However, this is not easy nowadays. According to a new study by Adjoined Consulting and SAS Marketing Automation, 77 percent of shoppers in 2006 defined themselves as loyal customers, a drop from the previous year when 84 percent said they met the definition.[4] Customers are more empowered and confident than before, and it takes true value to impress them.

Customer loyalty is built on both rational and emotional grounds. Although incentives such as price discounts, exclusive merchandise, or quality evoke rational values, the sense of recognition and appreciation of being a special customer and not just one in a large group is an emotional incentive that is highly effective. Think of a salesperson remembering your name, a card you receive with special offers on your birthday, or an invitation to a "by invitation only" store event. The emotional reward is priceless.

An emotional reward can also be tied to ethical and socially responsible initiatives adopted by the store. For instance, Target's REDcard rewards shoppers with price discounts, but because Target is an already a low-priced store, the impact of such rewards may not be very significant. Therefore, Target has decided to evoke loyalty through other emotional rewards resulting from its involvements in the community. Through its Take Charge of Education program, shoppers can choose the school they want their money to benefit. Target, in turn, donates 1 percent of customer's in-store and online purchases to the school. This creates a multilevel connection between the store, the customer, and the community. By shopping at Target, these customers feel they truly are making a difference.[5]

Store Experience

Shopping is an emotional experience that has evolved into a favorite pastime where customers experience the brand before making a purchase decision. The store experience is also sensual, is shaped by the physical appearance and feel of the store as defined by its layout, interior design, music, smell, and lighting. All of this combines to create what we may call a store **ATMO-SPHERE**—the equivalent of identity symbols of the product brand. In addition, the store experience is strengthened by the brand's personality. The personality is how the store behaves as a brand. This is highly manifested by its culture, how it is interpreted in policies, and the way its own employees interact with the consumer. Thus, in reality, the shopping **EXPERIENCE** is a manifestation of the store's identity as a whole, as shaped by a mix of store aesthetics (atmosphere) and the store personality, which is demonstrated by its culture, its employees, and the set of rules and policies that are ultimately inspired by its mission and vision statements.

So, based on what we've discussed so far, we can conclude that store branding is about choosing a retail model, defining its concept mix, and creating an emotional and functional experience through a unique atmosphere (look and feel) and personality (together form the store brand identity).

Store Atmosphere

A store atmosphere is created through the aesthetics and feel of the store as expressed in the store design, layout, graphics, colors, lightning, and so on. The store atmosphere plays a pivotal role in attracting customers into the store and influencing them to make a purchase. The whole experience needs to be enjoyable (emotional) and efficient (functional). And hopefully, as a result, the experience will be memorable enough for customers to return.

Layout

A major element of a store's aesthetics is the **LAYOUT**. A store layout needs to achieve the following:

- Minimize material handling costs.
- Increase productivity and profitability through better exposure of merchandise and ease of movement.
- Utilize space efficiently and eliminate bottlenecks.
- Utilize labor efficiently and facilitate communication and interaction among employees and between employees and customers.
- Reduce customer service time.
- Facilitate the browsing experience as well as the entry, exit, and placement of material, products, and people.
- Incorporate safety and security measures.
- Promote merchandise and service quality.
- Provide flexibility to adapt to changing conditions.

The psychological factor in store design and layout is important. Studies in consumer behavior and shopping habits offer a lot of insight on how customers are affected by layout and presentation details. For instance, an open layout allows shoppers to quickly scan the store visually and identify locations of interest—it's a welcoming and accommodating layout.

STRAIGHT LAYOUT

Figure 6.11

Straight layout

(Illustration by

Andrea Lau)

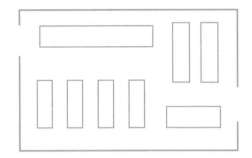

DIAGONAL LAYOUT

Figure 6.12

Diagonal layout

(Illustration by

Andrea Lau)

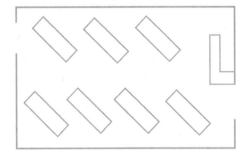

ANGULAR LAYOUT

Figure 6.13

Angular layout

(Illustration by

Andrea Lau)

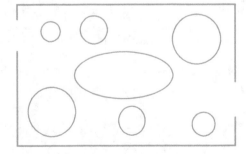

There are basically five types of stores plans. [6]

1. *The straight floor plan:* Suitable for any type of retail store. It is economical and utilizes the walls and fixtures to create small spaces within the retail store. (See Figure 6.11.)
2. *The diagonal floor plan:* Suitable for self-service stores. It offers excellent visibility for cashiers and customers and invites movement and traffic flow to the store. (See Figure 6.12.)
3. *The angular floor plan:* Suitable for high-end specialty stores. The curves and angles of fixtures and walls make for a more expensive store design, while the soft angles create better traffic flow throughout the store. (See Figure 6.13.)
4. *The geometric floor plan:* Among the most suitable for apparel shops. It uses racks and fixtures to create an interesting and nontraditional look without high cost. (See Figure 6.14.)
5. *The mixed floor plan:* Incorporates the straight, diagonal, and angular floor plans to create the most functional store design. The layout moves traffic toward the walls and back of the store. (See Figure 6.15.)

Merchandise Presentation

Merchandise presentation utilizes various types of fixtures and shelving in order to effectively expose and promote the product in an attractive and inviting way. Fixtures come in different shapes and forms, such as wall fixtures, tables, bins, or racks. Shelving may be more flexible and easier to maintain. Merchandise display can be done through hanging, folding, stacking, dumping in bins and baskets, and so on.

Merchandise presentations can evoke different mental images and create a different feel to the store, such as a sense of exclusivity or luxury.

GEOMETRIC LAYOUT

MIXED LAYOUT

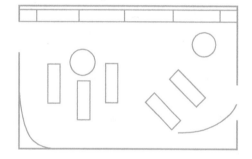

Store Windows

Store windows are a major communication tool. They promote the store's personality and, in a way, set the mood. As the Zara case study illustrated (see pp. 172–175), the company relies heavily on its store windows to promote the brand, given their lack of traditional marketing budget, which is almost 0.3 percent of sales compared to an industry average of around 10 percent. Instead, they rely heavily on the store windows, in-store experience, and word of mouth to promote their brand. Zara also has a specialized team that travels the world to train store employees on the designs and techniques in order to maintain an effective and consistent message through their stores.

Some store windows have grown to have a strong impact on product brands. In fashion, for a new designer to get his or her design displayed in the windows of Bloomingdale's or Bergdorf Goodman has always been a great achievement. Windows are truly a reflection of the store's personality as much as the designer's.

Other Store Design Elements

Store design refers to both the exterior and interior of the store, which combines elements of architecture and interior design. (See Figure 6.16.)

- The exterior store front must be noticeable and inviting. Logo and store name need to be visible, clear, and memorable. (See Figures 6.17 and 6.18.)
- Lighting highlights the store's mood. However, the aesthetic effect should complement the merchandise presentation and visibility.
- Sounds and smells play an integral role in creating a sensory element to the whole store atmosphere. Many retailers distribute sets of music CDs to all their branches, which the stores are then directed to play exclusively.

Store Personality

A store brand personality is the soul of the brand. The personality is an embodiment of the strategic vision and the brand promise, which in return is the force behind every decision made. It, therefore, reflects the concept, aesthetics, functionality, and the way employees behave. As a result, a personality develops over time and is manifested through interaction. It is the brand's soul and attitude.

Positioning Based on Experience (Personality and Atmosphere)

We have explained that a product brand can be positioned at two levels: the product level (in the form of the product mix) and the brand level (in the form of identity). Applying this to retail brands, the two levels of positioning are the store concept level (the business model with the relevant concept mix) and the experience level (created by the branding process). It should now be clear how all elements of atmosphere and personality work together to form a strong store experience, which in return defines the brand identity both physically and emotionally. The functionality and logistics of the retail concept lay the foundations for a store experience that is enhanced and defined by its atmosphere and personality in a way that is meant to complement the merchandise, the price range, location, and all elements of the concept mix.

The store experience can be based on various values.

- *An experience based on entertainment:* One such example is Niketown, highlighted earlier in this chapter (see Figure 6.19).
- *An experience based on expertise:* This is where the store evokes a high level of knowledge, expertise, and specialization. Customers visit the store not just to shop but to learn and be educated. This is common for highly specialized stores in the category killers segment (such as The Home Depot).
- *An experience based on sensual satisfaction:* This is where the "wow" aesthetic factor is manifested in its design and décor.
- *An experience based on a lifestyle:* The store demonstrates the lifestyle of the brand and creates the right environment or world for the shopper to experience the brand as it is intended. Designer flagship stores such as Ralph Lauren's store on Madison Avenue, New York, Louis Vuitton in Paris, or Giorgio Armani in Milan are designed and furnished with every detail that reenacts the brand's dream. The products, the layout, the music—everything creates a picture reflective of the brand's lifestyle.
- *An experience based on a bargain:* Discount stores such as Filene's Basement and Ross with their store layout, centralized checkouts, and most important, their merchandise and prices are a good example of this. (See Figure 6.20.)

For positioning through experience to be effective, it needs to be:

- authentic
- relevant to the merchandise image
- what gets shoppers interested

TABLE 6.1	PRODUCT BRANDS VS. STORE BRANDS
PRODUCT BRANDS	**STORE BRANDS**
=	=
Product Mix	*Concept Mix*
(Features + Price + Location + Service)	(Merchandise + Price + Location + Service)
+	+
Identity	*Experience*
(Symbols + Personality)	(Atmosphere + Personality)
	thus the experience also reflects the store's identity

200 PART TWO: THE FASHION BRAND

Finally, it is never sufficient to highlight the important role of employees in shaping the store experience. Employees are at the forefront because they directly interact with the end customer. Employees should be champions of the brand. They need to live it in order to sell it. In many ways they *are* the brand.

Communication

COMMUNICATION activities play a bi-directional role in the branding process. They communicate and reflect the positioning strategy and brand identity to the outside world and, at the same time, impact the process of identity building—either positively by reinforcing it or negatively by distorting it and reflecting conflicting messages.

The store brand is unique in its ability through its space and physical appearance (such as signs, fixtures, and so on) to become a communication channel in its own right. Internal (in-store) communication activities are an essential component of the communication strategy of any store, and they complement other external activities, such as advertising and publicity. Accordingly, we

conclude that there are two platforms of communication for any store.

- *Communication inside the store (internal):* Includes visual communication through store signage and visual merchandising, as well as experiential communication through interaction with employees.
- *Communication outside the store (external):* Includes advertising, direct marketing, PR, publicity, and other channels.

Internal Communication

Consumers are drawn to the store through the brand promise trumpeted in external communications. The brand promise in reality reflects the personality as the brand perceives it. When entering the store, the shopper experiences the brand: in the process of being transformed from a browser to a buyer, the shopper compares what has been promised to what is actually experienced and develops his own image of the brand accordingly (that is, creates his own positioning).

Transforming the customer from a browser to a buyer inside the store is usually achieved with

Figure 6.19

The Niketown experience can be both entertaining and interactive.

(Getty Images/Stuart Franklin/Bongarts)

Figure 6.20

At Filene's Basement, it's all about the thrill of a bargain.

(© 2007 Richard Nowitz)

a

b

Figure 6.21a, b

A comparison of Walmart storefronts displaying its (a) old logo, dividing "Wal" and "mart" with a star, and its (b) new one, which keeps the name undivided.

(© Kathy deWitt/ Alamy)

(Courtesy of Walmart)

and supporting visual elements. The name and logo must be catchy, memorable, and most of all, reflective of the business model and merchandising strategy.

The recent controversy over the new Walmart logo demonstrates the importance of the logo in the brand's life. Some believe it has an organic feel and an eco-friendly connotation; others think it is too generic and undistinguishable. From their side, Walmart describes the new logo as follows: "This update to the logo is simply a reflection of the refresh taking place inside our stores and our renewed sense of purpose to help people save money so they can live better."[7] (See Figures 6.21a–b.)

In-store signage: In-store signage covers many usages. (See Figure 6.22.) For example:

- *Institutional signage:* Describes the store policies, mission statement, and other relevant information.
- *Departmental signage:* Guides the shopper though each department.
- *Point-of-Sale (POS) signage:* Usually located on fixtures with information about specific merchandise items. (See Figure 6.23.)
- *Store graphics:* This includes large images and graphic panels that offer a great opportunity to show off merchandise with attention-grabbing images.

Other forms of in-store communication that appeal to the senses are:

- *Sound:* Music can highly complement the intended shopping experience.
- *Touch:* Use of specific materials such as glass, marble, or wood can convey certain feelings of warmth or modernity.

the help of in-store communication. As some data indicates, 80 percent of purchases are decided upon in-store, indicating the impact of the in-store experience on impulse buying. Accordingly, visual and experiential signals need to be clear and consistent with the perceived personality and targeted experience. When carefully balanced with the human element and customer service, visual communications can create an engaging and successful selling environment.

Examples of the tools of store visual communications are:

- *Name and logo (visual identity):* The first and most visible element in a comprehensive visual communications program is the retailer's visual identity, composed of the store name, logo,

Figure 6.22

A striking in-store graphic from Gap.

(*Andrew Harrer/ Bloomberg via Getty Images*)

- *Smell:* For example, Victoria's Secret sprays its perfumes in stores.
- *Lighting:* Lighting sets the mood and makes merchandise more appealing.

External Communication

External communication refers to marketing activities done outside the store in traditional and emerging media channels. External communication is utilized to achieve various goals, such as:

Figure 6.23

In-store displays can inform the customer about special promotions, such as this offer for 50 percent off the price of a top when you buy a bottom.

(© *Ilene MacDonald/ Alamy*)

- Inform shoppers of events and price changes.
- Inform potential shoppers of a new store or a new location.
- Inform shoppers of new merchandise.
- Increase in-store traffic through promotions.
- Enforce brand positioning though advertising or celebrity sponsorship.
- Interest new customers in the store and retain old ones.
- Respond to competition pressures.
- Create buzz and interest in the store: Benetton's provocative campaigns are a good example,

as well as H&M's association with famous celebrities and models.

Types of external communication include:

1. *Advertising:* A nonpersonal form of communication through different media channels. Advertising is useful for any of the three purposes of communication: persuade, inform, or remind.

2. *Promotions:* Utilizes media or nonmedia channels. Direct marketing is often used as a more personal approach to delivering promotional material to customers.
3. *Publicity:* Nonpaid coverage such as magazine's editorial. Publicity can be positive or negative; however, it is effective, as it seems impartial coming from a third party.
4. *Public relations:* Events and activities that are meant to enhance the retailer's image and champion its role in its community.

Advertising

Retailers don't usually spend as much on advertising as manufacturers do because the store itself plays a major role in communicating the brand. Nevertheless, advertising is still utilized by stores who foresee economic viability of the expense.

The approach to the advertising message can have different focuses.

- Reinforces how the store reflects a specific lifestyle.
- Builds a dream to which the customers aspire.
- Builds a mood around a product.
- Creates interest through humor.
- Demonstrates how the products relate to the consumer's everyday life.
- Demonstrates usage or functionality of a product.

ADVERTISING OPTIONS

The retailer has many different advertising options that include:

- *Newspapers:* Probably the most frequently used in retailing to either announce special promotional events or include promotional inserts such as coupons.
- *Television:* Advertising on national channels makes more financial sense to department and specialty chains with a national network of stores because of its cost and range of coverage. On the other hand, cable and local channels reach a more focused and segmented audience. TV advertising can be effective in generating higher traffic and sales due to its entertaining and demonstrative capabilities and qualities.
- *Radio:* Usually used to address selected customer groups to announce events with a relatively short lead time.
- *Magazines:* Major fashion magazines usually aim for large national circulation. Thus, advertising in magazines such as *Vogue* and *Harper's Bazaar* is more suitable for national chains or co-branding campaigns shared between retailers and manufacturers.

Promotion

There are many possible types of sales promotions such as:

- *Premiums:* Extra items offered with the purchase of a product.
- *Contests and sweepstakes:* Generate interest and excitement.
- *Loyalty programs:* Encourage repeat sales.
- *Coupons:* Encourage sales through price discounts.
- *Samples:* Generate interest through trial, such as perfume inserts in magazines or in-store samples.
- *In-store display:* Generate traffic and benefits from impulse buying.

Direct Marketing

DIRECT MARKETING (DM) allows for a more differentiated and segmented communication. As such, it is more personal and effective in building relationships with customers because they are treated as individuals, not as a bulk group. It is also easier to monitor and control. Another advantage to DM is that, unlike advertising, there is a lack of external noise effect from competitors, which can highly distort the effectiveness of the message.

Retailers use DM to send catalogs, coupons, e-mails, and newsletters. DM relies heavily on a large database of shoppers' details and an effective distribution system. It can also be used as a step toward future targeted advertising. There is always a common-sense belief that if a customer orders tennis shoes from a catalog, he or she might generally be interested in tennis supplies as well.

Personal selling is another example of DM. It is the most direct and personal of any retail activity, and the role of employees in building the store's brand image has been highlighted before and cannot be emphasized strongly enough.

Co-Marketing

CO-MARKETING refers to when manufacturers and other retailers market a brand together and share the cost of the advertising campaign. It is commonly used when certain brands or products are sold exclusively through certain retailers. This case is known as *vertical co-marketing*. On the other hand, *horizontal co-marketing* takes place when two or more retailers collaborate together in a campaign, such as promoting a new shopping center. (See Figure 6.24.)

Choosing the right communication mix depends on the goals and objectives the store hopes to achieve, such as:

- *Creating store traffic:* For which advertising, direct marketing, and internal visual communication can be effective.
- *Transforming store browsers into buyers:* For which in-store visual communication, employees, promotions can be effective.
- *Responding to competition:* Either or both of the previous bullet points can be effective.

Other Options

Stores can try to use unconventional methods of promotion that may create a buzz or attract attentions. For example, the Las Vegas Nordstrom

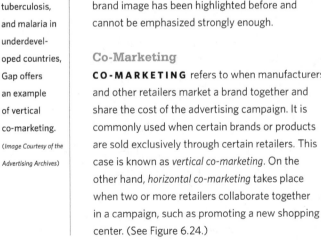

Figure 6.24

In teaming up with the RED campaign to fight AIDS, tuberculosis, and malaria in underdeveloped countries, Gap offers an example of vertical co-marketing.

(Image Courtesy of the Advertising Archives)

realized that the city lacks a major influential newspaper publication typical of other major cities, which they could use for running an advertising campaign. As a result, Nordstrom came up with a new campaign that they believed would be more effective. In a city that is a major tourist destination, taxi cabs are something that almost every visitor needs or sees along The Strip and are, therefore, an excellent channel of communication. With this in mind, they came up with a campaign that repainted city taxis with the store name and products.

Growth

Growth in retail operations can be achieved through:

- Opening of new stores
- Horizontal integration and acquiring of existing stores
- Online growth on the Internet (e-tailing)
- Growth through franchising
- Growth into global markets

Franchising

FRANCHISING simply refers to a retailer (the franchisor) offering a store owner (the franchisee) the rights to emulate the retailer's business model or system of conducting his business. Thus, a series of stores can be opened with a consistent concept, look, and feel throughout all franchised stores. Franchisees will usually pay a royalty fee, which is usually a percentage of sales or a combination of a percentage and a guaranteed minimum. In return, they also get training, marketing, and management support from the franchisor. As with

any business arrangement, there are a few advantages as well as challenges in franchising.

Advantages

From the franchisor's perspective, advantages include:

- An opportunity to expand the retail brand into new markets with minimal investment while maintaining the brand's image.
- A source of revenue. The structure of fees can differ, but in general it is a combination of a one-time fee and a percentage of sales that can be around 5 percent. Sometimes a minimum monthly payment is guaranteed even if monthly sales did not cover the royalty fee.
- Exposure and increase in brand awareness.

From the franchisee's perspective, advantages include:

- The freedom of being self-employed.
- A good way to start a business for entrepreneurs who want to own their retail business but lack the expertise and are not sure what to do.
- Support from the franchisor in the form of employee training, marketing material, and possible share of the cost of certain events or advertising campaigns.
- Benefits from opening a store with an already established brand name, image, and customers' interest.
- An opportunity to learn the business model and eventually go out on their own.

Disadvantages

From the franchisor's perspective, disadvantages include:

- Lack of control and possible difficulty in monitoring a large chain.
- Damage to the brand by any malpractice of any one of the franchisees. (Usually customers are not aware that these stores are independently owned, and the blame is directed to the brand as a whole.)
- Legal headaches in cases of disputes.

From the franchisee's perspective, the disadvantages include:

- Lack of freedom and constraints over new ideas.
- Some sense of insecurity, as franchise agreements are usually designed in such a way that a franchisee can be easily dropped if a conflict arises.
- Other franchisees' mistakes and mishaps that can affect store performance.
- Financial burden. All costs of preparing the store are the franchisee's responsibility. In some agreements, for instance, franchisees cannot return unsold merchandise to the franchisor. In addition, in some cases, minimum fees are still expected to be paid even if sales are down.

There are many brands that adopt the franchise model or a mix of franchising and other models (for example, private ownership) such as Esprit, Benetton, and Stefanel, just to name a few.

Global Growth

International geographic expansion is adopted by retailers for various reasons related to growth strategies and competition.

- It presents new growth opportunities in new markets. This opportunity is specifically important if the domestic market is already saturated with limited growth opportunities.
- Businesses with a unique business model or product may find lucrative opportunities overseas. H&M's concept proved successful in the different international markets it entered.
- Economic conditions can be a major factor as well, either to escape a domestic economic downturn or to benefit from an economic boom overseas. The recent rush by retailers and manufacturers alike to enter and be present in the lucrative and large Chinese market is a good example.
- Businesses can benefit from diversification of investment and resources as well as economies of scale in the case of retailers who produce their own private brands.
- In some situations, international markets are a good outlet for certain items that have not sold well locally.
- Strong local competition can be another driving factor for locating in various overseas markets.

However, global expansion for retailers comes with many of the same challenges we discussed in a previous chapter, such as foreign exchange fluctuations, taxes, regulations, and political instabilities, as well as shipping risks such as lead time and cost.

Important Issues to Consider

Retailers may be forced to rethink their pricing strategy overseas due to the previously mentioned differences and end up with price discrepancies that may create different positioning spots to the brand in different parts of the world.

Issues related to product adaptations are also important. Customers' size charts differ from one place to the other. The United States has a large population of oversized customers, while Japan requires mainly smaller sizes. A size "medium" in one country will be a "small" or a "large" in another. These differences create many challenges in production and inventory management.

Distribution and delivery is another issue to consider. The need for a fast and reliable distribution network is essential to meet different stores' needs in different locations. With differences in the levels of infrastructure development, transportation costs, and time zones, the challenges become quite apparent. Many store chains create various local distribution centers servicing specific market zones to facilitate the distribution process and cut down on time and cost.

Modes of Entry into an International Market

Entering and expanding into a global market can be done through different modes.

- *Wholly owned subsidiaries:* Most luxury brands own their boutiques. Although this is helpful from an image perspective, it is a costly venture. Experts estimate that in general, it may not be a feasible venture with sales less than $10 million. On the other hand, some laws in foreign countries may not allow full ownership by foreign entities.
- *Joint ventures:* Necessary in markets where the regulations or distribution system is too intricate to allow for independent market penetration and entry. The Japanese market used to be a good example. Giorgio Armani and Christian Dior were among the many brands that had to join forces with an established Japanese partner to secure a competitive presence in Japan.
- *Franchising:* Selling the business model in return for royalty fees. This minimizes investment and reduces direct control and risks in unfamiliar and foreign markets.
- *Unconventional locations:* Such as airports and duty-free stores. Through duty-free stores, brands gain access to multitudes of customers as they pass through airports around the world. (see Figure 6.25).

E-tailing

The Internet or "click-and-shop" model as a retail concept—commonly known as **E-TAILING**—covers all the previously discussed range of

Figure 6.25

John Couri, president and founder of Duty Free International.

(© Louie Psihoyos/ CORBIS)

models in addition to new ones that only exist online. In the next chapter, we will examine a few of the exciting new models that have emerged online by means of new technological advances. We have established earlier that positioning strategies need to be flexible to remain relevant. As shoppers' lifestyles change, so do their shopping needs and habits. Even in the world of brick and mortar, new models have developed to accommodate customers' new expectations. Niketown stores and Prada Epicenters, for instance, have created new shopping environments and experiences that respond to those new needs and transform shopping into a full sensual experience and a fun leisure activity.

When the Internet exploded in the nineties, it was a good example of a new retailing concept that utilized technological advances to respond to socioeconomic changes. The Internet presented a new retailing channel and shopping opportunity for retailers and shoppers respectively. However, it may seem that Internet shopping is more suitable for some products than others. In general, the greater the degree of variance in the product, the more difficult the online shopping experience will be. In spite of this, one of the greatest advantages of online shopping remains convenience. It is a shopping outlet that is open 24/7 and with global reach. This is not to say that going online is enough to transform the business into an international global operation; to make that claim, the online global presence needs to be supported by marketing and distribution strategies that understand the challenges and demands entailed. There are many decisions and measures that need to be taken into account to successfully run a global retail operation online. These include:

- Packing requirements and costs for overseas shipping.
- Shipping couriers options and costs.
- Taxation and tariffs.
- Delivery times.
- Languages of communication and service. For example, will you need to create mirrors of the site in different languages for different countries?
- Arrangements with suppliers, if necessary.
- Warehousing and inventory control.
- Payment options and constraints.
- Privacy and security measures.
- Updates and maintenance frequency.
- Integration of the online store with the physical brick-and-mortar store. For example, can customers order online and pick up or return an item in a store? (You can with Nordstrom, but not with Victoria's Secret.)
- Laws and regulations in different countries.

The implications of these decisions and measures on cost, price, and store margins are obvious.

Advantages of E-tailing

The Internet also solves a major problem of space restriction and shelf limitations. Your cyber real estate is cheaper and expandable. However, many customers may still prefer to physically visit the store first to get familiar with products before they decide to shop online; others may prefer to get informed about the range of products, prices, and store availability online before physically visiting the store. The former scenario demonstrates the existing challenges of shopping online, while the latter indicates how the Internet can be a convenient and time-saving alternative.

Online challenges include security challenges as well as the inability to physically try, touch, and feel products. Software developers are continuously developing new and more advanced security and data encryption solutions, and e-tailers have attempted to address the other issues of delivery and product trial. Today many e-tailers offer free and fast shipping options and flexible return policies, making it easier for shoppers to buy and try products with minimal risk. The amount of information generated by shoppers as a result of these interactions allows e-tailers to create databases that are valuable in creating high levels of personalized customer service, addressing each customer's or group of customers' specific need. The Internet is also an effective component of after-purchase service and relationship marketing through personalized e-mails, special offers, coupons, newsletters, and so on.

In addition, the possibility of integrating online marketing with offline activities creates an unprecedented opportunity for capturing the customer's attention at all times with an engaging, interactive, and personalized message that is focused, inexpensive, and much more effective. If handled wisely, it can improve brand awareness and loyalty tremendously.

By examining the success of the Zappos.com brand, we realize that it is attributed to a number of factors.

- Free, quick shipping demonstrated an enlightened understanding of the online shopper and the challenges of Internet shopping.
- Zappos.com possesses a clear understanding of the nature of the product.
- They understand that branding, especially nowadays in an environment where the

customer is empowered and well-informed, is based on trust (remember the promise) and the experience (remember the identity). They focused not just on the product and prices but on the experience itself and the relationship they wanted to develop with their customer. This experience was backed by a well-designed infrastructure that included a state-of-the-art warehouse and logistics of delivery.

- They adopted a great customer service approach. For instance, "If someone calls for an item that Zappos does not carry, the customer service rep is encouraged to help the person find somewhere online that does carry it. Zappos may not make any money of the sale, but the person goes away with a positive experience."[8] With a trademarked logo that reads "Zappos powered by service," the emphasis on service is highly evident as their core brand value and the heart of the company culture.
- Needless to say, Zappos also has a presence on Facebook and Twitter. They simply want to be where their customers are.
- Zappos.com works on maintaining a fun, young spirit that is strongly present on their site and appreciated by their customers.

There have been many initiatives to make the online customer service experience more personal and fulfilling; for example, the use of live chat with a customer service representative or visual communication through real-time streaming services, such as Skype.

Loyalty is not just about promotions or price bargains; it is, at the minimum level, about getting what is expected whenever and wherever the

BOX 6.1   ZAPPOS.COM

Figure 6.26

Zappos began
as an e-tailer
specializing
in shoes.

(Courtesy of Zappos)

Zappos began as a shoe e-tailer in 1999 (see Figure 6.26) after its founder, Nick Swinmurn, became frustrated while shopping for shoes in traditional stores. The initial success of Zappos was not attributed to its collection of shoes and prices but mainly to its service. According to Zappos.com, the company perceives itself as "a service company that happens to sell shoes." Zappos.com realized early on that with items such as shoes, customers prefer to touch and try the products first before making any purchase. It also realized that buying online, while rewarding in many ways, is hampered by shipping costs and time. Thus, it offered customers free overnight shipping both ways, allowing buyers to try on the shoes in the convenience of their home. And although nowadays it does not ship overnight (three to four business days instead) customers are still offered a 365-day return policy and 24/7 customer service with live online assistance, which is intelligently referred to as "customer loyalty service." Its strong approach to customer service has gained Zappos.com a great following based on word of mouth. On its Web site Zappos declares that its culture and value is based on "best" service, as well as being adventurous, creative, and passionate. Today Zappos.com is more than a shoe e-tailer; the merchandise mix has been extended to include clothes, bags, and accessories such as eyewear and watches. In addition, Zappos has introduced a new site called "Zappos Couture," (see Figure 6.27) which sells brands such as Juicy Couture, Elie Tahari, Adidas by Stella McCartney, Donna Karan, Missoni, and many others.

In July 2009 Amazon.com purchased Zappos for nearly $900 million.

Source: http://www.zappos.com

Figure 6.27

Zappos has
added the
broader Zappos
Couture, offering
a full range of
clothing brands
for both men
and women.

(Courtesy of Zappos)

customer interacts with the brand. However, better service, whether online or offline, is achieved by exceeding expectations. It's about the wow factor—giving the customer something to talk about for a long time and creating the desire to come back for more. Meeting expectations is the first step in loyalty, but exceeding them is the real deal maker. No brand can exceed expectations without understanding where it stands in the consumers' minds and what value they perceive, so wavering too far from the core values and personality of the brand is a major cause for losing loyalty. Unwavering does not mean inflexibility or stubbornness toward new growth opportunities; it simply reflects the need to remain true to the brand's promise and consistent with its values, which remains true online as well.

E-tailing, Merchandising, and Branding

Great merchandise is the key to success for most retailers, online and offline. Great retail brands are not built around advertising but on store experience and having the right merchandise available at the right price and time. If you want to create a successful e-tailer, you must create real value either through a well-conceived, broad selection of products along with better pieces and/or through a rich shopping experience built

around a narrower product selection. This is the core of good merchandising. An example of successful online merchandising strategies is offering consumers "solution selling." Solution selling refers to grouping and selling various products as solutions to needs related to an occasion, a hobby, or a lifestyle. This can be done much easier and more efficiently online than in a retail store because of the ability to link different sites together (it is like shopping at a few stores at the same time). These solution centers bring together cross-category selling opportunities, creating a new and profitable tool to retailers. Moreover, these solutions can eventually be customized to specific customer needs. By introducing new brands online, companies can take advantage of seeding, or building early awareness by offering new brands for trial online before they are available for purchase more broadly in stores. Thus, brands can initiate customers' interests early on and use the process as part of a market testing program.

Finally, it is important to remember that the basic elements of a brand's identity do not need to change on the Web, but the manner in which this identity is communicated will most likely change often. Therefore, the brand's relevance needs to be maintained in conjunction with the technology adopted.

Chapter Summary

- In spite of their differences, products and services share some similarities in their branding process.

- The service mix is the mix of attributes that define the retail store concept. They are: merchandise, price, location, and service.

- Retail store brands can be positioned at different levels and on different components of their service mix.

- Shopping is an emotional and sensual experience.

- Store personalities define how the store brand behaves.

- Store atmosphere is a mix of aesthetics that attracts customers and manifests its visual and sensual identity.

- Internal communication is an integral part of the brand communication strategy.

- Sales personnel play an important role in the branding process. They should be brand advocates.

- Franchising is a common policy for growth in the fashion retail industry.

Chapter Questions and Issues for Discussion

1. Compare services to products, and examine the difference and/or similarities in their branding process.

2. Define *retail concept*, and briefly discuss its role in the positioning strategy of a retail brand.

3. What are the advantages and disadvantages of franchising as a global growth strategy?

CASE STUDY: Barneys

Barney Pressman opened Barneys in 1923 in the neighborhood of Chelsea, New York, on Seventh Avenue and 17th Street, a neighborhood at the time with almost no notable stores or interest (see Figure 6.28). In the beginning, Barneys had a hard time getting manufacturers excited about the new store and found it harder to obtain merchandise. As a result, it started with merchandise obtained from closeouts, bankruptcy sales, or merchandise that manufacturers wanted to get off their hands. Barneys managed to survive with its used clothes and cheap merchandise in spite of margins being lower than industry standards (around 30 percent instead of 50 to 60 percent) because of its location and low rent.

The unconventional location meant that Barneys did not get much walk-in traffic but had to rely on loyal customers. Under the leadership of Barney's son Fred, the store took a different direction, buying merchandise more selectively, and by 1965 the store expanded to around 100,000 square feet while changing the look and feel of the store tremendously. Sales people were also chosen carefully for looks, not just skills. Fred started to look toward Europe for new merchandise and designers, and in 1970 Barneys opened its Barneys International House where it embraced European designers, such as Pierre Cardin.

In later years, times got tough and many specialty stores were forced to close down. That is when Barneys came up with the idea to hold a five-day warehouse sale with high discounts that could reach up to 50 percent. The event turned out to be a huge success and has become a kind of New York tradition. With the clout Barneys now had with suppliers, it managed to get specially discounted merchandise for this event and sell it with high margins, even at sale prices. Barneys seemed to always be a step ahead of the competition. Soon it realized how much quality mattered to its customers, and as the Italian industry had a turnaround in production quality, it decided to give up many of the French designers that were by now carried by most department stores in town and turn toward Italy. It was Barneys who discovered a then-young designer named Giorgio Armani and introduced him to the American market. Barneys gained the exclusive rights for Armani's name and design in New York and a say in the future licensing plans of the brand. This marriage between Armani and Barneys proved to be a success for both sides and established Barneys as one of New York's high-end retail destinations. By the mid-seventies, Barneys was performing better than many competitors with inventory of more than $50 million a year.

The Women's Store

In the mid-eighties, Fred's son Gene decided to open a Barneys women's store and embarked on promotional activities, such as a Chanel-sponsored event, in an attempt to attract uptown shoppers to the store. The store was meant to be fun and daring and continue the trend of discovering up-and-coming new talents, such as Azzedine Alaia, as well as embracing the hottest designers of the moment, such as J. P. Gaultier, Yohji Yamamoto, Thierry Mugler, and Romeo Gigli. Although other stores carried most of these brands, Barneys' store identity and image remained unique and distinguished through its special events, merchandise, and infamous iconic and sometimes shocking window displays designed by Simon Doonan (currently Barneys' creative director). In the mid-eighties, Barneys was making over $90 million in sales in its 170,000-square-foot store, or about $530 per square foot, and a gross margin of around 50 percent. However, although the women's wear store was extravagant and attractive, it remained a financial strain, so the Barneys family started looking for strategic business partners and turned to Japan, which in the eighties was seen as a strong flourishing economy eager to invest in America.

The Japan Years

In 1989, Barneys and the Japanese department store Isetan formed a joint venture. According to the deal, Barneys Inc. was formed, and Barneys was to open a chain of stores in the United States. Barneys Japan was also formed through Isetan, which held a license to use the Barneys trademark in Asia, including building stores in Japan, as well as having Barneys USA train Isetan employees on the Barneys method of retail operations with the hope of improving their stores' margins. The financial details of the deal seemed very favorable to Barneys, which would grow without relinquishing full control to Isetan. In a few years, Barneys opened about 14 stores, including locations in Chicago and Beverly Hills, as well as some less successful choices such as Houston and Troy, Michigan, where the stores shortly closed.

With the cheap long-term lease of its Chelsea store coming to an end 1996, and the failed attempts to buy the location, a decision was made to relocate the store to midtown. Finally, and very discretely, a choice was made for the location at 660 Madison Avenue (see Figure 6.29).

The Madison Avenue Store

Designing the new Madison Avenue store started lavishly with no limits or budget constraints. Marble, mosaics, mother-of-pearl-finished wooden shelves made in Indonesia, goatskin-laid wood-work—the list goes on. With problems of its own in the Japanese market and a strained relationship with the Barneys management, Isetan decided to go its own way. Meanwhile, the lavish spending on the Madison Avenue store continued, and by the time the store opened in 1993, Barneys was unable to pay its bills of about $40 million. Designers were not being paid, and many young designers stopped shipping their lines. In addition, many established designers struggled with the choice of the new location, given that they either already had their boutiques a few blocks away or already had their collection in nearby stores, such as Bergdorf Goodman, Saks Fifth Avenue, and Bloomingdale's.

Although the first day's sales were about $1.3 million, many mistakes snowballed, leading the store to file for bankruptcy in 1996. Some of the problems included:

- Lavish interiors (such as floor treatment at $300/square foot)
- The 600-square-foot restaurant entrance on first floor that deprived the store's potential sales of items such as perfumes and accessories that are traditionally known for their high markups of around 75 percent
- Last-minute expensive changes up to minutes before doors opened for the first time
- High employee theft: a porter reportedly walked away with a total of $100,000 worth of suits, and a $1,500 baccarat crystal leopard figurine was stolen four times
- Inability to make payments to vendors and designers

For the casual observer, Barneys' financial results may have seemed acceptable. For example, Barneys announced that its gross margin was a healthy 52 percent; however, its undisclosed expenses were 60 percent (over by $10 million). And although the Madison Avenue store was generating $140 million in sales, or about $655 per square foot, it was much less than projected and far less than nearby Bergdorf Goodman's $1000 to $1200 per square foot.

Merchandise

Another important factor was the store's decision to focus on high-priced designer clothes and stop carrying the traditionally more profitable moderate ranges such as Linea Rossi and San Remo, which were selling very well. The result was that Barneys focused on a very narrow market of rich men and stopped being the authority in menswear it once was. (See Figure 6.30.) Barneys also launched its CO-OP concept to offer casual apparel and accessories targeting a younger market. CO-OP originally started within its New York flagship store and eventually branched out into a chain of freestanding stores.

Bankruptcy and Beyond

Many of Barneys U.S. stores closed down, and by 1995 Barneys filed for bankruptcy. In 1997, the original iconic store in Chelsea closed for good. Barneys was first purchased by Jones Apparel and then in 2007 by Istithmar, a Dubai investment company. In 2009, rumors spread of a possible sale; however, Istithmar confirmed that it has no current plans to sell Barneys and that it is standing behind the brand.

Figure 6.29

Today one of Madison Avenue's high-style destinations, Barneys' controversial new store opened in 1993.

(Getty Images/ Spencer Platt)

CASE STUDY Questions

1. Evaluate the decision to relocate on Madison Avenue and how Barneys today compares to that of the early days in terms of strategy and brand image.

2. How would you compare Barneys' international growth strategy discussed here to that of Louis Vuitton's in Japan, as discussed in the chapter 3 case study?

Figure 6.30

Barneys' Creative Director Simon Doonan poses with his Donatella Versace in his Versace window display.

(© Diane Cohen/Everett Collection)

SOURCES

Doonan, Simon. 2007. "Barney's Green Grass." *New York Observer*. November 27. http://www.observer.com/2007/barneys-green-glass

Levine, Joshua. 1999. *The Rise and Fall of the House of Barneys*. New York: William Morrow and Company.

Steinhauer, Jennifer. 1997. "After Dressing Men for 74 Years, Original Barney's is Closing." June 18. *New York Times*. http://www.nytimes.com/1997/06/18/nyregion/after-dressing-men-for-74-years-original-barneys-is-closing.html

www.barneys.com

www.istithmarworld.com

ENDNOTES

1. www.thefreedictionary.com/retail+store

2. "Retail: What Future for Malls, Department Stores?" BNET (August 2003). http://findarticles.com/p/articles/mi_qa3908/is_200308/ai_n9300933/

3. Robert Reppa and Evan Hirsh, "The Luxury Touch," *Strategy + Business*. (February 29, 2007/Spring 2007, Issue 46). http://www.strategy-business.com/press/enewsarticle/enews040307?pg=all

4. "Does loyalty really exist?" Customer Insight Group, Inc. (2007), 2.

5. Ibid., 4.

6. Shari Waters, "Types of Store Layouts." About.com: Retailing. http://retail.about.com/od/storedesign/ss/store_layouts.htm

7. Business Week. "What Does Wal-Mart's New Logo Mean?" MSN Money (July 4, 2008). http://articles.moneycentral.msn.com/Investing/Extra/WhatDoesWalMartsNewLogoMean.aspx

8. Soren Gordhamer, "The New Social Engagement: A Visit to Zappos." Mashable (April 2009). http://mashable.com/2009/04/26/zappos/

**Traditional
marketing is not
dying, it's dead.**
—Sergio Zyman,
former chief marketing
officer of Coca-Cola

iBRAND:

The Age of Interactive, Wireless, and Virtual Brands

The previous two sections of the text examined a few new technologies that are changing many of our daily habits and the way we interact with each other. This section continues that discussion. We will start in this chapter by explaining some of these new technologies and models and exploring their significance. Then in the next chapter we will examine their direct impact on the general concept of branding.

The iBrand name we created for this chapter is inspired by the trend of terms prefixed with the letter "i" that was initiated by computer guru Apple and adopted by others (Apple's iPod, iPhone, Imagine Publishing's iCreate, and CNN's iReport, among others; see Figure 7.1). With its implication of user empowerment and consumer control, it seemed appropriate and rather inevitable to name this chapter **IBRAND**. Every technology examined and discussed in this chapter focuses on the concept of consumer empowerment one way or the other. As we will discover together in this journey, technology is reshaping our lives and the sociocultural environment in more ways than we ever imagined. And the truth remains that in spite of everything the Internet has brought to our lives, its potential has not been fully utilized, and the best is yet to come.

CHAPTER
OBJECTIVES

- Introduce the reader to new technologies and models such as mass customization and M-branding among others.

- Examine the fashion-related applications under these new technologies.

- Examine the new role of the consumer under the new technology environments.

- Explore the implication of these technologies on the branding process.

Figure 7.1

New technology is changing the face of fashion branding in a way that involves the customer as never before. Elie Tahari's iPhone app, for example, offers virtual viewing of its runway shows.

(Courtesy WWD/ Fairchild Publications)

The Interactive Brand: Mass Customization

Interactive branding refers to a situation whereby the consumer interacts directly with the brand or the process of creating and developing it. It is through the help of new technologies that it has become possible for consumers to play a direct and interactive role in shaping a brand as

he or she likes. A good example of this trend is the concept of mass customization (or MC). In this chapter we focus on mass customization, explain the concept, give examples of various applications, and then examine how this technology relates to the branding process. Let us start by understanding the concept.

Mass Customization vs. Mass Production, Pure Customization, and Personalization

It is essential that we start by defining the concept of "mass customization" and how it relates to and differs from concepts such as pure customization, mass production, and personalization.

Mass customization

MASS CUSTOMIZATION refers to the concept of allowing each consumer to customize or adapt products' features according to his or her needs within a standardized platform with an acceptable price premium.

According to this definition, mass customization gives consumers an option to customize features of a product, given that it is based on a mass-produced structure or frame.

Mass Production

The introduction of the machine and assembly lines during the Industrial Revolution allowed producers to supply large volumes of standardized products with lower costs. The result was a sea of sameness that was best summed up in the famous quote by Henry Ford, founder of the Henry Ford Group, when referring to the infamous Model T car: "Any customer can have a car painted any color that he wants so long as it is black."[1]

The apparel industry was equally affected by the Industrial Revolution and the wave of standardization as evident in the rise and growth of ready-to-wear (RTW) apparel. Although RTW was initially slow to grow, it eventually flourished as urbanism and a new class of professionals grew in the first half of the twentieth century. RTW was modern, suitable for the new lifestyle, and also affordable because it was produced in standardized patterns and sizes. It was under the pressures of standardization that a strong need for differentiation among products existed. As a result, the need for marketing strategies, advertising, and branding grew as necessary tools to achieve differentiation and competitive advantage among brands products.

Made-to-Measure or Pure Customization

Made-to-measure (MTM)—also referred to as bespoke or one-offs—and tailored garments have been the norm in the fashion world throughout history and up to the Industrial Revolution. In the past, most garments, if not sewn at home, were obtained from specialty neighborhood stores where customers were known by name and shopped for in-house or made-to-measure products. It was a pure case of customization whereby every piece could have been totally different and totally customized from beginning to end. It is a trend that still existed with the rise of ready-to-wear in the form of tailored menswear and women's wear clothes and, to some extent, in the grand houses of haute couture.

Personalization

Although this sometimes also refers to made-to-measure or bespoke commissioned products, it refers more accurately to the practice of personalizing a standardized product by adding monograms, initials, or emblems to products such as shirts, bags, wallets, and so on. In this manner, it is not pure customization because it is not a fully tailored or commissioned product, and not mass customization either because it does not involve inherent alteration of product's features. Personalization can also refer to personalizing the shopping experience or choice offerings, as in the case of recommending a few store items based on the personal data and preferences of the consumer (such as personalizing the product offering). This process does not refer to the production of the product as mass customization would, but rather to limiting the customer's choices to what better suits his or her style and personality from an otherwise large range of products. Clearly mass customization is a larger concept in which personalization can be just one element.

Lately we have seen how technology is playing a big role in taking personalization to a higher level. For example, a new range of body scanners is offering customers a uniquely personalized shopping experience by using their personal data and preferences to recommend selective and targeted choices from a large line of products.

Mass Customization in Fashion Products

There are examples of mass customization from various industries, which range from customizing your computer (such as Dell, in electronics) to customizing a novel with your own characters,

scanners to produce what they call the FitPrint—the printout the system produces with the user's exact measurements—only now it is not just used to help the customer select the best fitting jeans from the items already available in the store, but the data is transferred electronically from the retail location to the jeans manufacturer, where the garment pieces are custom cut by computer control. The customer can also choose from a selection of styles and washes and add details such as a pocket shape and design, stitching, and other personalization options. The completed custom jeans are shipped directly to the customer in three to four weeks.

Ollyfit

Olly is a children's shoe company that introduced the Ollyfit in its stores. The process starts by taking the exact measurements of every shoe and linking it to its computer system. After a child's foot is scanned, the system superimposes the child's foot onto the desired shoe and recommends a perfect fit that even puts into consideration room for future growth.

In addition to being attractive and fun services for customers, both of the Intellifit and Ollyfit examples also deal with one of the great fallacies of standardization—that one size fits all and that same sizes are truly standardized.

Mi Adidas

Adidas first introduced its new Mi Adidas concept in its Paris store. By visiting the store, customers can jog on a computerized catwalk where sensors embedded in the track record the exact pressure of their footfall and gauge their running posture. This data, combined with the customers' accurately measured shoe size is used to create a perfect fit.[2]

Figure 7.2

In an example of mass customization, a customer gets his measurements taken in the Intellifit booth.
(Associated Press/ WILL POWERS)

including their names, personal characteristics, and romantic environment (for example, personalnovel.de, in publishing). In the fashion industry, there are various examples that adopted the model with different levels of customer integration. The following are a notable few.

Intellifit

Intellifit is an American company based in Pennsylvania, which introduced the Intellifit Booth. As a customer steps into the booth, fully dressed, the machine collects over 200 body measurements through safe radio waves in as quickly as 10 seconds (see Figure 7.2). The customer then receives a confidential computer printout listing his or her exact measurements and recommendations of all the brands and sizes that fit him or her and are available in the store.

The company has taken the concept a step further by introducing the Custom Jeans Center in its Philadelphia retail store. The concept utilizes the body measurement technology used in their

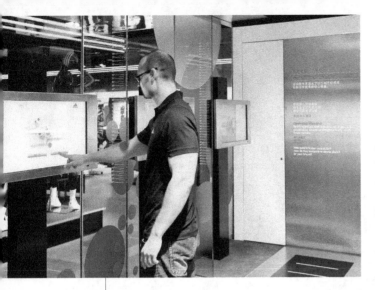

Figure 7.3

The interactive
miCoach Core
Skills area at the
Adidas Brand
Center in Beijing.
(*Adidas via Getty
Images*)

After the measurements are taken, customers choose the look of the shoe by pointing to a massive interactive screen (see Figure 7.3). By simply pointing at images on the screen, radio frequency identification (RFID) technology (highlighted later in this chapter) interprets their gestures, converting them to commands giving detailed information on the Adidas product. When the choices are made, the customer can see how the new shoe will look on him or her by using a three-dimensional virtual mirror, which allows the customer to "virtually" try on his or her own creations, checking out the shape, color, and cut from every angle even before the shoe has been produced (see Figure 7.4). Mi Adidas orders are produced in the same factories as the brand's mass production orders but are manufactured by small, multiskilled teams capable of producing the entire shoe. Total time for delivery to the customer from receipt of order is less than 21 days. The measuring and fitting process is free, but the ordered shoe costs from $40 to $65 extra depending upon the style. A similar example of such technology is used by Nike I.D.

Figure 7.4

The Virtual
Mirror for
Augmented
Reality from
Adidas scans a
person's feet and
presents them
with images of
how they would
look wearing
different sneaker
styles and
colors.
(*JOHN MACDOUGALL/
AFP/Getty Images*)

Threadless.com

Threadless.com is a community-centered, online-based company headquartered in Chicago. The concept of the company is allowing members of the threadless.com community, aspiring T-shirt designers, to submit T-shirt designs online; the designs are then put to a public vote. A small percentage of submitted designs is selected for printing based on the votes' results, then sold through an online store and lately a new brick-and-mortar outlet in Chicago as well. Creators of the winning designs receive a prize of cash and store credit. (See Figure 7.5.) Like all mass-customized processes, this flexible and open-to-creativity environment is controlled by a set of measures such as predefined basic silhouettes and sizes that form the basic canvas for customers' designs and the standardized platform as defined by the model.

The threadless.com model is interesting in the fact that it allows users to share their customized product with everyone else and have it up for sale. This way they manage to keep T-shirt prices low and affordable. It also creates a very inviting environment for users to continuously submit new ideas, make some money, and be a part of a growing community. Some other examples comparable to threadless.com are Look-Zippy.com and Spreadshirt.com.

Figure 7.5

Aspiring T-shirt designers and their designs on threadless.com.

(*Courtesy of Threadless. com*)

We can conclude that mass customization is a middle-of-the-road solution between mass production and pure customization or made-to-measure. Under mass customization, manufacturers use a common, fixed platform (an element of mass production), allowing them to produce the basic platform or structure of the product in large quantities and with relatively controlled costs, while still being flexible enough to allow the customer to interact and participate in the development process and customize specific features of the final product (an element of made-to-measure).

What to Customize?

In previous chapters we have categorized the fashion industry into various segments ranging from luxury products to mass-market brands. The remaining question is which of these industry segments is more suitable or ready for a process of mass customization?

Luxury Brands

It is important to remember that in this chapter we have distinguished between the concepts of mass customization and pure customization (or made-to-measure), as well as personalization. A good example to demonstrate these differences comes from Louis Vuitton, the leading luxury brand. Louis Vuitton offers its customers three different options and services that range from personalizing to fully customizing their line of bags and luggage:

- *Personalization:* LV offers personalization services on ready-to-purchase luggage and other products. Services include painting monograms on hard-sided luggage as well as hot stamping on tags, smaller leather goods, or soft-sided bags. Customers can choose from different font styles and colors. All these services are complimentary. (See Figure 7.6.)

- *Made-to-order products* (LV's equivalent application to MC): This service is available for both hard sided and soft bags. Customers are allowed to "choose from models available in several materials, and variations can be made to the lining, external material, and metallic pieces."[3] Customers are then given a price and time frame for the completion of the bag. After a 50 percent deposit has been paid, work on the bag will start, which might take four to nine months for completion, based on the type of bag ordered. The bag is then sent to the customer's store for pick up.

- *Made-to-measure products:* This service differs from the previous two services by including a designing stage that takes two to four weeks to create a design based on the customer's requests. It also comes with a much higher cost and could take up to 12 months for completion.

Luxury products and the whole experience that comes with owning one has always been about exclusivity and the feeling of being unique, special, and different from the crowd. And if you desire an exclusive made-to-measure item (or service), you expect it to come with a large price premium. The premium is usually so high that it shifts this item or service into a different segment both in terms of price as well as target customer. For example, a Louis Vuitton customer may expect to pay over five times the price of a ready-made bag for a made-to-measure customized one. This point is crucial to our argument because, as highlighted under the challenges section of this chapter, one of the main criteria of mass customization is that although it comes with a price premium, it should never be too high to shift the product into a different segment, targeting a different market or hindering current customers from obtaining it if they are willing to pay a reasonable extra amount.

ISSUES TO CONSIDER

- Exclusivity, personalization, or pure customization attainable with luxury goods are not the same as offering a mass-customized luxury product.
- The issue of the effect of MC on risking a brand's image as a result of a mismanaged process will be more relevant for luxury brands than any other fashion category. Accordingly, MC for luxury goods will probably be available under a more controlled environment and with more constraints on what can be customized and how far customization can go.
- MC offers consumers an additive level of exclusivity. Exclusivity is probably the main driver for purchasing luxury goods (in addition of course to the anticipation of quality) and will be so for customizing a luxury brand. It remains to be seen, however, why a traditional luxury brand customer who can afford a fully customized made-to-measure item would settle for a somewhat lesser exclusive option.
- Some argue that luxury products' customers are not our common e-shoppers. And that given the general nature of luxury products, their cost, and exclusivity, the distant Internet environment does not seem very suitable. Looking at the Louis Vuitton examples, we will notice that although the customization options are referenced on their Web site, the process itself takes place in their stores on a one-to-one basis. It is just the personalization option of

Figure 7.6

Louis Vuitton allows you to personalize your purchase by adding your initials. (*Courtesy George Chinsee/WWD/ Fairchild Publications*)

adding your initials or monograms (the simpler and less exclusive of all options) that is available online and for free.

- The rise of the new luxury brands referred to in an earlier chapter and the new breed of luxury consumers might be the biggest drive behind the mass customization trend in the luxury segment. Rising from the middle-segment market, these new up traders are younger, hipper, technology savvy, selective, and practical.

F. Piller highlighted an interesting observation made by Claudia Kieserling, founder and president of Selve, a leading shoe brand in the area of mass customization, when she said, "Luxury is a key characteristic of mass customization. No matter what price you ask, consumers see it as pure luxury," or we can add, at least as something special.

Mass-Market Brands

Mass-market brands and consumer goods should be generally comfortable with adapting MC and inviting customers to participate in shaping and designing the product. In this segment, products are more accessible and affordable; the customer base is more diverse and more value-for-money driven. A customer of a mass-customized pair of Levis or Adidas sneakers is willing to pay the premium for a product that has a better fit and value. Of course the pleasure of exclusivity is a plus. This is usually a customer who shops around before making a purchase decision and is more accustomed to window shopping, online browsing, and e-commerce.

ISSUES TO CONSIDER

- Once again, MC should not shift the price of the brand to a higher segment.

- Mass-market brands may benefit more from new technologies, such as the Internet and virtual communities, than luxury brands probably would, as well as a younger and hipper customer base that is more Internet savvy.
- More value for money and a better product are among the main drivers for choosing a mass-customized product in this category.
- MC also offers customers of such products the opportunity to trade up to a more exclusive brand.
- MC can be a major differentiation strategy in a very competitive market segment that suffers from sameness and copycats. A MC option can actually help prolong the life of an initially less-exclusive brand and in a way create an attractive brand extension that is supported and harnessed by its users.
- When proven beneficial, we should expect a bigger shift toward online mass-customization options in the nonluxury segment. An increase in adopting online solutions and new technologies will be inevitable. Brands will want to stay competitive and be the first to lure customers into engaging in a fun and addictive process of brand manipulation. It might be their only alternative for long-term survival.
- The fact that nonluxury fashion brands are generally of a low to medium price point might be of a great advantage as far as mass customization is concerned. A more affordable cost eliminates an entry barrier for users. Think of the T-shirt customization example explored in this chapter. Because the process is affordable and financially low risk, customers might give it a try for fun, as a venue to express

their creativity, or to fulfill a hobby. Of course, in the case of threadless.com, there is also the incentive of making money as well by having the customized T-shirt available for public purchase.

Mass Customization in Fashion Retailing

The examples of Adidas and Intellifit demonstrate good applications of mass customization in products, which in return impacts the retailing environment and increases the level of personalizing the shopping experience. Yet the possibilities are actually much bigger. Until today a totally personalized shopping experience has been an elite, high-priced service offered by exclusive boutiques or high-end specialty stores, such as Bergdorf Goodman or Neiman Marcus. Yet we have seen how new technologies such as RFID can make a personalized and customized experience available to each and every one of us. Consumers can interact with dressing room windows and TV screens plotted around the stores to decide when and what to try on, make purchase orders, get advice on styles and trends, and seek assistance if needed. These features, coupled with an alternative to shop virtually or online if desired, create a new level of consumer control and a myriad of choices and solutions that can be totally customized to your taste, time, and character.

Secondlife.com

In 2007, Italian fashion designer Giorgio Armani opened a virtual store on Secondlife.com, the 3D virtual community Web site. He modeled the virtual store on his flagship location in Milan. He even created an avatar of himself. Although the store is in a virtual world, it demonstrates the growing popularity of such environments among consumers and Internet users; such an approach allows the brand to relate to its customers and emotionally connect with them as it shares their interests and speaks their language. It shows that the brand is hip, modern, and relevant. And of course it is a gateway to Giorgio Armani's official e-shopping Web site. In addition to Giorgio Armani, Christian Dior chose secondlife.com to display an exclusive collection of jewelry on the virtual community's islands (virtual locations that are visited by users), demonstrating how the marketing potential of these environments can be quite important in the future.

There are estimated over 2 million users (or residents) of Second Life (SL). Thus, it is obvious that apart from their entertainment appeal these virtual worlds can have a serious business impact on developing and marketing brands. For instance, Mary Ellen Gordon from Market Truths, an online research agency, demonstrated that certain products such as athletic shoes have a very high level of brand awareness on Second Life. Gordon also presented relevant consumer behavior statistics[4] that showed:

- 57 percent of Second Life users (or residents) consider buying a real-life product as a result of a recommendation they received from someone in Second Life.
- 55 percent recommended a real-life product to someone they chatted with in SL.
- 25 percent have checked a product in real life after seeing it in SL.
- 9 percent have purchased a product in real life after seeing it in SL.
- 8 percent have bought a real life product in SL.

This data demonstrates the great marketing potential and branding relevance of these virtual worlds in real life and on real products. Another example of an interactive and collaborative online community that offers users the tools to create virtual worlds is SceneCaster.com.

iStorez.com

iStorez.com is a Web site that allows users to create their own customized shopping mall. It is the online equivalent of window shopping,[5] where users can browse thousands of storefronts (a storefront is an extension of a retail store's Web site) from hundreds of stores while iStorez presents the most updated and relevant storefronts based on the users' preferences and criteria. The iStorez storefront creation engine is based on the Web 2.0 technology. iStorez differentiates itself from other comparison shopping sites in delivering a customized shopping experience that dynamically changes based on what a visitor is looking for or a seasonal theme. In addition, shopping comparison sites are usually visited when users have narrowed down what they want to buy and are comparing prices and features, while iStorez allows them to browse around and "window" shop in a virtual mall they have created themselves. iStorez is clearly a good example of mass customization through creation of your own shopping environment or mall, as well as personalization of the shopping offerings.

Stylefeeder.com and Stylepath.com

These are two similar models that create virtual window shopping experiences and learn from your habits and preferences to make suitable recommendations. Stylepath also allows you to virtually decorate rooms from a selection of real furniture.

Your Own CyberSelf

Compucloz and My Virtual Model (Public Technologies Media) offer a similar concept and allow the users to create their own CyberSelf, a 3D virtual model based on their physique and body features. (See Figure 7.7.) The model is an application that, when used by the host Web site, allows shoppers to input their measurements to create their own model and use it to try on various products to see how they would fit on their bodies. Lands' End is a brand that has utilized the Public Technologies Media technology on their Web site.

It is important to note that in the area of retailing, the distinction between personalization and mass customization may be a bit blurred. A simple way of looking at it is that personalization mainly tries to answer the question of what to buy, whereas customization answers the question of how to buy.

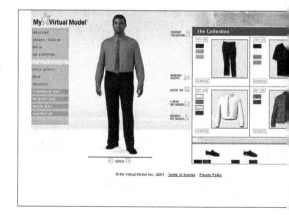

Figure 7.7

Myvirtualmodel. com creates a digital mannequin of yourself to let you see how you will appear in clothes before you decide to purchase them. *(My Virtual Model Inc./ Newscom)*

230 PART THREE: THE FUTURE OF FASHION BRANDING

Mass Customization and Technology

In reality, mass customization is not a new concept; the term *mass customization* was introduced in 1987 in Stanley M. Davis's book *Future Perfect*. Yet it owes its current rise to more recent technological advances, such as the Internet, software development, Web-based applications, and telecommunication innovations that are enabling customers to interact and integrate with the developing process and thus complete the circle for the model to function.

The Internet has proven to be a great platform for linking consumers and producers. And the development of what became known as Web 2.0—the newest generation of the Internet—has made it easier to create Web-based communities, blogs, wikis, and virtual environments in a manner that makes the process attainable and effective. In addition, technologies such as radio-frequency identification (RFID) promise a new era of data gathering and the creation of a new mass-customized shopping environment that could redefine the retailing experience of the future.

Issues to Consider

- As just mentioned, the Internet has been a great platform for applying mass customization by allowing customers to interact with the brand and its producer. However, not all kinds and segments of fashion brands have embraced the technology in the same manner or with the same level of integration. This is discussed later in this chapter.
- If mass customization is a manifestation of the increasing power of the consumer in the twenty-first century, then the Internet and other technological advances have been instrumental in such a change of power in the branding game together with other social and economic developments, including general increase of wealth, globalization, and economic growth in various parts of the world such as China.
- Not all consumer segments respond to technology advances and embrace them in the same manner or with the same degree. This point will be discussed later as we examine the application of mass customization in the luxury segment.

Mass Customization and the Fashion Branding Process

Based on our discussion of branding in chapters 2 and 3, we developed a branding process that can be summarized in the following four major stages:

1. The brand decision (involves the 3Cs: company; customer; culture)
2. The positioning strategy (incorporates the VIP model: value-identity-product mix)
3. The brand communication
4. Growth (or other) strategies

Let us examine how mass customization relates to these branding stages.

The Brand Decision (3Cs)

- From a consumer's perspective, MC offers users a high level of empowerment and control over the brand they cherish. For the first time, consumers are not just on the receiving end of the branding process but are part of it. They are not just brand users but literally *partners*.

- As a result, mass customization is an instrumental tool in what has been known as *brand democratization*, which is the trend toward more accessible and approachable brands by a wider and newer group of customers.
- The Internet and online applications have proved to be good platforms for customer input and interaction, which diminishes (not necessarily abolishes) the need for other costly channels (such as brick-and-mortar retail outlets), as well as opens the door for a wider integration among parties involved. In a way, it is B2C (business to consumer) meets B2B (business to business) meets C2C (consumer to consumer) meets C2B (consumer to business), all in one virtual environment.

The Positioning Strategy (VIP)
- MC offers a high level of brand differentiation, which in return is a strong element for developing a competitive advantage.
- If well managed, mass customization can offer consumers the right product with the right features and fit, which in return means a higher level of customer satisfaction and diminishes the need to shop somewhere else. The result is customer loyalty, which is the ultimate goal of any marketing strategy.
- Mass customization creates value through economies of scope rather than the economies of scale principles associated with mass production. Economies of scope refer to the economic benefits resulting from producing more than one product. Economies of scope create both revenue opportunities through incremental revenues and the adaptability and flexibility to pursue new and profitable channels.

- The opportunity to outsource certain functions, such as design and creative work, might have a positive economical impact on the manufacturer, as it may reduce the need to possess certain technical or creative skills as well as allowing for the redirecting of resources to other aspects of operations, such as production innovation.
- On the production side, the model is clearly a suitable platform for the concept of just-in-time (whereby raw materials are ordered and delivered when needed) and thus delivers better inventory management and cost reduction benefits.
- In a situation where the product is mass customized through a sourcing community (also known as open innovation) where many users can participate in developing and upgrading the product (think of the threadless.com brand in fashion or the Linux brand in computer operating systems), the product is actually in a continuous state of innovation and development. This is a process that would otherwise cost a great amount of money, time, and research effort on the organization's part. It is interesting that innovation and the future development of the brand in this case is sponsored and crafted by the actual end user who possesses the direct need for the product, a situation that can hardly be imitated with any level of forecasting, market research, or focus groups.

The Brand Communication
- From a marketing perspective, the model delivers a marketer's dream come true, whereby the end product is predetermined, predesigned, and predemanded by the end user, which might

hypothetically mean that the producer is making a product that is presold. This impacts the communication and promotion message and the marketing strategies in general.

- Adopting mass customization should impact both the content and mode of brand communication. In terms of content, brands generally highlight their distinctive features that give them their competitive edge as well as emphasize the brand's value. In other words, it promotes their positioning proposal. However, under MC, the features are not as totally predictable because they are altered and finalized by the end users themselves. Accordingly, the focus of the communication message is to remind potential users of the brand value and invite them to participate in a highly gratifying experience of collaborating in developing the product. This gives the message a service focus, not a product one. It's about the experience, not the features; your version of the brand, not ours; how you want the brand to be, more than what we propose. It's all about you, the *customer*. This promotion and communication tone is very strong, personal, and effective in building a strong level of customer loyalty and positive brand image.

- Based on the last point, a mass customized product requires a personalized communication message. Thus under MC, new communication channels such as personalized e-mails, newsletters, text messages, customizable Web pages, and so on are all suitable channels under this model (more new options will be discussed later in the chapter).

- Mass customization of products will inevitably pave the way to the mass customization of

marketing and promotion. In reality, this already takes place in the form of viral marketing. Viral marketing or, as some call it, *buzz marketing*, is based on a C2C (consumer to consumer) environment where the users in a way "hijack " the brand (to be discussed further in chapter 8) and take over the marketing process themselves through message sharing, networking, and word of mouth. The result is a snowballing effect that creates a buzz that is wide reaching, effective, and very low cost. It's a situation whereby the main role of the brand's marketing team is to create the environment, and possibly manipulate the content or initiate an interest, yet the process itself remains in the hands of the users. Just like customization, viral marketing transforms the users from passive receivers to active contributors in the marketing process and in brand ownership. This is not to ignore the role of the brand, though, because viral marketing has to be initiated by something that attracts the users' interest. A strong offer, an important announcement, or exciting news should trigger the interest and get the ball rolling. Let's never forget that any brand, whether it is online or offline, has to be built on true value that is meaningful to the user.

The Internet has witnessed many successful examples of viral marketing in recent years through online communities, blogs, and videos created in support of brand examples such as Barbie, Nike, even British singing sensation Susan Boyle.

Growth Opportunities

- The MC model could very well thrive on a network of workshops to satisfy its low quantity of ever-changing products. Workshops and small business units should flourish under this model, creating new business opportunities for young entrepreneurs and smaller operations. In the Mi Adidas example, the shoes are produced within the same factories by a smaller group of skilled workers, a model reminiscent of the preindustrialization era, borrowing from the customized world of tailoring and haute couture.

- MC allows the brand to grow by offering new options to existing customers and attracting new ones. It's a form of brand extension that expands the brand offering as needed by its end user. In addition, the Internet being a common platform for MC gives the service a global reach that would have been hard to attain in a traditional brick-and-mortar environment.

Challenges under
Mass Customization

- The biggest challenge is the mind-set change. The fashion industry is one that has historically strived on secrecy, egoism, and creative dictatorship. Designers and managers who are used to a culture of total control and a highly protective environment may not easily accept an environment of branding democracy, nor comprehend the possibility of letting an outsider take control, manipulate, or hijack a brand they have been building and protecting for years.

- In an open environment such as that created by mass customization, possessing a level of control is not only challenging but necessary to maintaining the brand's integrity. Every brand strives to consistently maintain the image it creates. Yet if customers are allowed to manipulate the brand and reshape the product to their liking without any control measures, the brand image may be vulnerable and easily tarnished.

- Control also refers to measures needed to manage the growing customer database and facilitate smooth feedback channels demonstrating a quick response in order to maintain customer retention and long-term loyalty. In a different environment, special orders are not the norm, and customer feedback is occasional and usually available if and when a customer is asked. Yet under the new environment, every order comes with a unique set of requirements and personal data. This wealth of data has to be well managed and rechanneled in a more dynamic and personal style of service that keeps developing every time the customer returns for a purchase.

- Adopting mass customization is not an immediate guarantee of 100 percent sales. A good example is threadless.com, which as mentioned earlier, bases its T-shirt production on popular vote. Yet popularity did not always reflect actual sales numbers. The same problem encouraged Look-Zippy.com—a French site with a similar model—to develop a measure of control by which they post the selected models online for two weeks where customers can place their orders, followed by production (another example of control measures).

- Mass customization might result in a higher price due to the higher cost brought about by meeting the specific needs of every customer, such as setup cost or skilled labor. Yet these costs are counterbalanced by efficiency in forecasting and product development, postponement of activities until an order is placed, and better customer retention. In addition, customers are usually involved in customization with an expectation and willingness to pay a suitable premium for their new gains, given that it does not imply a switch into an upper market segment[6] (for example, the price premium is not so big as to shift the product to a higher market segment).

The previous examples show that mass customization as a model can be a rewarding branding and competitive strategy in the twenty-first century. As with any model, it has its challenges and limitations. Yet what makes it lucrative is its ability to embrace new technologies and respond to the consumers' growing desire for empowerment over what, when, and how they buy products. The model has also proven to be a flexible one that can be applied in variations, allowing it to quickly react to new challenges as they develop, and transform these challenges into lucrative and profitable options, helping the brand to survive and become profitable.

The Wireless Brand: RFID and Mobile Technologies

Digital and electronic technologies have allowed products and services to be designed, packed, delivered, and experienced in new and different ways like never before. The pace and complexity of options have increased and, with them, the speed of brand success or failure. In the world of wireless technology, the Internet continues to establish new business models that already have and will alter the way we approach marketing in general—and specifically branding—in the near future. The following sections discuss examples of **WIRELESS TECHNOLOGIES.**

RFID

RFID stands for radio frequency identification. The technology is built around the concept of putting cheap and tiny tags that contain a radio transmitter/receiver on physical objects. These tags are then used to allocate the objects. The tag can be attached to anything and can carry different sorts of information about the item. A radio reader device can be mounted anywhere or carried around the store and can read every tag within range, thus monitoring and keeping track of every tagged item while transferring this data to any computer. One of the important features of this system is its reasonable cost. The tags, for instance, can be around 20 cents or higher; however, once prices drop to single digit cents, they would be even more economically feasible to adopt for lower priced products. The advantages and applications are numerous and without any human labor involved. The first obvious application of RFID is inventory control. In addition to placing the devices in stock rooms and warehouses, stores can create what is being dubbed as *smart shelves*. For example, when a customer picks an item off a store shelf to purchase it, the information is immediately transmitted wirelessly to inform the warehouse; before you know it, the item is replenished with no need for phone calls, written forms, or long waiting time. Smart shelves help achieve this through sharing information between the tags on the shelved product, the reader devices, and the computer network. Many stores have already either adopted this system or are in the process of doing so, such as the GAP.

Figure 7.8a

This interactive magic mirror provides a selection of different viewers' garment suggestions as well as their votes on the various pieces. *(Bloomberg via Getty Images)*

Figure 7.8b

Rather than simply showing this woman's reflection, this magic mirror displays an image of a completely different garment from what she is wearing. *(Bloomberg via Getty Images)*

The technology and concept can be taken a step further and be adopted in a multitude of applications and services that will not only streamline the retailer operations but enhance the customers' shopping experience and highly personalize it. Marketing enthusiasts and writers such as Rick Matheson have explored many of the promising and fascinating applications of RFID. Here are a couple of interesting examples.

- TV screens can be placed around the store with RFID readers attached so that after a customer picks an item off the shelf, screen readers close by capture the item's data and initiate a series of special offers and updates relevant to that item or its category. The same experience will be repeated with almost every customer, leading to an unprecedented level of personalization and target marketing. Barnes & Noble is among those exploring this option.

- Imagine smart garment labels that can communicate with your washing machine and transmit the appropriate washing instructions for the garment, such as the right water temperature and drying instructions.

- This wireless technology might eventually lead to similar chips embedded in our credit cards or wallets so that we do not need to check out at store registers anymore. When we leave the store with the items, they are wirelessly intercepted along with our credit card information and automatically charged. Not only will this make it easier and faster for customers to shop, but may eventually reduce rates of store theft as well. Wireless checkout is still in the testing stages, but once again the potential is amazing.

- Nanette Lepore, a New York-based designer, has been at the forefront of experimenting with new technologies that enhance her customer's shopping experience at her SoHo store. For instance, she has been testing what is known as magic mirrors—in-store mirrors that interact with the RFID tags placed on her garments. When you hold or wear a garment in front of the mirror, the magic mirror senses what the item is, then the "transparent video monitor housed within the mirror's glass reveals itself to play animated scenarios featuring the brand's whimsical Lepore Girl mascot upselling accessories and complementary items."[7] (See Figures 7.8a–b.)

- When Prada opened its first epicenter stores in New York and Los Angeles, it adopted RFID to create a highly personalized and unique experience not only for the customer but for the employees as well. Employees held wi-fi-based tablet devices that scanned RFID tags on garments; this way they could check inventory, make recommendations based on previous sales, trace garments, and detect where they had been misplaced. They could also monitor which part of the store had a higher level of traffic. In addition, the tags could trigger nearby screens to display relevant runway clips and make recommendations to buyers based on the items they picked and previous buyers' votes. In the dressing room, shoppers can obtain information on garments using an interactive touch screen display. This information is conveyed to the screen via RFID tags attached to garments throughout the store. While the customer tries the clothes on, the magic mirror takes time-delay video and replays the action in slow motion so the shopper can take in the full effect.[8] (See Figure 7.9.)

- Wireless systems can be used to link back-end databases to loyalty programs. So, for instance, when a customer walks into a store, he or she may enter a code that in essence alerts the store that he or she has arrived and is ready to receive special promotions based on their previous purchase history as saved in the database.

- Shopping carts can be equipped with wireless touch screens that provide detailed information about products and where to allocate them in the store.

These amazing examples demonstrate the great potential of the technology and how it can change not only the way customers shop, but how retail operations are run and brands managed in the future. However, like any new technology and application, it comes with a few challenges and concerns.

Figure 7.9

A woman uses a touch screen in a dressing room at the Prada Epicenter in New York:

(*Catrina Genovese/Time & Life Pictures/Getty Images*)

237

Challenges under RFID

RFID technology can be utilized in different retailing environments. (See Figure 7.10.) The biggest challenge is the question of privacy. The fact that, through RFID, stores can monitor everything we pick and scan every item that may already be in our pockets and purses as long as it has a built-in tag raises legitimate privacy issues and recalls fears of a Big Brother consistently watching our every move.

Another challenge that stores such as Prada face is the ability and willingness of traditionally trained employees to adopt and learn these new technologies and operate in a totally different retailing environment. The challenge highlights the unquestionable need for intensive training, not only in how to use these new devices but regarding their impact on the whole operation, especially the level of customer service.

M-Branding

M-BRANDING, or mobile branding, refers to the use of mobile technologies and devices such as our cell phones and PDAs. Wireless devices such as cell phones are the most intimate and personal devices any of us has ever acquired, even more than a laptop or PC. It is the only device that you carry everywhere and all the time, and it is probably the first thing you check when you wake up every morning. It is a device that has highly penetrated the market; almost every single member of the family probably has a cell phone or PDA of their own. It is also interesting to note how mobile users are generally more willing to pay extra dollars for their mobile services and downloads (such as ring tones) than they are for other online services they would get through their laptops or PCs. Examples of current marketing and branding mobile applications include the following.

Mobile texting is becoming quite a phenomenon all over the world and especially in Europe and Asia. Its effect is comparatively less in America because, for the most part, the American society is based on commuting, which may consume a large amount of time during the day. Nevertheless, a recent study by Forrester Research shows that 85% of U.S. users between the ages of 18 and 30 (also known as Generation Y) frequently use text messages, compared to 57% of all adults. Texting has been effectively used by many organizations in various ways as seen in the following examples.

- When Bravo.com introduced its new fashion program "The Fashion Show," hosted by designer Isaac Mizrahi, it allowed viewers to participate in the voting process online, which they could also do using their cell phone (similar to the "American Idol" format), thus transforming viewers from passive observers into participants and co-owners of the whole competition. In addition, it offered games, show updates, and the ability to view the final collections as well. The same channel offered

Figure 7.10

At the Tokyo department store Mitsukoshi, RFID technology is used with cosmetics to show virtual before and after faces of their customers.
(*YOSHIKAZU TSUNO/ AFP/Getty Images*)

with the new generation of iPhone 3GS, which includes built-in support. The sensor tracks your run, then sends the data to your iPod. In addition, as you run, the device informs you of your time, distance, pace, and calories burned. Your data is saved on Nikeplus.com where you can monitor your progress as well as access information about products and athletes associated with Nike.

- *Style.com:* This Web site's iPhone application gives the user access to hundreds of designer collection photos and exclusive videos. Style.com reported over 1 million ads served via iPhone in a single month[9] (Fashion Network has a similar app).
- *Ralph Lauren:* An innovative marketing effort was initiated for his 2009 collection by introducing an iPhone app especially for his Fall 2009 and Spring 2009 collections, allowing users to explore the Ralph Lauren collection and view highlight videos, a look book, special video slideshows, as well as use a store locator for the United States and international markets. (See Figure 7.12.)

photos, ring tones, and wallpaper to subscribers of the Rachel Zoe program, all available for downloading on their mobile cell phones.

- Mobile phones are already being used in some parts of the world such as Asia to communicate with vending machines by dialing a number on your phone, making a purchase, and paying at the same time, all through your phone. There might come a day when we do not need to carry wallets or credit cards anymore because our mobile phones will suffice.

The new craze for iPhone apps has created a plethora of applications that can have marketing potential, such as the following.

- *Near to everywhere app:* This is an application that allows users to shop malls and get updates and location of stores.
- *Nike:* Nike introduced its very popular Nike+iPod application for both the iPod and iPhone, which was meant to replicate the online Nikelab experience. You just put the sensor in your Nike + shoe that comes with a built-in pocket. (See Figure 7.11.) No need to connect the device

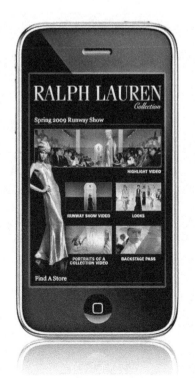

- *Net-A-Porter.com:* The fashion-forward e-tailer launched NET-APP, which allows users to shop using their iPhone or iPod touch. The application is free and updated every Monday and Wednesday. In addition to the shopping, it hosts a number of interesting features:
  - Browse through the latest fashion products and trends with detailed information (such as sizes, fit, prices, and so on) on products with a high-quality customizable photo library.
  - Read the Net-A-Porter weekly fashion magazine.
  - Access product-specific details, including size and fit information.
  - View content that is relevant to the user's location (such as prices in various currencies).
  - E-mail product information to friends.
  - Send an e-mail to a team of fashion advisors offering guidance on sizing, fit, and expert style advice.
  - View and add items to a personalized Net-A-Porter wish list that users can access on their desktops.

ScanLife

ScanLife offers a new software application that allows more interactivity through the mobile phone. After installing the application, users can scan a 2D bar code that is placed on products, hang tags, magazines, or any flat surface using the camera of their cell phone. When scanned, the information triggers actions such as directing the user to a Web page with specific information about the product or where he or she can download materials such as coupons, store location directions, price list, and more. Thus a window

shopper, for instance, can target an item he or she sees in a window after closing hours and immediately be directed to information about the item such as availability, sizes, prices, watch video relevant to the garment, read reviews, and eventually have the option to purchase it online from their phone. (See Figures 7.13a–b.)

Presence Application

Presence is an IBM product that allows stores to detect shoppers who have already signed up to the service once they enter the store and accordingly offer them individual coupons and special offers in real time. The application, in addition to offering a highly customized service to shoppers, offers retailers a wealth of information about the shopping habits of their customers and how they respond to special offers and discounts.

Beaming

Beaming refers to a technology that allows companies to use billboards and displays to beam information to PDAs and cell phone devices via infrared or Bluetooth ports. Similar to the RFID examples, you can wave your cell phone or PDA device at an item in a store and view comparison prices of the item online or get different relevant information. This technology is already being used in Japan. Another application for this technology allows billboards placed on highways to intercept FM frequencies of passing cars. Based on your radio station of preference, they start displaying ads relevant to your taste. The system is smart enough to differentiate among cars and not pick up the same signal twice. The same technology can be used in other locations where billboards can send videos, games, and other applications to cell

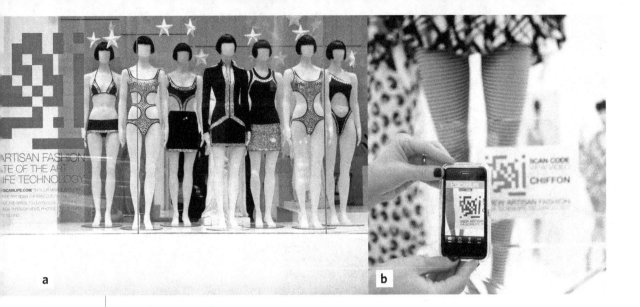

a   b

Figure 7.13a, b
(a) A shop window promoting the store's use of ScanLife.
(b) All you need is a phone, a camera, and the ScanLife application to access numerous forms of information regarding a product.

(© Michael Falco)

phones through Bluetooth technology. With the users' permission, billboards can complement their displayed messages with these more interactive and fun applications.

Beaming technology is also being tested for use inside stores, beaming interactive content with product and store information on walls, floors, and any other solid surface, adding flexibility to how and where to inform and interact with the customer.

Audio Targeting

Audio targeting refers to directing sound in the same manner that a laser beam directs light. These ultrasonic beams create a sound bubble that can be directed to specific objects or individuals in its path. When the bubble hits a wall or an object, it transmits audible frequencies that are heard only by whoever is passing through these audio bubbles in a very narrow range and targeted frequency, so that it feels like wearing personal headphones. The greatest application for such a technology is the ability to send different audible messages to different targets and create a highly customized message. So in a way, two people can be passing by your store but

each receives a different promotional message or offer. Or you can transmit different messages in different aisles or segments of the store that are heard only by whoever is passing there. An example of this technology is the HyperSonic® Sound technology (HSS) from the American Technology Co. The ultrasonic emitters use ultrasonic energy to reflect sounds and voices in very specific areas and remain focused in a narrow column of sound. (See Figure 7.14.) This effect is produced without the conventional speaker's excess baggage—there are no voice coils, cones, crossover networks, or enclosures. Sound does not spread to the sides or rear of an HSS unit, eliminating the problem of uncomfortable and unwanted noise pollution produced by conventional speakers.[10] A listener can stand anywhere within the audio beam range and hear the marketing messages. According to the company, HSS technology can be used to:

- deliver sound to areas that are either physically impossible to access or too costly to install conventional loudspeakers,
- isolate sound to a specific region or person, and
- communicate highly intelligible messages over long distances.

Figure 7.14
Audio tar-
geting allows
sound to be
directed within
an extremely
focused area, or
sound bubble.
(Courtesy of
International Robotics,
Inc.)

Wireless Technology and the Fashion Branding Process

Let us examine the impact of wireless technologies on the fashion branding process.

The Brand Decision (3Cs)

- The greatest impact of wireless technologies and all technologies referred to in this chapter lies in their potential for high interactivity and the fact that they establish a two-way channel of communication that is dramatically different from how one-directional traditional marketing has been.
- Because of these technologies, customers are not just on the receiving end anymore; they are partners in a way that will eventually shape and redefine the brand involved.
- Wireless technologies, such as mobile phones, have transformed our personal habits and level of communication as individuals. In return, they help to reshape our culture, expectations, and needs in a manner that affects everything we interact with, including the brand.
- Cultures are dynamic, and through viral marketing and real-time interactivity, wireless technologies do not only shape them, but communicate them and spread them as established values and habits as well.
- From a company perspective, wireless technologies support the virtual organization model and the flat dynamic structure where feedback is crucial and quick. It also offers new income opportunities from new services as well as from lowering costs by introducing new cheaper marketing options. It also offers a great source of consumer data and profiles. But above all it brings the organization closer to the customer and establishes a more intimate relationship built on continuous dialogue and personalized services.

The Positioning Strategy (VIP)

- Just like MC, these communication channels provide more than just communication; they serve as a platform for branding and value generation through their level of personalization.
- One of the biggest advantages of the high level of personalization achieved under this environment as well as MC is their ability to narrow the gap between corporate brand positioning and the brand image as established in the consumer's mind. As consumers get what they want and expect from the brand, and the brand successfully assists them in achieving that, the brand promise is manifested, the image is solidified, and loyalty, which is the best measure of success, becomes more attainable.
- Creation of apps and interactive application are in a way a form of brand extensions. They offer new growth opportunities and exposure for brands where they can not only be promoted but generate income as well (selling ringtones, videos, subscriptions to special services and

updates, new outlets for shopping and placing orders, and so on).

- Wireless applications also have a direct impact on establishing, promoting, and polishing the brand's identity. Co-branding such as that between Samsung Phones and Giorgio Armani, for instance, enables the brand to reinforce its visual identity in a modern and relevant way that may be more effective than placing the logo on a traditional printed ad.

The Brand Communication

- The intimate relationship we develop with these little wireless devices has a strong impact on

THE FUTURE OF CUSTOMER SERVICE?

Figure 7.15

The poster of the film *Minority Report*, a dramatization of a "futuristic" technology about to actually exist.

(*20TH CENTURY FOX/ Album*)

In the Tom Cruise/Steven Spielberg sci-fi movie *Minority Report*, Cruise's character has a surgeon replace his eyeballs with someone else's in order to avoid being tracked by police through retinal scanning. In the futuristic world of *Minority Report*, retinal scanning enables everything from collecting subway fares to tracking consumer behavior. At one point when Cruise's character enters a store, the holographic image "reads" his replacement eyes and cheerfully greets him, "Hello Mr. Yakimoto, welcome back to the Gap. How did those assorted tank tops work out?"

The fictional technology of Hollywood is about to exist in the real world through a technology called Human Locator, an interactive visual system developed for advertising and entertainment by Freeset, a Canadian creative technology consulting firm. Human Locator detects when humans are near, tracks their movement, and then broadcasts messages directed at them from a nearby screen.

Drawing on cutting-edge computer visualization techniques to track full body movement in real time, it allows consumers to actively participate in and interact with advertising. It works with most video displays or projectors and can output video, animations, audio, and motion graphics. At the same time, the system provides advertisers with measurable viewer data.

Sources: www.freeset.com; www.humanlocator.org

Figure 7.16

Armani co-branded with Samsung to produce the Night Effect Soft Bank 830C Emporio Armani mobile phone, released in 2009.

(KAZUHIRO NOGI/AFP/ Getty Images)

marketing and branding strategies. It opens the doors wide open to a world of highly personalized and targeted messages that are not only relevant, instantaneous, and up to date, but a fraction of the cost compared to most traditional marketing channels.

- The mobile environment is capable of delivering information and promotional offers in different ways and formats such as text messages though SMS and e-mails as well as video, audio, ring tones, games, and so on. The messages sent can range from information and announcements, to offers, coupons, or other practical information and news. Another great advantage is the possible seamless integration between mobile technology and the Internet in the form of Internet and e-mail access, tweeting, and more, through the mobile phone.
- Mobile devices can also play a major role in viral marketing through the share of videos and text messages.
- The new environment is more suitable for a pull rather than a push approach, whereby the focus is to address consumers and motivate them to take initiative and be interested in pulling (demanding) the product and starting a viral marketing round. (In a pull marketing strategy, the consumer usually *pulls* the goods they demand for their needs into the market; accordingly, marketing activities target the final consumer. In the push strategy, the suppliers *push* them toward the consumers who may not be aware of it and accordingly, the manufacturer concentrates some of their marketing effort on promoting their product to retailers to convince them to stock the product.)

- Mobile applications such as iPhone apps are being used to broadcast live streaming of fashion shows. Dolce & Gabbana, for instance, have decided to make this move in 2010 as a step to follow their earlier move to go live online and on their Facebook page. It is another example of the democratization of fashion and a manifestation of the role and impact today's ordinary consumer has in the fashion scene.

Growth Opportunities

Wireless technologies and relevant applications (such as iPhone apps) create new brand extension and growth opportunities. They extend the brand's presence in the user's lives in an exciting and interactive manner that in return reinforces the brand image and generates value. What is interesting is that users are also part of this growth and extension strategies because they are capable of developing their own apps and platforms that could support and showcase the brand.

Wireless technologies can be easily integrated with other technologies, such as the Internet as will be discussed later, and accordingly can also play a role in extending the global reach of the brand.

The co-branding example of Armani and Samsung demonstrates the repositioning opportunities such technologies can offer to older brands by making them more hip, current, and relevant to modern users. (See Figure 7.16.)

Challenges of Wireless Technologies

As with any marketing process, the information used needs to be useful, and the value proposed needs to be real and relevant to the consumer. Accordingly, incentives and promotional offers need to be meaningful.

The entertainment value should not be ignored. Interactivity and entertainment can make the message more engaging and exciting in order to encourage the user to respond.

Just like on the Internet, the consumer should not be a victim of spam and unsolicited material or be enticed to subscribe to newsletters without a clear and easy way to opt out and unsubscribe. It is also always advisable to seek their approval and permission before getting them engaged in such activities. This way, the customer feels respected and perceives the promoter as honest and professional. The result is a better chance for building a trusted, long-term relationship.

Always be aware of new trends and technologies. The iPhone apps craze and Twitter mania prove that today's customers get bored easily and are always on the lookout for new cool trends.

As mentioned earlier, one of the biggest benefits of the new media is its ability to micro-segment markets and highly personalize marketing messages. Thus, it is essential to clearly identify customers and determine the best ways to customize and personalize messages.

Never ignore the power of real time. Real-time streaming with updated news and information is attractive and can easily capture users' attention and interest.

As with any service, activities need to be backed up with good and effective customer service that offers quick responses and solutions.

Consider integrated mobile campaigns with other activities, such as online activities or in-store promotions. This approach keeps the user engaged, interested, and entertained. An example mentioned earlier about dressing rooms' magic mirrors that can be wirelessly connected to Facebook applications is a concept that could be easily emulated and adapted by a mobile app.

Word-of-text is a term that is quickly replacing *word-of-mouth*. Yet as much as we need to envision the potential of this medium, we also need to understand its limitations and deal with it. Text messages, for instance, are challenging in their focus and length. With a limitation of 160 characters in most languages, you will need to learn how to send a message and make your point across effectively within such constraints.

The Virtual Brand: The World of Social Networking

The Internet differs from many previous technologies in that it is not as centrally controlled as other channels were, such as TV or newspaper. It offers a more open environment because we live in **VIRTUAL COMMUNITIES** that we create with people we choose and trust. Buyers nowadays trust other Internet users' (who are virtually strangers) opinions and feedback regarding a service or a product more than those of real world experts. We now live in virtual social communities and probably interact with each other more through blogs and social networks than we do in the real world. Thus, the impact of such networks cannot be ignored. Even if some models are fads that are destined to be replaced by new ideas, the truth remains that a culture has been shaped and has changed us forever. Here are some examples of virtual environments.

Blogging

Blogging stands for *Web logging*, which is a form of online personal publishing that allows individuals and companies to articulate and broadcast their message in cyberspace.[11] The significance of blogging is that it is personal, fast, casual, and intimate. It also differs from other Internet publishing channels in its frequency and interactivity. Its real-time effect, simplicity, and interactivity have allowed users to express themselves and their opinions in a very casual way. The result has been the rise of the social networking phenomenon that started with a community of blogs referred to as the blogosphere and transformed into the new wave of social networks, such as MySpace, Facebook, and Twitter. Obviously not all blogs are valuable; however, some have becomes sources of debates, serious discussions, and valid critiques. It is estimated that more than 11 percent of Internet users read blogs, making blogs more and more attractive to marketers.

A significant outcome of blogging is the creation of a platform for consumers to group, form communities, and openly share views and comments on different products and brands. Although the challenges are clear, as they may end up criticizing the product or brand, they can also allow users to embrace the brand and take ownership of marketing it and become its champions. It's the same concept again of brand hijacking and viral marketing. What has been amazing is the amount by which users have grown to trust these blogs as their point of reference. For example, Nikeblog.com is a blog that is not affiliated with Nike but was created by Nike customers (referred to as "sneaker heads") who claim that Nike is their favorite brand. The blog offers product news, discussion, and opinions about Nike and other brands as well. They also offer coupon and shopping links to various sneaker styles in addition to a Facebook and Twitter presence.

On the other hand, businesses have found an opportunity in blogging by participating in a more casual dialogue about the brand that is more trust-building and frank. Guidelines for effective blog marketing may include:

- Write and update interesting and relevant content on a regular basis. There's no substitute for attracting attention than publishing content worth sharing.
- Contact existing customers, marketing partners, and industry peers and let them know you've launched a blog. Profile them in a blog post to give extra meaning and incentive for visitors to pay attention.
- Link to other influential blogs.
- Contribute posts to other blogs. Comments posted on other relevant and influential blogs with a similar target audience may be helpful in building visibility, as these comment forms will usually include the opportunity to link back to your blog.
- Integrate the blog with other social channels such as Facebook, Twitter, and YouTube.
- Include blog links on your Web site as well as everywhere you post your Web site address both online *and* offline.
- Have employees add the blog URL to their e-mail signatures as well as online profiles (on sites like LinkedIn, Facebook, and Twitter).
- Promote your new blog and the value of its content via e-mail to prospective customer lists.

- With PR efforts such as media relations, approach journalists with press releases and other material. Always include a link to your blog in those communications.
- Bloggers can also make money directly by tapping into the money-generating power of affiliate advertising, such as the Amazon's affiliate advertising program, which pays bloggers if a reader buys a book reviewed on a their blog.
- Advertise your blog through links on relevant sites or sponsored links on search engines.
- Remember that although visitors' traffic remains the lifeblood of any blog, not all bloggers make money directly from their blogs. Rather, their blogging may lead to money-making opportunities such as consulting gigs, business connections, or book contracts.

Social Networks

The blogosphere has evolved in recent years into the new phenomenon of social networks such as Facebook, MySpace, and Twitter. These new platforms are redefining the manner in which we communicate and relate to the world. On the business level, they have opened a Pandora's box of marketing tools and options that go beyond the mass-marketing thinking of decades ago. In a recent study by *BtoB* magazine and Business. com,[12] 56% of marketers indicated that they intend to increase their investment into social media, and 44% already reported positive effects for their sites. Respondents also indicated that their top goals for spending on social marketing are to:
- build brand awareness (81%),
- increase traffic (77%),
- generate leads (67%),

- better engage with customers (66%), and
- improve search results (57%).

Other important reasons for a company or a brand to participate in a social network is to be part of their audiences' world and interests, in addition to benefitting from low-cost marketing. However, before a company rushes into being part of this environment, it needs to approach it as seriously as it would any other marketing endeavor. They can always start by asking the following questions:

- *What are my primary goals and objectives? What about my secondary goals?*
- *Does my target audience spend time on these social networks? Which ones? How often? What do they do? And what are their expectations?*
- *What do I need to do to attract my audience and retain their attention?*
- *What resources do I need? How much will it cost? Do I have the technical skills needed to run and maintain my presence?*

To better appreciate the significance of these questions, let's examine two of the most visited of these networks: Facebook and Twitter.

Facebook

Facebook is a free social network where subscribers can create their own blogs and fill them with information and updates about their personal lives and interests. They add and communicate with friends by sharing photos and stories, as well as joining different networks of common interests and locations. Similar to other social networks, Facebook is easy to use and very intimate in nature. In social networking, the most important parameters are the size of your network and the number of people who are part of it.

In addition to individuals, many companies have joined the bandwagon of social networks such as Facebook and utilized it as a marketing channel in various ways, such as:

- Inform readers with updates and latest company news.
- Offer contests and promotions to encourage visitors to link to the blog.
- Participate in groups that interest and attract their target customers.
- Create a database for future e-mails and newsletters.
- Use the entertainment factor with tools such as videos, games, and music to offer fashion updates and generally make the experience exciting and worth revisiting.
- Receive feedback and initiate a dialogue about the brand and its products.
- Use all of these activities to build up interest and confidence in the brand.

Examples of brands that had a strong and early presence on social networks are Nike and Diane von Furstenberg (DVF). The DVF page, for instance, offers news, photos of fans and women in DVF dresses, and a fan-of-the-week application where fans can share ideas and photos of themselves in DVF outfits. (See Figure 7.17.)

In April 2010, Facebook announced a set of new social plugins that were meant to enhance the level of online social interaction and, in return, the level of integration between businesses and online shoppers. For instance, the new open graph protocol introduces a tagging system that allows applications and networks to map users' real preferences and choices. Plugins such as the Like button and the activity stream, among others,

keep track of visitors' preferences and activities in real time, so online users will easily be able to find out their friends' favorite store, music, jeans brand, and so on. Businesses have quickly foreseen the business potential of these new applications. A good example is Levi Strauss & Co., which took measures to use such plugins to integrate its business with Facebook, allowing users to tag products they like, and introducing its Friend Store in which consumers logged into Facebook are able to view their friends' preferred products.[13] This level of integration makes information sharing more accessible, relevant, and dynamic, which will in return create more focused marketing strategies as well as enrich the shopping process in general.

Twitter

Twitter is an example of microblogging. It is a text-based blogging network, but with limitations of 140 characters per entry. It's considered by many to be the next generation of instant messaging. Twitter has gained wide acceptance in a short time due to its capabilities as a real-time platform for self-expression. Twitter is considered a social network because users can add or remove friends as well as attract a group of fans and followers. It is the most "real-time" of all networks and the fastest to spread news and updates. New features are being tested that may allow users to segment fans and group them. The key element to Twitter is to keep the followers interested as you share your news, thoughts, and updates. No wonder that tweets of celebrities are very popular because they give regular individuals the opportunity to get closer to their favorite star's inner thoughts and lives. Designers such as Karl Lagerfeld use Twitter to share their thoughts and views. In one tweet, Karl Lagerfeld described life in the fashion world as a short life where you live six months at a time. As a matter of fact, although this intimate and very personal perspective of Twitter is the most intriguing, it is also the most challenging because users tend to forget that it is still a public platform and that anything said can be used against its user. It also means that it is an extension of our personal lives. People talk on Twitter as they talk in everyday conversations. And the fact that you can access the Internet with your mobile phone and tweet makes it more convenient and accessible at every hour of our lives. For Twitter fans, it is highly addictive and engaging, which means it can also be a very effective marketing channel, especially given the indications showing that most Twitter users are also engaged in other social networks, such as Facebook. As a result, Twitter is used by many to increase traffic and direct visitors to their blogs where they can get more info and details on specific subjects.

Brands are using Twitter in many ways, such as in keeping events' attendees up to date with time, location, delays, and all sort of details and information. It is a great way to document events as well,

making it a kind of virtual real-time diary.

There have also been various success stories of job hunting through Twitter. Job seekers have used tweets to explain their move, who they are, and what they are looking for; they offer a link to their blogs with details about themselves and get feedback and job leads as a result. Thus, Twitter is more than a one-way stream of information. It can be an effective platform for dialogue and interaction through responding to readers' comments and links to other networks.

Virtual Environments and the Fashion Branding Process

Let us examine the impact of virtual environment on the fashion branding process.

The Brand Decision (3Cs)

- The Internet and its virtual environments have the potential of integrating all previously mentioned technologies and creating a platform of collaboration and shared brand decision making between the brand producer (company) and the customers. Customers are empowered and can easily communicate with the company and the brand at various levels in an engaging environment and on daily basis.

- Activities on virtual worlds and communities are a great source for information about consumer behavior and profiles. This data is precious in guiding companies through critical branding decisions, such as market segmentation, positioning strategies, and relevant communication strategies.

Figure 7.17

Diane von Furstenberg takes advantage of the Twitter craze to update DVF fans on events, new products, and more.

(Courtesy Fairchild Publications)

- Similar to mobile technologies, virtual communities reshape our social habits and define our new culture. As culture reshapes, so do our needs and the products and services we seek to satisfy them. Virtual communities (VCs) created an environment of options, variety, a culture of mix and match, and a new sense of community. Consumers today trust and seek the advice of other community members and bloggers more than they do professionals or traditional sources.

The Positioning Strategy (VIP)

- Virtual communities are instrumental in brand positioning. They provide platforms where ideas, suggestions, and support for the brand are initiated and shared. They offer a wealth of information that companies can use to enhance their strategies. However, they are also places where verdicts of the brand are strongly and bluntly shared. Just as favorable, viral marketing through social networks is a fast (and cheap) and effective promotional tool, though negative stories, reviews, and shared bad experiences can hurt the brand with a faster and stronger impact than could have happened before.
- VCs as well as wireless technologies offer the company a great opportunity to reposition the brand if needed by listening and responding to targeted customers' needs as well as integrating their new lifestyle. Older brands can come across as more relevant and part of the current "cool" culture.
- VCs can reinforce the brand's identity in terms of both its personality and visual identity. It presents the brand as modern and fresh, as well as offers opportunities to showcase its visual identity in a clear and attractive way.

The Brand Communication

- Virtual worlds offer a direct and real-time channel of communication between the company and the user as well as between different users, allowing a more effective spread of messages and ideas (once again, showing the importance of viral marketing).
- Related to the previous point, VCs also allow the creation of brand communities that become brand advocates and play an instrumental role promoting the brand or even killing it. The example of Nikeblog.com mentioned earlier is a good one.
- Companies have adopted the brand community concept by creating their own blogs and Facebook/social networking site pages, and made these sites work to promote the brand and support it. For example, Adidas introduced the Your Area tab on its Facebook page. It allows its almost 2 million fans to view content from their local countries where they buy sneakers and other products. The page includes links to photos, videos, news, a store locator, and promotions, making it very interactive and engaging.
- Another interesting impact is that of communities together, with streaming capabilities, on the future of fashion shows. The late Alexander McQueen was a pioneer in bringing high fashion through live streaming to the Internet. The show, done in collaboration with SHOWstudio.com, was broadcasted with six video cameras operated by using motion-control technology that captured the models walking down the catwalk from various angles in order to deliver to the online viewer as close to a real-life watching experience as possible. With many others to follow such as Burberry, Marc Jacobs, Ralph Lauren, and Calvin Klein, each in their own way, many marketing professionals

are starting to question the future of traditional fashion shows as a marketing and communication platform, which may in return have its effect on traditional print advertising and editorial coverage that have always thrived on these shows. The role and look of future fashion shows will change as part of the changing marketing environment. Technology will democratize fashion shows as they target new and different groups of customers. As live technology expands the outreach of fashion shows, it also eliminates the elements of news and exclusive coverage, which other media such as magazines live on. It is just another example of how technology will reshuffle the roles and goals in the world of marketing, and the time may come when virtual fashion shows will totally replace traditional ones.

- In chapter 8, we will discuss in more detail how virtual environments alter the traditional communication model and place these social networks in a strategic position to play a direct role in forming, altering, and delivering the promotional message of the brand in collaboration with the company or on its behalf.

Growth Opportunities

- Similar to other technologies, VCs create new brand extension and global growth opportunities, especially for retail brands as they offer new e-commerce and marketing solutions that are supported and reinforced by the end user and in many cases created by him or her as well.
- VCs could also play an important role in global growth and brand globalization in general. The level of interactivity, information sharing, integration, and entertainment they deliver could easily diminish cultural and geographic

barriers, as well as create an engaging and inviting experience for many to share.

Technology Integration

One of the most fascinating things about all the previously mentioned technologies is the potential for **TECHNOLOGY INTEGRATION**—the possibility of integrating all of them to create a rich, interactive, entertaining, and personalized environment for the user. Everything is so interlinked on the Internet now that among Twitter, Facebook, MySpace, YouTube, and all the other social networking sites on the Web, you have many different vehicles to promote and get your brand and message out there.

For instance, IconNicholson Social Retailing® created (and trademarked) *social retailing*, a technology that integrates in-store shopping with online social networks in order to target young adult shoppers and respond to their new shopping habits. It is basically the technology behind the magic mirrors discussed earlier. With social retailing, interactive mirrors can send live video feed to any cell phone or e-mail account selected by a shopper.

The same feature will allow shoppers to check what may be available on the store's Web site that is not available in-store, with the option of making the purchase right there in the dressing room. Some other examples include:

- *Polyvore.com:* Polyvore is a fashion site that describes itself as a "fashion and social shopping platform that's redefining how people around the world experience, create and shop for fashion on the Internet."[14] It allows users to mix and match images of garments by simply dragging from any Web site online to the fashion sets they create on Polyvore.com. Users can use the images to create sets of outfits that demonstrate their personal style and that they can eventually purchase, promote, or share with friends. The sets are displayed on the site and can also be shared on blogs or social networking sites. (See Figures 7.18 and 7.19.) The site is easily integrated with users' Facebook profiles, for example, and users are able to use personal items they may have uploaded from their cell phones, such as to their Facebook pages and showcase them in their sets. Sets are displayed and shared by users and organized in groups based on themes, allowing people with common tastes to interact. In addition, Polyvore highlights new trends, news, contests, and style advice in a blog-style format. Brand producers and designers can also use the site to showcase their designs by setting up a feed with their products as well as to benefit from the exposure they get by the sets the users create. According to Polyvore, they have an estimated audience of over 3 million "trendsetters and tastemakers," as they call them, with 118 million page views per month. The average user is a 22-year-old female on the cutting edge of fashion. Polyvore's appeal lies in its ease of use, level of integration with other Web sites and social networks, as well as the community and social networking environment it creates for its users. This model demonstrates a workable level of integration between various platforms and models. It is e-commerce meets blogging meets social networking meets designers' showcase, all in one place.

- *Rivolta Shoes:* Rivolta Shoes is a good example of the integration between mass customization and M-branding. Rivolta produces and sells customized high-quality, tailor-made shoes by replacing the traditional method of tracing customers' feet on paper with a digital scanning device. The store personnel perform a 3D scan of the customer's feet to record their perfect shape. The customer is then able to customize all of the shoes parameters and try them on virtually in front of a special virtual mirror, all in real time. The company also has plans to create an iPhone application where customers can design and purchase their shoes anywhere they are. Being a luxury item, the shoes are quite expensive (close to $2,000), but the experience is also a good example of the new level of service luxury brands can offer in the new environment.

The Impact of Technology Integration on the Branding Experience

One of the biggest impacts of technology integration on the brand is in the way users can experience the brand. A platform of these technologies integrated together creates a richer, more engaging, and interactive environment like never before. Environments where customers can experience the brand, manipulate, evaluate, promote, and utilize it all within a mix of both real and virtual worlds. For example, the previously mentioned Secondlife.com is a demonstration of virtual environments where users move and interact with places and objects through the use of avatars (virtual characters). The prospects of these virtual environments have been the focus of many new studies that aim at integrating various technologies to create more interactive and seamless experiences that may eventually blur the lines between what is real and what is virtual. Advances in animation movement (think of the movie *Avatar*) will soon be brought to these applications, allowing online avatars to not only have a more real-life movement and look but be better integrated among applications. For example, users will eventually be able to move their avatars between virtual worlds so that a visitor to Second Life can walk into another virtual world carrying their possessions with them. It is really like going shopping in a virtual mall, moving from one location to the other while matching and comparing items. This level of seamless integration will open the door for new shopping habits and the ultimate goal of integrating real-life shopping with a virtual one. One of the greatest future developments anticipated in this area is the introduction of "virtual reality touch." A haptic technology (haptic is from the Greek haptesthai, meaning to touch; in technology it refers to the science of the sense of touch) is being tested at Queen's University, Ireland, that will bring the sense of touch to the virtual world. The field of haptic technology will allow a future where shoppers can feel the products they want to buy online. This technology is already being seen in some racquet-based sports games in Nintendo's Wii where players can feel the weight and impact of the ball. Thus, if we revisit our example of the Giorgio Armani store in Second Life, we can imagine a time when you can visit the virtual store, touch and feel the weight and texture of the garment,

carry it (virtually) to another location where you can check a matching accessory, try them all on your avatar, then maybe send a photo to your friends' cell phones to have their opinions before you make the final purchase online or send the info to your local store for you to pick up on your way home—all taking place without leaving your seat.

The Power of the "i"

The technology examples mentioned in this chapter may quickly be replaced by, or developed into, more advanced applications, as is always the case with technology. However, what these new technologies and examples have established are a few important trends that are here to stay, such as the rise of the consumer and user as the true marketer behind the brand. They also demonstrate how market segmentation can be taken to a more microlevel as a result of the need and ease of the personalization of the marketing message. Thus, market structures and segments, consumer habits and roles, and the dynamics of the branding process are all changing. The forces are shifting faster toward empowering the consumer. It's the power of the "i" and the birth of the iBrand.

Chapter Summary

- New technologies and models are empowering and redefining the role of the consumer in the branding process.

- As the role of the consumer changes, so do the dynamics of the branding process.

- New technologies also create new growth and communication opportunities.

- The concept of positioning may need to be revised under the new models.

- Technology integration creates a new environment of interactive shopping experience that may eventually blur the lines between our real and virtual worlds.

Chapter Questions and Issues for Discussion

1. Given the discussion on mass customization, the model seems to hold new opportunities for young entrepreneurs considered to establish a new business. Highlight the advantages and challenges of the model from an entrepreneurial perspective.

2. Compare the way luxury and mass-market brands adopted the new technologies. What are the opportunities and challenges that each segment may encounter?

3. Based on the chapter arguments and your personal analysis, how would you interpret the term *iBrand*?

KEY TERMS

IBRAND

MASS CUSTOMIZATION

M-BRANDING

RFID

TECHNOLOGY INTEGRATION

VIRTUAL COMMUNITIES

WIRELESS TECHNOLOGIES

CASE STUDY: Boo.com

"Unless we raise $20 million by midnight, boo.com is dead."
Ernst Malmsten, boo.com CEO, May 17, 2000

Boo.com was the brainchild of Swedish entrepreneurs Ernst Malmsten, founder of Bokus.com, a European online bookseller, and Kajsa Leander, a fashion model. (See Figure 7.20.) They were eventually joined by Patrik Hedelin, an investment banker at HSBC Holdings who had worked with Malmsten earlier on Bokus.com. Together the three founded Boo.com in 1999 with great anticipation, media fanfare, and the financial backing of some of the world's heaviest investors, such as LVMH and JPMorgan, only to pull the plug within six months of the launch.

The Concept

Boo.com was envisioned as the Amazon.com equivalent for fashion and sportswear, a world-leading e-tailer for prestigious brands such as DKNY, Polo Ralph Lauren, Nike, Fila, Lacoste, and Adidas. However, Boo was not just about the products sold, but the shopping experience, global reach, and new technologies. It was meant to be more than just a shopping Web site; it was supposed to represent *a lifestyle*.

The Product

Boo.com was to offer its mix of top and trendy fashion and sportswear products at full retail price in an engaging Web site offered in multiple languages. The site was to enable shoppers to view every product in full color and from various angels on three dimensional models, along with the ability to zoom in and rotate them to examine all details. Items could be searched by color, brand, price, style, and even sport. And with the goal of catering to a global clientele, the site featured a universal sizing system based on size variations among brands and countries. The site

also introduced Miss Boo, an animated avatar that interacted with visitors by giving styling advice based on specific activities or geographic location. One of the site's most appealing services was its quick delivery within one week, with free returns from any location through its 24-hour operating service center. To emphasize the lifestyle concept of Boo.com, they launched *Boom* magazine, which was available online in different languages and contained articles about movies, music, fashion, sports, and editorials, all of which reflected the urban lifestyle Boo.com aimed to represent.

The Customer

The Boo.com team did not really do much traditional market research at the early stages of their venture; instead they relied on the vague idea of who their customer might be and the pioneering proposal on hand. The team perceived their target customer to be between the ages of 24 and 40 and saw themselves as the perfect profile. However, in a meeting with Jerry Fiedler, chairman of Leagas Delaney Advertising Agency, Fielder advised them to focus on the 18-to-24-year-old customers. As he explained, this group includes the influential trendsetters in the market—younger customers like to dress like they are 18 and those above 30 who dress like they are 24. He also advised them to visit department stores to learn about their merchandise mix and the power of different brands: to compare which brands were showcased in their windows (mainly expensive and exclusive young designer clothes to gain fashion credibility and entice customers into the store) with those actually filling most racks (the more mainstream brands).

The Identity

Boo.com relied on three elements to create a sensory, exciting quality and modern identity for their brand. These were its name, Web design, and character Miss Boo.

The Site Design

The team spent a lot of time perfecting the aesthetics and visual appeal of the site. They created a modern hip design with a distinctive orange color and soft modern fonts dominating its look. As their only selling outlet, the site was the company's window to the world and therefore perceived by the team as a major marketing tool. However, many believed that so much emphasis on marketing appeal eventually hampered the functionality and practicality of the design.

The Name

The name is probably the most intriguing of all the site's attributes. Choosing the name was not an easy task: Their goal was to pick one that was easy to pronounce globally and would work well in various media. Toying with various options, such as "sneaky.com" among others, the team finally stopped at Bo.com. Bo was a name inspired by movie actress Bo Derek, famous for her role in the movie *10*, whom they perceived to portray a retro image. The name was appealing because it was short, easy to remember and pronounce, and meant nothing in particular. However, the domain Bo.com was already taken, so they decided to add another "o," ending up with Boo.com instead.

Miss Boo

Miss Boo was a virtual sales assistant meant to guide visitors through the site, offering advice, and creating a fun interactive experience. Miss Boo was an important identity component because she was the face of the company. Accordingly, the challenge of deciding on her looks and style was neither easy nor cheap. One of the most controversial decisions to make for

Figure 7.20

Boo.com founders Kajsa Leander and Ernst Malmsten.

(© Lars Tunbjork)

Miss Boo was the style and color of her hair. Miss Boo was meant to reflect the site's lifestyle and character while appealing to its international clientele without representing just one race or group. To assist in her styling, therefore, they hired international hair stylist Eugene Soulemain, known for his work with Hollywood stars and fashion houses like Prada. In addition, they hired Glenn O'Brian, a well-known New York style commentator, to make Miss Boo's statements cool and fun and, most important, possess an international appeal rather than one specifically European. For example, when asked "How old are you Miss Boo?" she offers the flip response, "None of your business, but I'm legal." And to the question, "What's your background?" she cleverly threw back, "For somebody two-dimensional, my background is remarkably deep."

Proposed Values

The new venture and business model seemed like a very attractive proposal with promising values and benefits for all its stakeholders, such as its customers, suppliers, and investors.

- *For customers:* Boo.com aimed to offer customers around the world a unique shopping experience. The goal was to be the first global retailer of sportswear and fashion on a customer friendly, cutting-edge site, with 24/7 worldwide access to an unlimited selection of brands that would otherwise be difficult to find in one place. This was to be backed with excellent customer service and a system of quick delivery with free returns.
- *For suppliers:* At a time when e-tailing was in its infancy, Boo.com offered suppliers global reach and an online outlet that was not meant to be a discount site.

- *For investors:* The team managed to secure the financial backing of some of the world's biggest investors, including LVMH from France, the Benetton family from Italy, investors from the Middle East, and financial institutions such as JPMorgan, among others. At a time when everything related to the Internet was attractive, and big investment decisions were being made based on potential rather than accurate and detailed financial analysis and projections, Boo.com was particularly attractive for its aggressive vision, innovative technology, global reach, and growth potential, especially because most online businesses back then were mainly national operations. After all, "e-commerce was supposed to be global," declared a JPMorgan executive. Accordingly, the company was attractive enough to secure $130 million in investments and at one point was valued at $390 million.

Communication

"...the biggest, boldest bet in the short history of electronic shopping."
— Herald Tribune

The team believed that with their business model and an aggressive promotional strategy the company would create what they called its "big bang" rate of growth, achieving an estimated customer base of 500,000 by the end of their first year. They focused on a PR strategy that gained coverage in influential consumer and trade publications, such as *WWD* and the *Financial Times*. And with an estimated $25 million dedicated to advertisements in expensive, trendy fashion magazines such as *Vogue* and *Vanity Fair*, as well as on cable television and the Internet before their Web site had been launched, they managed to attract about 350,000 e-mail preregistrations from people who wanted to be notified of the site's launch date. Boo.com was greatly anticipated and perceived by many as the biggest new thing on the Internet.

The Challenges

Initially, Boo.com was meant to launch in May 1999 with an IPO to follow in six to nine months. However, in spite of all the excitement, Boo was hit by a wave of challenges both at the business model level as well as at the technical, operational, and financial ones, forcing it to postpone the launch date more than once.

Some of these challenges can be summarized as follows:

- Inventory management was challenging, because the model Malmsten had adopted earlier with Bokus.com—in which it purchased items only after they were sold online rather than carrying any inventory in advance—could not work for Boo.com. Most suppliers would not agree to sell their items on an order-to-order basis because this would have required that they always keep these items available in their warehouses. Given the seasonal nature of the fashion product, this system would never have worked. Suppliers prefer advance orders that allow them to manage their inventory accordingly rather than fill their warehouses with old seasons' merchandise.
- Another hurdle with merchandise was that some suppliers such as New Balance did not respond favorably to their initial partnership proposal because they already had an international presence or representation with other partners.

- In order to overcome the anticipated reluctance of online customers to purchase fashion products they hadn't tried on or touched first, Boo.com decided to offer customers free returns from any location. For an international operation with an operational network in various countries, this meant they had to be prepared to cope with a very high level of returns because customers in these cases tend to order different items in different sizes and colors to try them on before making their final decision (which is also a common problem with the catalogue industry).
- Postage paid, free return policy also meant dealing with different mailing systems and costs, which seemed a bit complicated, especially on the European side.

Here is how it worked: All European orders were packed from the warehouse in Cologne, Germany. When a French customer placed an order, French postal service La Poste labels would be put on the box so that it appeared as if it were shipped directly from France. Meanwhile, the package would be transferred with other items from Cologne to a location in France, where it was then sent through regular French mail. In the case of returns, the item was to be sent to a given French address where all returned items were collected and sent back to the warehouse in Germany. This unique approach meant that every sale was, in a way, taxed three times because the company's headquarters and servers were in London with operating offices in France and its distribution center in Germany.
- Some experts questioned the viability of their concept, selling both fashion and sportswear items in one place. To them it was not clear if Boo.com was to be positioned as a fashion

company or a sports one. And when the reply was "both," they believed it would never work, given that each industry approaches its market differently. For instance, the sports goods market is known to be particularly specific and focused in its marketing and distribution channels.

- With the large amount of product to sell came the huge task of developing a database that would accommodate around 50 pieces of descriptive information referring to the size, color, and price of each product in more than one language and currency.
- The biggest challenge of all was technology. Although some of the proposed technological applications may seem common and easy to adopt today, in 1999 they created a series of bottlenecks and headaches:
  — For most existing e-tailers at the time, such as Amazon.com, the technology platform was built in-house as they started small and then gradually grew. Yet in the case of a global operation such as Boo.com, it had no choice but to rely on another party to develop the needed infrastructure that would accommodate a multilingual version of the site with a ballooning database to cover different price, tax, and postal options based on each country.
  — As Boo.com's Web site was the only selling outlet for the company, it needed to be attractive, sophisticated, with plans to heavily use 3D, animation, Flash applications, java scripts, photos, and a range of frills. Yet back in 1999, many of these byte-hungry technologies were in their infancy, and most Internet users still connected through dial-up with a maximum speed of

54k. A reporter expressed the frustrating experience in his own words: " . . . 81 minutes to pay too much money for a pair of shoes that I'm still going to have to wait a week to get." Even the constant presence of Miss Boo seemed to be an annoying feature to some. (See Figure 7.21.)

- Another major access problem and technical embarrassment that haunted the system was the inability of Mac computers' users to complete their orders.
- The project management was a nightmare, given that at one point they were dealing with about 18 different technology companies from all over the world with no central architect. The result was an unavoidable range of system bugs and glitches.
- The huge database was not well managed nor synchronized, leading to product mismatches and confusion that eventually meant customers would not be able to buy the right product or obtain the right information.

The End of Boo.com

With many technical issues and frustrations, Malmsten launched PROJECT LAUNCH, an operational plan meant to tackle seven main areas: bug fixing, business testing, technology operations, merchandising operations, order fulfillment, customer operations, and operational resourcing.

Among the measures taken was delaying the launch date, which also meant cancelling many of the planned marketing events and ads. However, the greatest challenge was raising about $60 million to finance the three-month delay. The plan yielded some positive results. When the site finally

Figure 7.21

Boo.com's virtual
sales assistant
Miss Boo was
an important
element of the
site's identity.
Here she entices
potential
customers to
get involved by
taking a quiz
that "she" has
created and
potentially win
$1,000 worth
spending money
on the site.

(Boo.com)

launched on November 3, 1999, it hosted around 50,000 visitors on the first day. However, they had only a 0.25% conversion rate, meaning only 4 in every 1,000 visitors placed an order. The low conversion was partly due to the still-existing technical difficulties and confusion in placing orders. The site was buggy, even causing some visitors' computers to freeze, and about 40 percent of the visitors could not even gain access.

Although the company managed to work on and solve many of these glitches, as well as more than double the conversion rate to 0.98 percent before Christmas, the negative publicity buildup was inevitable. The high costs and excess spending did not help either. Boo.com spent lavishly, had a presence in more than 18 countries, and for a company that employed over 350 people when it started with 30, Boo was overstaffed with overpaid employees scattered in its international offices. Accordingly, in its first 18 months, the company had managed to spend $135 million of investors' money.

Sales were lagging badly and the company running out of cash. Their ad agency BMP filed claims and UPS refused to distribute unless paid in full. Boo.com began selling clothing at a 40 percent discount and laying off employees as well as cancelling Kajsa's baby project, *Boom* magazine.

In a final attempt to salvage the business, Malmsten considered making available to outside companies the spare capacity of Boo.com's technological and logistic platform capable of handling a growing number of orders and shipments in Europe and the United States within five days. The new restructuring plan required an urgent injection of cash, and the new funding target was $20 million to be raised by midnight, May 17. Yet by that deadline, the company had only managed to raise $12 million, which was not enough. Addressing the board members in a phone conference, Christopher Heather, Boo.com's legal council, warned, "I hope everyone understands what this means: if you don't put up more money, the company will go bust." The long silence that followed said it all. The same day, Malmsten hired a liquidating firm. On May 18, the Web site was shut down. The headline in the *Financial Times* article read, "Boo.com collapses as investors refuse funds." The article then declared, "Online sports retailer becomes Europe's first big internet casualty." Boo.com was closed.

CASE STUDY Questions

1. Compare Boo.com to an existing e-tailer (such as Zappos.com) and evaluate their differences and similarities.

2. Using the concepts learned thus far in this book, create a brand profile for Boo.com, highlighting its concept, value, identity, and so on. From a branding perspective, why did it fail?

SOURCES

Chaffey, Dave, and Fiona Ellis-Chadwick, et al. *Internet marketing: Strategy, implementations and practice.* Harlow: Pearson Education Limited, 2009.

Lanxon, Nate. "The greatest defunct Web sites and dotcom disasters," Crave: The Gadget Blog from CNET UK, January 5, 2008. http://crave.cnet.co.uk/gadgets/0,39029552,49296926-3,00.htm (accessed April 5, 2010).

Louis, Tristan. "Boo.com goes bust," tnl.net, May 19, 2000. http://www.tnl.net/blog/2000/05/19/boocom-goes-bust/ (accessed March 24, 2010).

Malmsten, Ernst, and Erik Portanger, et al., *Boo hoo*. London: Random House, 2001.

Slatalla, Michelle. "Boo.com tries again, humbled and retooled." *New York Times*, January 11, 2001. http://www.nytimes.com/2001/01/11/technology/online-shopper-boocom-tries-again-humbled-and-retooled.html?pagewanted=1 (accessed April 2, 2010).

Sorkin, Andrew Ross. "From big idea to big bust: The wild ride of Boo.com." *New York Times*, December 13, 2000. http://www.nytimes.com/2000/12/13/business/from-big-idea-to-big-bust-the-wild-ride-of-boocom.html?pagewanted=1 (accessed June 27, 2009).

ENDNOTES

1. Henry Ford, *My Life and Work* (Whitefish, Montana: Kessinger Publishing, 2003), chapter iv.

2. Marina Kamenev, "Adidas' High Tech Footwear," *BusinessWeek*, November 2006. http://www.businessweek.com/innovate/content/nov2006/id20061103_196323.htm

3. www.louisvuitton.com

4. Alicia De Mesa, *Brand Avatar* (London: Palgrave, 2009), 33.

5. www.istorez.com

6. F. Piller, K. Moeslein, and C. Stoko, "Does Mass Customization Pay? An Economic Approach to Evaluate Customer Integration," *Production Planning & Control*, 15, no. 4 (June 2004): 435–444.

7. Rick Mathieson, *Branding Unbound* (New York: AMACOM, 2005), 147.

8. Ibid.

9. Jason Jobson, "Fashion Apps: The New Wave of Mobile Fashion PR," The Fashion Rag (March 12, 2009). http://www.piercemattiepublicrelations.com/fashionprdivision/2009/03/fashion_apps_the_new_wave_of_m.html

10. Product Overview, LRAD Corporation. http://www.lradx.com/site/content/view/13/104/

11. Tomi Ahonen and Alan Moore, *Communities Dominate Brands* (London: Futuretest, 2005), 101.

12. *PC Today*, November 2010, 9.

13. Ross Tucker. "Memo Pad: First In Line,." *WWD*, April 22, 2010, 15.

14. http://www.polyvore.com

8

Redesigning the Brand

In this chapter, we will examine the effects of the new environment created by technologies and innovations discussed in chapter 7 on the brand concept and branding process. In previous chapters, we formulated a definition that captured the essence and purpose of the brand as we traditionally knew it—a brand is an entity with a distinctive idea expressed in a set of functional and experiential features, with a promise of a value reward relevant to its end user and an economic return to its producers (through the building of equity). A successful brand has a strong identity (mentally and physically), is innovative, consistent, competitively positioned, and holds a matching positive image in the consumer's mind.

We also established that the three major players or co-authors for the brand are the culture, customer (or user), and company, so that we have a simple equation:

Culture + Company + Consumer = Brand

- *Culture:* Culture dictates new social trends, beliefs, and behaviors. It defines what is "cool" and acceptable by various age groups and market segments.
- *Company:* The company is the producer of the brand and the one that bears the ultimate financial and marketing risks as well as the creative, production, and logistic responsibilities of developing the brand.
- *Customer:* Brand customers experience the brand, consume its products, and, therefore, play an important role in the life of the

- Explore the implications of new technologies and models discussed in chapter 7, such as mass customization, on the nature and definition of the brand.

- Examine how technology relates to the 3Cs that co-author the brand.

- Learn the concept of micro or satellite brands.

- Explore the new role of positioning under the new environment.

- Explore the importance of experiential branding under the new models.

- Emphasize the need to redefine the brand.

263

brand. For starters, a brand is developed with the end users in mind and with the goal of satisfying their unfulfilled needs. In addition, the users are the ultimate judges of the brand, and it is they who decide the brand's true and final positioning, based on their experiences with it, among other factors.

In addition to these points, we have examined in the previous chapter a few new technologies and innovations, such as mass customization, social networks, and wireless technologies. We've established that these technologies have a direct influence on the roles each of the co-authors play in the branding process. The increase in the level of consumer **EMPOWERMENT** is a consistent and important outcome, as we have seen. We have also noticed how the adoption of a new model, such as mass customization, demonstrates an interesting and significant paradigm shift in the way and level by which companies manage their brands and interact with the final user.

However, the two critical questions remain: How do these innovations and technologies affect the brand concept? And do we need to re-examine the branding process as a result? To answer these questions, we need to take a closer look at the impact of these forces on the brand elements we have just highlighted.

The Impact of New Technologies and Models

It is essential that we examine the impact of these new technologies, discussed in the previous chapter, on the brand concept by exploring how they affect each of the three major influences and authors of the brand: the 3Cs (company, customer, culture). The way technologies affect and reshape these three influences and brand sources will result in reshaping the brand itself and the way we experience it.

Culture and Technology

The relationship between culture and technology is clear and easy to detect. Cultures are dynamic, ever evolving and adapting. **TECHNOLOGY** plays a direct role in redefining habits and values, and thus reshaping cultures. So if technologies impact our lives, behaviors, and social habits, then brands that adopt and introduce these technologies have an equal impact as well. Think of how Microsoft, Apple, or DuPont have changed our lives in many aspects with their innovations and products. The new technologies and solutions discussed in chapter 7 have clearly created a new environment of technological accessibility that has redefined how we interact with each other and with our products. Indeed, the Internet and other recent innovations have altered our social habits and behaviors and created new levels of social communities and human relations. Consumers who used to be highly passive and mainly located at the receiving end of the branding equation are now given the tools, platforms, and choices to become more active in the decision-making process. In short, the new environment has simply redefined the roles of the players in the branding game.

As a result, businesses are facing a new reality and culture of consumer empowerment, whereby instead of dictating and sometimes manipulating, companies have to negotiate, respond, and share with consumers and outsiders what they have been fiercely protecting for years. This includes the creative elements of their brands. And for the fashion industry, it is a major challenge indeed. However, the timing seems to be right for both sides. Consumers, on one hand, in an age of self-consciousness and independence (noticeably among women), are looking for better options to express and satisfy their needs and get what they *really* want. Producers, on the other hand, need to stay competitive, different, and relevant to their customers. Brands are getting too similar, and competing on the basis of product features alone, as we mentioned, is a short-term strategy because features are easily and quickly copied. Thus, the need for new alternatives and solutions is both necessary and inevitable. Equally inevitable and significant is the implication of such changes on old-school marketing strategies and principles, which may be deemed irrelevant and outdated, and therefore in need of being revisited, reexamined, and probably redefined, as we will soon discover.

Customer and Technology

As mentioned earlier, the customer or user has always played an integral role in the branding process. The user is the drive and inspiration behind the brand, and it is the user who eventually decides on the brand's positioning through the image he or she creates for it. However, by examining these roles, you will notice that the customers' direct presence is at the early stages, before the brand is born through market research measures, as well as at the end of the process, after the brand is developed, marketed, and its products sold and used by them. Thus, the customer is mainly absent from the process between these two ends. However, what new applications

and technologies, such as mass customization, have done is reposition the users in the center of the process and transform them into true and active co-developers. In addition, other innovations such as social networks and blogging have allowed customers to play an even more direct role in marketing the brand themselves. Their role in the brand marketing process is not just to offer a positioning verdict but to directly influence the marketing process itself and determine its positioning path. The idea of users taking over the marketing process has led to the introduction of a marketing concept known as *brand hijacking*.

Brand Hijacking

The term **BRAND HIJACKING** is used in two references that are similar at their core. It refers to a situation where a brand is meant to target a specific market segment and user group but gets picked up and popularized by a different one. One example is army-attire-inspired fashion, like cargo pants, which were popularized and made fashionable by the youth segment. (See Figure 8.1a.) Other examples are the Hummer SUV, or even scooters, which were initially marketed with women in mind but became a cultural icon for a whole generation in the sixties, especially in Europe. (See Figure 8.1b.)

Brand hijacking also (and most commonly) refers to consumers taking over the marketing and promotion of the brand and its products through various forms of viral marketing, as witnessed in blogs and other social networks such as Facebook and YouTube. Think of how file sharing software such as Kazaa and Napster were so popular, gaining an enormous following without any major marketing activities from their

(a) Commonly used by the military for their rugged properties like hard-working fabrics and multiple pockets, cargo pants were adopted as a fashion trend in an example of brand hijacking. (© Deborah Feingold/ Corbis)

(b) Another military example, the Hummer, was also "hijacked" by the general public as a popular vehicle. (© Transtock/Corbis)

creators. It was the enthusiastic online community of users, through word of mouth, developing free plugins and skins (the visual appearance of any software application such as the color and design of your Winamp player, Windows Explorer browser, and so on) to enhance the program's usability and appeal that created a marketing success story without relying on traditional methods of campaigning or advertising. And think of the many personal video clips made popular worldwide through YouTube and social networks. Brand hijacking through viral marketing or communication is a major development and indeed a true challenge for companies to come to terms with. Although we are starting to witness an increasing level of acceptance, companies had (and many still have) a hard time letting go, allowing customers to take over and market the brand themselves—and to view that as an opportunity rather than a threat. To do this, companies and managers need to dismantle old mental models of business and marketing practices and adapt to the new environment. The classic notion of being in control of every marketing aspect is quickly becoming outdated and irrelevant. Just think about the music industry and how it reacted to music downloads and peer-to-peer applications (such as Napster). Instead of adapting to the new reality and designing a new model that would embrace it, they decided to fight it to protect the old business ways they knew. The results were disastrous: decline in sales, user outrage, and the emergence of more and newer ways of sharing and downloading music. It took an innovative brand like Apple to introduce a new model in the form of iTunes, which offered an acceptable and realistic alternative, acknowledging

a

b

the users' needs and demands for choices and control. The concept of brand hijacking can be viewed as a form of open source marketing (as in open source software) whereby users contribute to the development of the product (in this case, the marketing strategy). Marketing consultant James Cherkoff referred to an interesting example from 2005 when an advertising video created by an outsider for Volkswagen's Polo car was posted online. The ad was shocking, well made, and ended being viewed by millions of people. Yet Volkswagen's reaction was to demand a public apology and call the lawyers, a course of action straight from the old school. In fact, it demanded back the source material from the makers of the ad.[1]

Tim Gaskin is a San Francisco-based pop artist who is famous for painting images of celebrities juxtaposed with logos and symbols of brands to which they've been linked. In 2005, he hand-painted a wall mural for The Hotel des Arts in San Francisco, known for showcasing the original fine art of emerging artists from around the world. The hotel's painted rooms are world-famous exhibitions that receive international acclaim and respect. Gaskin's painting was a pop art project with Madonna's profile superimposed over a background of the Louis Vuitton logo. (See Figure 8.2.) The work was highly admired and received a good amount of press coverage. Yet Louis Vuitton's reaction to the project was a warning from its anticounterfeiting director demanding that the hotel remove the mural and threatening legal action against the artist, accusing him of "trademark infringement and dilution." (The hotel stood by its mural and supported the artist's right for free artistic expression.)

Figure 8.2

Pop-artist Tim Gaskin's mural of Madonna's profile super-imposed over a background of the Louis Vuitton logo at the Hotel des Arts in San Francisco. Despite general acclaim, the piece was attacked by Louis Vuitton, who demanded its removal.

(© Susan Seubert)

The reactions of both Volkswagen and Louis Vuitton raise a very simple yet important question: Why did these companies react this way? It is understandable that a company needs to protect its logo and trademark from dilution, misuse, and counterfeit activities, but are these two examples in any way comparable to counterfeiting? In the case of Louis Vuitton, what harm did Louis Vuitton encounter when its logo has been used by a celebrated artist in a one-of-a-kind painting? (Its prototype was valued by the artist at $5,000.) What harm would Louis Vuitton have encountered if it had embraced and celebrated the artwork, perceived it as an acknowledgment to its status and brand power, and viewed the work as a priceless act of publicity? How is this different from product placement in movies and video clips, which brands have to pay for? The major difference is control: the fact that these companies did not have control over the process as they are used to having. Although this paranoia of losing full control has some good reasoning behind it, it simply will not survive in the new environment of the *iBrand*. Companies and brands must dismantle their old mental models, open up and share resources with users, redefine their marketing strategies, and reevaluate them in order to compete. Of course, this does not mean giving in to any misuse of the brand's identity that would damage its image, heritage, and status. It simply means understanding that today users both can and will be a part of the marketing process. Companies need to see this as a tremendous opportunity, where their brands' users have a direct stake in the brand—rather than perceive it as a threat. It can be a recipe for great customer satisfaction and loyalty. As we've already mentioned, a few companies are beginning to understand and appreciate this trend, as demonstrated by their quicker adoption of new innovations seen in chapter 7; however, they still have a long way to go in treating these new channels not just as mere advertising extensions of traditional channels but as interactive platforms where they can share ideas and converse with their customers. It will definitely be more challenging in the fashion industry (especially the luxury segment), which has historically thrived on secrecy, egoism, and creative dictatorship. Will it eventually manage to survive in an environment of brand democracy? Can an industry that created the *super designer* and the *super model* embrace the rise of the **SUPER CONSUMER**? Most important, does it, and many other industries, really have a choice?

The Company and Technology

We have established that there is a need for companies to dismantle old mindsets and business models in order to survive and compete in the twenty-first century. And we have seen a shift in the customer/user's role in the branding process, which in return means a change in the branding process of the company as well. The new role of companies will become clearer as we get a closer look at how these technologies affect the most precious asset the company has: the brand.

The Brand and Technology

Based on what have discussed already, how would a technology such as mass customization affect the brand? We already understand that a brand has, in its core, a product with one or more distinctive functional features that posses a strong identity and deliver a value to the user.

We have also seen that mass customization allows each user to alter many of the products by manipulating and changing its features. However, manipulating and changing products' features do not in themselves alter the brand; otherwise, every product update would mean creating a new brand. Yet they do impact the brand in the form of creating new brand extensions, or rather a series of microbrands. Think of microbrands as a group of satellite brands that are variations of the mother brand.

Microbrands

By definition, a mass-customized brand (MC brand) is a brand where every consumer decides on the distinctive feature of his or her customized item. On the other hand, an open innovation environment refers to an environment of community sourcing, whereby every new input element might add to or tweak an existing distinctive feature. In both cases, the end result is a variety of distinctive features and variations of the "mother brand." This variety of features ends up creating what we may call a series of "micro" (or satellite) brands, where a **MICROBRAND** is a limited yet distinct version of the original (or mother) brand.

It is important to remind ourselves that mass customization is a middle-of-the-road option between cookie-cutter mass production and total bespoke, made-to measure, one-of-a-kind products. There is still a level of commonality and control, which makes it necessary to link these brands to the mother brand and create a common base and identity that links these satellite brands together. It is a confirmation that they are still the

same family of siblings, but simply not the twins they used to be. This is why mass customization is usually done at the product level but not at the identity level, which needs to remain intact as the umbrella or backbone that defines the mother brand and maintains the brand personality and ultimately its core value.

Accordingly we can say that satellite microbrands are a set of sub-brands with a common unifying identity and feature base, yet with a score of distinctive features customized and defined by the end user; these customized features create a unique experience with an equally high level of satisfaction among users and ultimately a higher level of loyalty to the mother brand. Microbrands are harder to predict because they are actually created and shaped by the user.

We have described microbrands as a form of brand extensions, yet there is a difference between brand extensions and microbrands. Brand extensions are about creating new and totally different products under the same brand, but here the newly created products share a commonality of purpose; for example, my customized Adidas running shoes as well as yours are still running shoes, your customized Levis jeans are still jeans, and so is every mass-customized product, but each in its own way. They are simply variations on a theme. Thus the key issue is that these changes, whereas they may alter the product features and enhance its functionality, should not alter the brand meaning and value. If you and I can create our own Adidas running shoes, we will get different shoes but not necessarily a different experience or brand value; on the contrary, we should have a closer level of experiential satisfaction. This is referred to as experiential branding.

Experiential Branding

In earlier chapters, we mentioned that what branding really does is create an experience; while products are consumed, brands are actually experienced. Thus, we can conclude that the goal of any brand and its marketing strategies is to "deliver the elements that would trigger these experiences. The belief is that the same set of experience components delivered to a group of people who share similar sensory perceptions, emotional drivers, personal histories, and living environments will trigger effectively similar experiences in each one of these people."[2] This is referred to in marketing as *experiential segmentation* and *experiential branding*. **EXPERIENTIAL BRANDING** is "the discipline of understanding and defining brands in terms of the way they are experienced, in order to differentiate them in the most powerful dimension: relevance (nothing is more relevant than an experience)."[3]

In reality, this seems hard to achieve, not just because each user is subject to different external factors (or noise) but because the products (which are traditionally a constant) are subject to different users' perceptions (a variable); thus, while you and I may be buying the same exact product, we most likely will have different experiences. However, if we refer again to our customized Adidas running shoes that are attainable because of new technologies, we have a situation where the product and its features are not identical anymore, and the product is no longer a constant. Yet, most likely, each of the users is getting an almost equal level of emotional satisfaction. Thus, although the branded product would be defined differently by each user, it would satisfy all users in a closer way.

Experiences are generally measured by the level of satisfaction, and in this case the users' experiences generate closer levels of satisfaction than could have been achieved before, when the same product was meant to satisfy different people under different perceptions.

It is important to remember that although mass customization alters the products features and thus functionality, these alterations caused to the features are never meant to be big enough to shift the product into a different category (running shoes fail to function as such and accordingly move into a different category); to achieve this, customization has to be handled with a certain level of control and limitations, which is exactly what mass customization is all about. Therefore, the emotional reward and satisfaction would outweigh the discrepancy in functionality and features and manage to generate an equally satisfying experience for all users.

So now that we have an understanding of how mass customization relates to the brand, we can conclude by saying that technologies such as mass customization do not necessarily create a new brand out of an old one but rather extend it into microvariations that may look and function slightly different yet deliver a better and rather consistent experience to all users.

Positioning

So how does all this affect the concept of positioning, which we have determined to be an essential concept to branding? It seems that under the new environment, the few elements the company can fully control are the initial features, or the product base, along with the identity, tools, and options it allows the users to customize. Thus, the role of the company is really shifting more toward being a service provider or a facilitator. And just as the major focus of all service providers is the users' experience, positioning based on experience and the emotional value of the brand becomes essential and paramount. The concepts of product positioning and brand image may seem irrelevant for the most part because they are predetermined and established by the user before the product is even fully developed and consumed. Therefore, as a product, the brand is inherently positioned or prepositioned by the ultimate user, which as we mentioned in chapter 7, should be a marketer's dream come true because the end product is predetermined, predesigned, and predemanded by the end user. This might hypothetically mean that the producer is making a product that is presold.

To some people, this idea of a brand with a score of distinctive features rather than one or a few common distinctive features might seem like a contradiction to what a brand is all about. Yet in reality, the idea of having just one key benefit is neither a reflection of how products are invented nor really a reflection of how people choose, buy, and appreciate them. It is mainly a requirement of a certain type of hard-sell advertising.[4] This has been the way things worked in a mass-produced environment in order to differentiate among similar products, which is obviously irrelevant in the new model. As a result, marketing and advertising strategies need to change in a way that is more responsive and accommodating to the new environment and the nature of the newly created satellite brands. Under MC, a brand is inherently

differentiated, and the sum of distinctive features created by the series of satellite brands does not qualify for the current mass-produced, hard-sell advertising strategies and marketing campaigns. There is a need for a more direct, personal, and focused approach to communication and marketing messaging, which some of the new alternatives discussed in chapter 7 seem to support.

Image

An image is best defined as how customers envision the product. Under MC, an image would seem to be more strongly derived from the level of innovation and flexibility of the customer's interactive experience than from its distinctive features. Features are still relevant, of course, but the level of integration, flexibility, and innovation of the platform will be of a higher relevance simply because features, being an element of design, are now under the users' control and for the most part determined by the user himself. So what the customer/user is really looking for is a suitable and innovative environment that will make the experience and process simpler and more effective. Is it easy to manipulate the product? Does the platform or software offer necessary tools for manipulation? Does the system crash? Does the system offer a responsive and effective feedback mechanism? And so on. As we mentioned earlier in this chapter, the positioning proposal will be highly experience-focused and, accordingly, such issues will be key elements in defining the branding experience and eventually determining the image. Thus, we can say that

Figure 8.3

The classic

communication

model.

(Illustration by

Andrea Lau)

COMMUNICATION MODEL

whenever the customer's intervention is high, the image tends to be more innovation-dependant (experiential-positioning focused), whereas it is more features-driven (product-positioning focused) when the customer's intervention is minimal. This will be clearly evident in the case of brands that possess some kind of a monopoly or "secret" formula, as in the case of pharmaceutical products (such as a secret anti-aging formula) or the case of Coca-Cola. These brands will be less susceptible to the customization of their monopoly feature, which in return will remain the core of the branding experience (and positioning strategy). The Coke taste or the secret beauty formula will remain an attractive feature as long as it is out of reach and cannot be manipulated. If consumers are ever allowed to manipulate them, what would be attractive to consumers are tools and platforms available for them to alter and manipulate the product.

On the other hand, from an innovation per-spective, what mass customization and open

innovation among other technologies create is a state of continuous innovation and development, a situation that is too hard and too costly to imi-tate otherwise. Once again, if the product core is continuously innovated (as in open innovation) or augmented (as in mass customization) by the help of the user, the company will focus many of its resources on the innovation of its platform (which can also be open sourced at certain levels) and on its role as a process, a service provider, and facilitator. This does not necessarily mean that the company is totally abdicating its full responsibilities in the development process, but it is surely sharing many of them.

The Relationship Redefined

The most dramatic implication of these changes remains the redefinition of the relationship between the producer and the customer, as well as the role of each in this new relationship. The new relationship is that of a partnership. This partnership changes the dynamics of brand development because the role of the producer shifts from a product maker to mainly a service provider, as we just mentioned. Within this framework, the *promise* of consistency is an element of service, *image* is a function of technical innovation, and the *relationship* is that of sharing rather than dictating. This, by all measures, is a major paradigm shift. This shift in roles necessitates a new level of communication based on a two-way dialogue and interactive conversation. Accordingly, the old-school marketing model of communication seen in Figure 8.3 may need to be revisited.

According to this model, communication is, for the most part, one directional, and the customer/user is rather passive. However, we've seen that in an environment of mass customization and the Internet's social networks and communities, the marketing message is not only received, but altered, reset, and resent by the users. The fact that users listen to fellow bloggers and social network partners and turn to them for advice, reviews, and feedback more than they would listen to companies or "official" experts demonstrates a new level of message filtering that did not exist before and that ultimately reshapes the message itself. Experts Tomi Ahonen and Alan Moore have proposed a new communication model depicted in Figure 8.4 that seems to suit our argument very well.

In the revised model, virtual communications

Figure 8.4

The revised communication model as depicted by T. Ahonen and A. Moore in *Communities Dominate Brands.* London: Futuretext Limited: 2005.

(Illustration by Andrea Lau)

REVISED COMMUNICATION MODEL

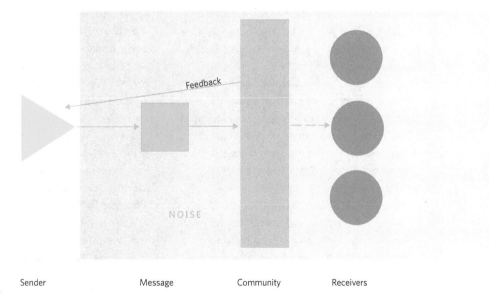

Feedback

NOISE

Sender   Message   Community   Receivers

act as a message filtering channel, where the receivers within the community who share common interests and mutual trust evaluate the message and either approve, amend, or replace it. They give feedback to the sender (the company) at an early stage and in a continuous (bi-directional) manner through various means such as chats, blog, entries, and so on. The users communicate with each other and with the sender (the company) for questions, clarifications, or recommendations. Before we know it, the message is redesigned and enhanced by the users on behalf of the brand and shared and looped by all interested parties.

Redesigning the Brand?

Based on what we have discussed, it seems inevitable that we consider revisiting the brand definition under the new environment to interpret these new relationships and influences. One interpretation that would focus on the effect of mass customization as a new and rising trend is: A brand in a mass-customized environment is an experiential proposal manifested in unique product variations within a web of satellite micro-brands created through a partnership between the manufacturer and the users, whereby the manufacturer establishes a brand identity, product base, and the platform and technology necessary for the user to co-design and define the desired variations. A mass-customized brand is inherently competitive, innovative, and pre-positioned with the goal of an economic return to its producer and a higher level of emotional and experiential value to its end user.

By comparing this to our initial definition, we have a couple of important observations:

- Although the nature and structure of the brand may differ under the new model, its goal for financial return and generation of value remains the same.
- The role branding plays in minimizing our purchase risks would seem to decline with the increase of user input. This may impose a few threats as the customer gets more confident and ready to switch and try other alternatives. That may indicate a lower propensity to brand loyalty, but it really means that brands need to work harder and use innovative tools to maintain the customer. Keeping up with technological advances that facilitate the customization process and offering more and easier options can be one way to do this. Loyalty remains all about service.
- Our initial definition implies that effective positioning is only achieved by some brands, especially the successful ones; under the new model, however, every satellite brand is inherently pre-positioned, most importantly by the end user himself. On the other hand, the mother brand is positioned on the basis of experiential and emotional grounds more than on a product one.
- Many of the signs attributed to successful brands in the first definition, such as innovation, consistency, and positive image, are inherent in the new satellite brands and are most often influenced by the end user himself, which can lead to a higher (and probably unprecedented) level of satisfaction.
- Finally, under the new model, the brand is in a continuous state of innovation that is, for the most part, relevant and with less financial burdens.

Thus it is safe to say that new technologies and models can actually strengthen the brand, improve its image, and increase customer loyalty. On the other hand, they impose new principles for communicating and interacting with the customer, a stronger focus on experiential value, redefinition of the concepts of positioning, consistency, and distinctiveness, and above all redefining the relationship between the brand, the company, and the end user.

This attempt to understand the impact of these new technologies on the brand and to redefine it accordingly should not by any means be seen as the ultimate "new" definition of the brand; it should instead be seen as a wake-up call and an invitation to examine the new meaning and role of the brand in the twenty-first century.

KEY TERMS

BRAND HIJACKING

EMPOWERMENT

EXPERIENTIAL BRANDING

MICROBRANDS

SUPER CONSUMER

TECHNOLOGY

Chapter Summary

- The definition of the brand may need to be revisited as a result of new models such as mass customization.

- Positioning may be deemed irrelevant under mass customization.

- The new models lead to the creation of a series of microbrands that are variations of the main (or mother) brand.

- Experiential branding is of extreme relevance in the new environments.

- The most significant impact of new technologies is the way they redefine the relationship between the brand and end user, and how they empower this user.

Chapter Questions and Issues for Discussion

1. How does technology redefine the role of the end user in the branding process?

2. How does the concept of experiential branding relate to the branding process as described in part 1?

3. How do microbrands compare to corporate brands and brand extensions?

ENDNOTES

1. James Cherkoff, "What is Open Source Marketing?" WebProNews, February 4. 2005. http://www.webpronews.com/topnews/2005/02/04/what-is-open-source-marketing

2. Laurence Bernstein, "Experiential Branding and the Consumer Experience Myth," Canadian Marketing Blog, April 15, 2009. http://www.canadianmarketingblog.com/archives/2009/04/experiential_branding_and_the_1.html

3. ibid

4. John Grant, *The Brand Innovation Manifesto* (West Sussex, UK: John Wiley & Sons, 2006), 16.

Glossary

ATMOSPHERE: The physical appearance and feel of a store, defined by its layout, interior design, music, smell, and lighting. (Ch. 6)

BRAND: An entity with a distinctive idea expressed in a set of functional and experiential features with a promise of a value reward relevant to its end user, and an economic return to its producers (through the building of equity). A successful brand has a strong identity (mentally and physically), is innovative, consistent, competitively positioned, and holds a matching positive image in the consumer's mind. (Ch. 1)

BRAND AUDIT: The stage where the organization assesses the brand's performance and measures customers' reactions. The evaluation of a brand's performance uses quantitative and qualitative data such as sales records, customer feedback, turnover, sales per square foot, complaints, returns rates, publicity, and so on. (Ch. 3)

BRAND EXTENSION: A means of expansion through increasing the range and type of product lines under the brand's umbrella. Brand extensions are not to be confused with line extensions: where brand extension refers to introducing new product lines or categories that did not exist before, such as introducing a menswear line to a previously known women's wear brand, line extension means adding new product items to an existing line of products, like adding short-sleeved shirts to a shirt line. (Ch. 3)

BRAND HIJACKING: This term refers to two situations. First, it is where a brand is meant to target a specific market segment and user group but gets picked up and popularized by a different one. Second—and most commonly—it refers to consumers taking over the marketing and promotion of the brand and its products through various forms of viral marketing, as witnessed in blogs and other social networks, such as Facebook and YouTube. (Ch. 8)

BRANDING: A multifunctional process that highlights a proposed value for a product and transforms it into a real consumer experience. (Ch. 2)

CHAINS: Stores with multiple branches. Specialty store chains sell one or multiple brands, yet the focus is on a segment or a category such as women's ready-to-wear, lingerie, and so on. (Ch. 6)

CO-BRANDING: The practice of using multiple brand names together on a single product or service. This form of alliance should have potential economic and commercial rewards to both parties. Co-branding agreements should cover marketing strategies, confidentiality issues, licensing specifications, warranties, payments and royalties, indemnification, disclaimers, and termination terms. (Ch. 3)

CO-MARKETING: When manufacturers and other retailers market a brand together and share the cost of the advertising campaign. (Ch. 6)

COMMUNICATION: The promotional mix available for expressing the brand's presence, identity, and value through advertising and other channels. The goal of brand communication is to convey the positioning proposal, polish it, and persuade the consumer to purchase the brand's products. (Chs. 3, 6)

CONSISTENCY: The maintenance of standardization and conformity. (Ch.1)

COPYCATS: Private labels that basically imitate the styles, color stories, and details of an established manufacturer brand and offer their alternative at a competitive price. (Ch. 5)

CRAFTSMANSHIP: The birthplace of luxury, as it originally embodied all the associations with luxury, such as artistry, scarcity, and uniqueness. Craftsmanship is all about handwork and manual labor, which produces a high level of quality that is not perfect, but is unique and hard to replicate or reproduce, unlike machine-produced pieces that are standardized and identical. (Ch. 4)

CREATIVITY: Amongst luxury brands, creativity is their biggest differentiator and comparative advantage. To deliver an ongoing flow of newness and artistry, creativity is critical to a fashion house's continued success. (Ch. 4)

DEPARTMENT STORES: Technically, a retailer that sells both soft goods (apparel) and hard goods (appliances and furniture). In terms of distribution, these are stores where brands and their products are ordered and managed by the store and are among other brands displayed. (Ch. 6)

DIRECT MARKETING: Where promotions utilize media or nonmedia channels, direct marketing is often used as a more personal approach to delivering promotional material to customers. It relies heavily on a large database of shoppers' details and an effective distribution system to build relationships with customers who are treated as individuals, not as a bulk group. (Ch. 6)

DISCOUNT STORES: Stores that sell known brands at discounted below market prices. These no-frills stores offer minimal services and in-store experiences in return for cutting their costs and passing part of these savings on to customers by adopting a low margin/high volume policy. (Ch. 6)

DISTINCTIVE FEATURES: Any brand is a product at its core, and any product is built on a feature or a set of features that are meant to solve a problem or satisfy a need. (Ch. 1)

EMPOWERMENT: The advent of new technology has led to a dramatic increase in the level of consumer empowerment in the branding process. The roles of the players in the branding game have been redefined, and companies now have to negotiate, respond, and share with consumers and outsiders, giving up the control they have always fiercely protected. (Ch. 8)

ECONOMIC RETURN: A brand's financial return to its producers through the building of equity. (Ch. 1)

ENTITY: In defining a brand, we prefer to use the term *entity* instead of a *product* or *service* because this term is more inclusive—it might refer to a product, a person, a country, and so on. The term *entity* also has both a legal insinuation and a reference to a potential market value and financial worth. (Ch. 1)

EQUITY: A brand's market value is a function of the brand's equity that it accumulates: the greater the equity, the more valuable the brand. Recognizing that a brand delivers something more than a generic product does, equity can be regarded as that extra "something" attached to a brand that adds value over and above the objective characteristics of a product. (Ch. 1)

E-TAILING: The Internet, or click-and-shop, model as a retail concept. (Ch. 6)

ETHICS: Our moral standards, or what we perceive to be right and wrong. (Ch. 1)

EXPERIENCE: The shopping experience is a manifestation of the store's identity as a whole, as shaped by a mix of store aesthetics (or atmosphere) and the store personality, which is demonstrated by its culture, its employees, and the set of rules and policies that are ultimately inspired by its mission and vision statements. (Ch. 6)

EXPERIENTIAL BRANDING: The discipline of understanding and defining brands in terms of the way they are experienced, in order to dif-ferentiate them in the most powerful dimension: relevance (nothing is more relevant than the experience). (Ch. 8)

EXTERNAL MARKETING: External interac-tion with the market. This interaction includes both

early stages of market research and later activities aimed at marketing and selling the brand concept to the rest of the world. (Ch. 2)

FLAGSHIP STORES: Usually the biggest and most impressive of a chain of retailers, generally located at the brand's headquarters or in major centers of the world. (Ch. 6)

FRANCHISING: A retailer (the franchisor) offering a store owner (the franchisee) the rights to emulate the retailer's business model or system of conducting his business. (Ch. 6)

FREE-STANDING STORES: A retailer found on major streets and in malls or shopping centers. (Ch. 6)

GENERICS: A dying breed and not very relevant to the fashion industry, these refer to no-name products such as shampoos and soaps that were sold at large discounts next to branded products in supermarkets. (Ch. 5)

IBRAND: The brand in the age of the Internet, with its implications of user empowerment and growing consumer control. (Ch. 7)

IDEA: The concept, the vision of the brand, or the initial dream upon which a whole venture is created. The idea is usually regarding a proposed solution for a certain problem or to satisfy a need the targeted user may have. (Ch. 1)

IDENTITY: Created by two elements or compo-nents: personality and symbols. The identity allows the customer to easily identify the brand both visually and mentally while differentiating it from other brands. (Chs. 1, 2)

IMAGE: The mental perception of how the buyer sees and understands the brand's identity and value. (Ch. 1)

INNOVATION: Change and rejuvenation in response to economic, technological, and generational needs and developments. (Ch. 1)

IN-STORE BOUTIQUES: Fully individualized stores located inside department stores, which can be either a space rented by the brand or run and managed by the department store itself, while employees are picked and trained by the brand. Also known as shops-in-shops. (Ch. 6)

INTERNAL MARKETING: The need to sell and market the brand's concept inside the organization before attempting to do so to the outside world. (Ch. 2)

LAYOUT: A major element of a store's aesthetics, which should also accomplish a number of goals, such as minimize material handling costs, utilize space efficiently, and eliminate bottlenecks, reduce customer service time, and so on. (Ch. 6)

LIFESTYLE BRANDS: Brands that successfully identify themselves with a lifestyle and a marketing segment to the point that their name or image is mentally triggered when the segment is mentioned. (Ch. 4)

LOCATION: The retail location signifies the level of shopping convenience and availability.

Mass-market versus luxury brands take very different attitudes toward location: mass-market brands are extremely flexible in choosing store sites, hoping to reach the widest audience possible, whereas the luxury sector views location as a sign of a brand's exclusivity, so options are much more limited. (Ch. 6)

LUXURY: The term *luxury* connotes something that provides pleasure or comfort but is not actually necessary, and the types of adjectives generally associated with it are *expensive, creative, trendy, exclusive, high quality*, and so on. Historically, the term implied *custom-made*, whereas in modern times, small independent crafts shops have been replaced by major luxury groups. Today, a luxury brand is one that consistently delivers a unique emotional value and possesses the capacity of creating a lifestyle experience through a strong identity, a high level of creativity, and closely controlled quality, quantity, and distribution, all of which justifies asking for a premium price. (Ch. 4)

MASS CUSTOMIZATION: The concept of allowing each consumer to customize or adapt products' features according to his or her needs within a standardized platform with an acceptable price premium. It is a middle-of-the-road solution between mass production and pure customization or made-to-measure. (Ch. 7)

MASS-MARKET: Brands that are mass-produced. Accordingly, these brands' values usually stem from price, functionality, and their value for money rather than experience, emotions, or lifestyles attached to luxury brands. (Ch. 5)

MASSTIGE: A category of premium brands that are neither at the top of their category in price nor related to other brands. They occupy a sweet spot in the market between mass and class, commanding a premium price over conventional products but priced well below super-premium or old luxury goods (examples include Bath & Body Works and Zara). (Ch. 5)

M-BRANDING: Refers to branding and marketing activities utilizing mobile technologies and devices such as our cell phones and PDAs. Also known as *mobile branding*. (Ch. 7)

MERCHANDISE: The product mix that is offered for sale. (Ch. 6)

MICROBRANDS: Limited yet distinct versions of the original or mother brand. More specifically, microbrands are a set of sub-brands with a common unifying identity and feature base, yet with a score of distinctive features customized and defined by the end user; these customized features create a unique experience with an equally high level of satisfaction among users and ultimately a higher level of loyalty to the mother brand. (Ch. 8)

PERSONALITY: A personality humanizes the brand and is developed through the accumulation of culture, vision, stories, product mix, and behavior. It sums up what the brand is all about and identifies the true emotional value and brand promise. Personality is the essence of positioning at the brand level because it represents the image you hope the customer will recall when the brand is mentioned. (Chs. 2, 6)

POSITIONING: How the company proposes the brand should be perceived in reference to its competitors or how it emphasizes the brand's distinctive advantages so that it stands out in the market to differ from specific competitors. Positioning is a process or strategy that can be summarized in the following four questions: A brand for what benefit? Who is the target, the potential customer? What are the differentiators that support and can create such a benefit? Who is the competition? (Chs. 1, 2, 6)

PREMIUM: Standing at the highest end of the spectrum of mass-market brands, premium brands are characterized by elements of craftsmanship but are not completely handmade or artisan in nature. Also referred to as *aspirational* or *new luxe* brands. (Ch. 5)

PREMIUM PRICE: Luxury brands are known for their premium prices in part because a premium price contributes to the exclusivity factor, but there also is a financial necessity: luxury products are expensive to produce, manage, and market. In addition, they are usually in short supply, in high demand, and are price inelastic (demand is not highly affected by price changes), all of which contribute to these brands' premium price strategy. (Ch. 4)

PRIVATE LABELS: Brands owned by a retailer and not a manufacturer. The definition of private labels has expanded to refer to both private labels sold next to manufacturers brands in multibranded stores (such as Club Room at Macy's or Target's Isaac Mizrahi collection) as well as private brands sold solely in their exclusive stores (such as Gap and Esprit). (Ch. 5)

PROMISE OF VALUE: Assures that the values attributed to the brand will be delivered. This promise is a contract with the customer, a guarantee of value, and a reducer of risk. (Ch. 1)

RELAUNCH: A strategy by which the brand is reintroduced after a period of demise or lack of market interest. (Ch. 3)

RELEVANCE: Confirms that what the brand is promising as a value makes sense to the consumer and that it is a proposal convincing enough to make them purchase the brand, selecting it over its competitors. (Ch. 1)

REPOSITIONING: A plan by which the brand redefines its market position, target customer, and strategy. (Ch. 3)

RETAIL CHANNELS: The range of concepts or business models designed to target various segments, incomes, and shopping habits, such as specialty stores, department stores, category killers, and discount stores. (Ch. 6)

RETAIL CONCEPT: The business model and retail philosophy adopted by the brand. (Ch. 6)

RETAILING: The major service side of fashion. In general, products and services follow the same principles and rules of marketing and branding, aside from obvious differences such as the human element where individuals delivering the service, such as sales personnel, are at the core of the brand. (Ch. 6)

REVITALIZATION: An approach whereby the brand is refurbished and modernized yet is meant to stay relevant to its existing customer with the possibility of gaining new groups. For the strategy of revitalization, innovation is a major tool. (Ch. 3)

RFID: Stands for radio frequency identification. The technology is built around the concept of putting cheap and tiny tags that contain a radio transmitter/receiver on physical objects. The system is used to monitor and keep track of tagged items while transferring this data to any computer. (Ch. 7)

SERVICE: Refers to the retailing operation of the fashion industry. Yet as a function of retailing, *service* mainly refers to customer service policies that are adopted both at the time of purchase and after. Customer service is important and relevant at every price level because it is a major driver for customer loyalty, which in return is a reasonable measure of success. (Ch. 6)

SERVICE MIX: The mix of attributes that formulate the retail concept or define the retailing business model as a service operation. It includes the merchandise, the price range, the location, and level of customer service. (Ch. 6)

STAR BRANDS: According to Bernard Arnault, chairman and CEO of LVMH, a brand needs to possess four characteristics to become a star brand: timelessness, modernity, fast growth, and high profitability. (Ch. 4)

STAR DESIGNERS: In the world of luxury, designers are usually transformed into superstars and in many ways are seen as *being* the brand themselves. With their talent and character, star designers are a major marketing force behind the brand and in many ways help define the personality of the brand. (Ch. 4)

SUPER CONSUMER: The empowered consumer in today's world of technological innovations. Unlike in the past when branding was strictly controlled by the company, these customers are now taking over to reshape and market the brand on their own terms. (Ch. 8)

SYMBOLS: Visual and physical attributes meant to communicate the esthetics, personality, and soul of the brand and aim to trigger specific mental associations and signals. They may take various forms such as a name, logo, color, and packing design. (Ch. 2)

TECHNOLOGY: The constant innovation of tools, applications, and devices that play a direct role in redefining our habits and values and thus continually reshape our culture. (Ch. 8)

TECHNOLOGY INTEGRATION: The combined use of different technologies to create a rich, interactive, entertaining, and personalized environment for the user. (Ch. 7)

VIRTUAL COMMUNITIES: Internet environments, such as blogs and social networks, that have reshaped our social habits and defined our new culture. They are instrumental in brand positioning, providing platforms where ideas, suggestions, and support for the brand are initiated and shared. (Ch. 7)

VISION: The concept and dream behind the brand. The starting point is realizing there is a necessity for a brand to exist and a potential for reward. Also referred to as the brand decision. (Ch. 2)

WIRELESS TECHNOLOGIES: Include RFID, M-branding, beaming, and audio targeting. These bring an organization closer to the customer and establish a more intimate relationship built on continuous dialogue and personalized services. (Ch. 7)

Index